# MIRACLE AND NATURAL LAW
## IN GRAECO-ROMAN
## AND EARLY CHRISTIAN
## THOUGHT

# MIRACLE
# AND NATURAL LAW

## IN GRAECO-ROMAN
## AND EARLY CHRISTIAN
## THOUGHT

### ROBERT M. GRANT

Professor of Theology,
University of the South,
Sewanee, Tenn.

WIPF & STOCK · Eugene, Oregon

Wipf and Stock Publishers
199 W 8th Ave, Suite 3
Eugene, OR 97401

Miracle and Natural Law in Graeco - Roman and Early Christian Thought
By Grant, Robert M.
Copyright©1952 by Grant, Robert M.
ISBN 13: 978-1-60899-751-0
Publication date 5/1/2011
Previously published by North Holland Publishing Co., 1952

# PREFACE

To express adequate gratitude for all the assistance I have received in completing this study would be impossible. It would be impossible, however, not to mention those to whom thanks is especially due: Professor A. S. Pease of Harvard University, Professor J. H. Waszink of the University of Leiden and Professor A. D. Nock of Harvard, all of whom have criticized and corrected my manuscript. The remaining errors are, of course, my own. I am also grateful to the authorities of Harvard College Library, the Koninklijke Bibliotheek ('s-Gravenhage), and the Bibliotheek der Rijksuniversiteit te Leiden. Moreover, to complete this book would have been impossible without the generous assistance, over a period of years, of the Carnegie Foundation for the Advancement of Teaching and the University of the South, the John Simon Guggenheim Memorial Foundation, and the United States Educational Foundation in the Netherlands.

Perhaps it should be said that when I speak of "science" I mean primarily the more or less systematic study of the workings of nature, especially as this study is related to reports of wonders of various sorts which seem to upset the system. It should certainly be said that the recovery of the Hellenistic sources of Cicero is a more difficult task than some of my ascriptions to Posidonius or Panaetius would suggest; but the influence of Posidonius can hardly be denied.

R. M. G.

's-Gravenhage 1951—Sewanee 1952

# CONTENTS

## PART I

### SCIENCE

## PART II

### CHRISTIANITY

# ABBREVIATIONS

| | |
|---|---|
| AJA | American Journal of Archaeology |
| AJP | American Journal of Philology |
| ARW | Archiv für Religionswissenschaft |
| ATR | Anglican Theological Review |
| BPW | Berliner philologische Wochenschrift |
| CSEL | Corpus Scriptorum Ecclesiasticorum Latinorum |
| DL | Diogenes Laertius |
| HTR | Harvard Theological Review |
| JBL | Journal of Biblical Literature |
| JR | Journal of Religion |
| JTS | Journal of Theological Studies |
| PG | Patrologia Graeca |
| PL | Patrologia Latina |
| RAC | Reallexikon für Antike und Christentum |
| RE | Real-Encyclopädie der classischen Altertumswissenschaft |
| RSR | Recherches de science religieuse |
| RTAM | Recherches de théologie ancienne et médiévale |
| SO | Symbolae Osloenses |
| SVF | Stoicorum veterum fragmenta |
| TAPA | Transactions of the American Philological Association |
| TWzNT | Theologisches Wörterbuch zum Neuen Testament |
| VC | Vigiliae Christianae |
| ZNW | Zeitschrift für die neutestamentliche Wissenschaft |
| ZP | Papyri Graecae Magicae |
| ZWT | Zeitschrift für wissenschaftliche Theologie |

# PART I
# SCIENCE

# FRONTISPIECE—PART I

A statue discovered at Rome between the Via Nomentana and the Via Tiburtina represents an anonymous figure as a philosopher and head of a philosophical school. From the list of his works on the base of the statue he is to be identified with the Christian bishop and teacher Hippolytus, early in the third century. The statue and the list of works show the extent to which scientific and philosophical studies were valued in early Christianity. The statue itself reflects to a considerable degree the realism which was soon to disappear in a more subjective style.

# 1

# NATURE

The relation of early Christianity to natural science is a somewhat complicated subject, but it is one which must be examined in order to understand the attitude of early Christians and others toward the credibility of miracles. When theologians tried to justify their accept-ance of the miraculous they often argued that miracles were really in harmony with nature or, while not contrary to the workings of nature, "supernatural". Other theologians held that they were actually "con-trary to nature". It is therefore necessary to find out what Greek and Roman writers believed about nature and its workings.

We shall not be concerned so much with what scientists were able to discover about nature as with what philosophers and other writers taught. The direct influence of ancient scientists, except physians, on ancient civilization was extraordinarily slight, and when ideas about science reached the ordinary literate person they had been expressed in the form of generalizations. We shall examine some of these generalizations, such as the idea of laws of nature and conceptions of matter and motion, in order to trace their origins and their influence, and in order to see the extent to which philosophy was erecting castles in the air.

We must also consider the use of these generalizations by historians and others who discuss the question of credibility, as well as the extent to which scientific ideas had entered into Greek and Roman education and into the thought of Hellenistic Jews and Christians. Only after this preliminary study (Part I) can we proceed to examine the miraculous and its defence by theologians (Part II). In this way we shall hope to give something of an answer to the question raised in a recent book on the god Asclepius. [1]

> The problem of miracles, as they were understood in antiquity, has never been studied in detail. Most books dealing with the questions involved are satisfied with stating that the ancients believed in miracles and that ancient and modern concepts differ in this respect.

[1] E.–L. Edelstein, *Asclepius* (Baltimore, 1945), II 157 n. 43.

In the history of Greek philosophy the word "nature" ($\phi\acute{v}\sigma\iota\varsigma$) is used in a wide range of meanings. Among the pre-Socratic philosophers, in Plato, in Aristotle, in Epicurus, and among the Stoics the word has no single meaning but carries with it several ideas. In the *Physics* of Aristotle four meanings are listed, but in the later *Metaphysics* we find seven. Even in a single analytical philosopher, then, the word "nature" has no uniform definition.

We are fortunate in possessing five recent studies of the history of the idea of nature to guide us through this complicated field. First is the general article of Hans Leisegang in the twentieth volume of the *Real-Encyclopädie* of Pauly–Wissowa (1941). [1] He deals with the meaning of *physis* in philosophy and science to Aristotle; the ideal of life "according to nature" and the corresponding idea of "nature" among Cynics, Stoics, and Epicureans; *physis* and *natura* in the philosophical, poetic, and religious literature of the Hellenistic age and of late antiquity; and special meanings of the words. Second is Fritz Heinimann's *Nomos und Physis* (Basel, 1945), which bears the subtitle *Herkunft und Bedeutung einer Antithese im griechischen Denken des 5. Jahrhunderts*. [2] It is a very thorough study of the origin and development of the antithesis between "nature" (a chapter is devoted to the idea of nature) and human political ideas or conventions. At the end of the fifth century the antithesis was sometimes developing into a synthesis. Heinimann gives examples of this development from Euripides and Thucydides. Third is an excellent article on the Greek idea of nature ("Der griechische Naturbegriff") by H. Diller. [2] This article examines the concept from the time of the pre-Socratics through Plato and Aristotle, the Peripatetics and the Stoa, to Posidonius and ultimately to Neoplatonism. Posidonius was the first to include within nature the irrational powers of the soul. His idea finally revolutionized the Greek conception of nature. Fourth is the rather general treatment given by R. G. Collingwood in his book *The Idea of Nature*, published at Oxford in 1945. Only the first part of his book is concerned with Greek philosophy, and he deals especially with the pre-Socratics and with Aristotle. Fifth is the discussion of nature by W. Nestle in *Vom Mythos zum Logos* (second edition, Stuttgart, 1942). This study is especially valuable for our purpose because Nestle is concerned with the way in which rational thought in Greece

[1] *RE* XX 1130—64.  [2] Cf. the review by F. Solmsen in *AJP* 72 (1951), 191–95, for some corrections.  [3] *Neue Jahrbücher* N. S. 2 (1939), 241–57.

gradually overcame older mythical concepts of the gods and the world. [1]

The earliest example of the word *physis* in Greek literature is in Homer, where it refers not to "nature" in general but to the special characteristics of the magical plant *moly* (*Od.* viii. 303). In the pre-Socratic philosophers it means most frequently the essence of something, less frequently the power or arrangement of "nature", and— infrequently—the origin of something. This least frequent use is the basic one, for *physis* is derived from the root *phy-*, to grow or become. *Physis* means the process of growth, a growing thing (the totality of growing things), and that which originates the process. It also comes to mean the "normal" healthy state of a living and growing thing.

With the rise of the study of foreign peoples in the fifth century "nature" comes to be contrasted with "law". Some differences between peoples are ascribed to nature, others to law or convention. Finally the "law" in this contrast is regarded as the opinion of the many, widely accepted but largely false. [2] In this sense, law is opposed to nature. On the other hand, some writers value law more highly than nature. They believe that the life of primitive man was disorderly and needed law to set it in order. [3] At a later date, the Cynics and Stoics reversed this view and regarded the advent of law as a step downward from the "natural" life of early mankind.

The pre-Socratics do not speak of anything as "contrary to nature", although the opposition of law to nature implies such an idea. In four testimonies to their thought, which must of course be used with more caution than explicit quotations, we find such an expression. It means nothing more than that men can act "contrary to nature" when they violate unwritten laws of conduct. [4] But we cannot be sure that the pre-Socratics themselves expressed this idea.

In Plato we often find the antithesis of "nature" and "law", but as he is not primarily concerned with "natural philosophy" except in the *Timaeus* we shall not expect him to advance the technical precision of the term *physis*. He often uses the expressions "according to nature" and "contrary to nature" in reference to human behavior. This use reflects the idea of nature as a normal, healthy state. What is just and good and temperate exists "by nature" (*Rep.* vi. 501 b). Some-

[1] The idea of nature is also discussed by B. Snell, *Die Entdeckung des Geistes* (Hamburg, 1946), 217–34.  [2] Heinimann, *op. cit.*, 89, cf. 153.  [3] *Ibid.*, 147–50.  [4] On these laws cf. R. Hirzel, *Agraphos Nomos, Abh. d. sächs. Akad.* 47 (1900–03).

times Plato uses *physis* for "the really existent", and the Platonic ideas can thus be called *physeis*. [1]

It is Aristotle who systematically defines the word *physis*. His most careful analysis is found in the *Metaphysics* (iv. 4, 1014 b 16–1015 a 19), where he gives seven definitions. *Physis* is (1) the genesis or growth of growing things, (2) the part from which growth begins, probably the seed, (3) the internal principle of movement in natural objects, (4) the unformed and unchanging matter from which natural objects are produced, (5) the essence or form of natural objects, (6) essence or form in general, and (7)—the primary (Aristotelian) meaning—the essence of things which have a principle of movement in themselves *qua* themselves. As we have said, Aristotle's thought on this subject developed gradually; in the corresponding passage of the earlier *Physics* (ii. 1, 192 b 8–193 b 18) we do not find the second, sixth, and seventh definitions. The definitions look more complicated than they actually are. They can be arranged under the usual three headings of the nature or essence of something (4–7), the healthy or normal state dependent on the growth-process (1–3), and a power working within natural objects (1, 3). In this sense any Greek writer could accept Aristotle's definitions.

Aristotle can speak of some things as coming into being "by nature", some "by art", and some "spontaneously" (*Met.* 1032 a 12). By nature a man begets a man; by art a man builds a house; [2] spontaneously certain animals reproduce without seed, or "by chance" (a subdivision of spontaneous production) an unskilled person may accidentally cause a cure by imitating the physician's art. What comes into being "by nature" always comes into being for a purpose. "Nature does nothing without purpose." Similarly, coming close to identifying God with nature, Aristotle says that "God and nature do nothing without purpose". [3]

In this case, why are there monstrosities in nature? The answer is to be derived from a comparison with art, for in art there are failures when the scribe makes mistakes in taking dictation and the physician gives the wrong medicine (*Phys.* 199 a 33). Therefore it is obvious that such errors can occur in nature. Some principle has been corrupted. We cannot say that such a result is due to chance; it is

---

[1] Leisegang, *op. cit.*, 1147.   [2] Art partly imitates nature and partly completes what nature is unable to effect (*Phys.* 199 a 15).   [3] We shall discuss these passages in dealing with matter and motion (c. 3).

due to spontaneity. Something takes place "by nature" but "contrary to nature" (*Phys.* 197 b 32). The same problem is discussed in more detail in the treatise *De generatione animalium* (770 b 10). The monstrosity (*teras*) is admittedly "contrary to nature", contrary not to the whole of nature but to nature as it is generally. In a certain sense it is "according to nature", for when we consider nature as it always and necessarily is, nothing takes place contrary to it. And "none of the things which are by nature and according to nature is disorderly, for nature is the cause of order for all things" (*Phys.* 252 a 11).

Aristotle's theoretical analysis of nature was accompanied by a lively interest in scientific study, especially in the field of biology, which was maintained in the Peripatetic school for at least two generations. Theophrastus wrote scientific treatises on plants and on other subjects, and his successor Strato of Lampsacus was renowned in antiquity for his concentration on natural science, which led him to be called "the physicist". [1] In contrast to Plato and the Stoics he regarded nature as a power which lacked intelligence, and against Aristotle he rejected a teleological explanation of nature's workings. He agreed with Aristotle, however, that nature itself contained the causes of coming into being, of growth, and of decay (fr. 33 Wehrli). [2]

On the other hand, Epicurus' interest in nature was considerably greater than his understanding of it. He wrote books on Nature, i.e. on the substance and arrangement of the universe, and apparently criticized the Platonic idea of the original "nature" or being. At one point he addresses Nature personified in a hymn of praise: "Thanks be to blessed Nature because it made necessities easily obtainable and things hard to obtain unnecessary" (fr. 469 Usener).

Nature is not to be forced but obeyed (Gnomol. Vat. xxi).

Elsewhere, however, he defines the "nature" of the universe as "bodies and the void" (fr. 75), and once borrows from Democritus the term *physeis* as equivalent to atoms (*Sympos.* fr. 6). He also uses the term "nature" for "being" or for "existence", as well as for what is normal or "natural." It is the same confusion which we have noted in other authors.

Epicurus, like contemporary Stoics and Cynics, expressed the romantic-ethical appeal to live "in conformity with nature," [3] or to

---

[1] This title was also applied to the pre-Socratic naturalists. [2] Cf. *Phys.* 192 b 15.
[3] This idea was introduced into Stoicism by Cleanthes; cf. W. Wiersma, *ΠΕΡΙ*

"follow nature". This appeal was accompanied by the portrayal of the life of primitive man and of the animals, which live and lived according to nature and have not acquired the sophisticated laws of later mankind. Thus Epicurus tells us that desires which are neither natural nor necessary lead merely to vain glory (D.L. x. 149).

Among the Stoics the term "nature" is used very loosely. It is the whole of existence, it is God, it is Zeus, it is the rational principle of the universe, it is the first cause, it is providence, it is a spirit or a fire. [1] Zeno defined it as an artificent fire leading the way for coming into being. [2] He thus combined the primal fire of Heraclitus with the Aristotelian emphasis on nature as becoming. He also said that fate, the motor power of matter, could be called indifferently providence and nature. [3] A more complete definition is found in Diogenes Laertius (vii. 148), who says that the Stoics speak of nature sometimes as embracing the universe and sometimes as producing things on earth. They define nature as "a self-moved condition (*hexis*) which follows inseminated rational principles and produces and preserves its products in definite periods of time, and produces effects which correspond to their causes". As the producer of a succession of causes it can thus be identified with fate and necessity. [4] Nothing takes place except according to nature and its rational principle. [5]

Cicero (N.D. ii. 81–82) gives us four definitions of "nature", two of which are Stoic. (1) Nature is a certain non-rational power producing necessary motions in bodies. This definition is probably based on the Peripatetic Strato. [6] (2) Nature is "a power possessing reason and order, leading the way and setting forth what the cause of each thing should effect as a result. No art, no hand, no artist can imitate its skill, for the power of a seed is so great that, even though it is very small, if it falls into a 'nature' which takes it and holds it, and acquires matter by which it can be nourished and increased, it will thus form and produce something in its own species. The products (a) are nourished through their own roots and (b) can move and feel and obtain and produce like things from themselves". This is a development of the definition given by Diogenes Laertius. (3) According to the Epicureans, nature is everything; it is bodies and

*ΤΕΛΟΥΣ: Studie over de leer van het volmaakte leven in de ethiek van de oude Stoa* (Groningen, 1937), 25–44.

[1] SVF II 1076; cf. Leisegang, *op. cit.*, 1153–54.　[2] SVF I 171.　[3] SVF I 176.
[4] SVF II 1076.　[5] SVF II 937.　[6] Cf. fr. 32–33 Wehrli.

the void. (4) The fourth definition is the one Cicero himself favors.

> When we say that the universe is constituted and governed by nature, we do not speak of it as wood or stone or anything of the sort which has no nature to hold it together, but as a tree or an animal.

This definition implies that the universe is not held together by its condition (*hexis*), for this is what holds together the bodies of stones or wood. Its constitution is due to "nature", as in the case of plants, and "nature" is identified with "soul", which holds animals together. [1] The definition comes from Posidonius rather than from Panaetius; [2] it is evidently "vitalist" and reflects the Stoic, especially Middle Stoic, conception of the universe as an animate being.

In the same period we find the rise and gradual diffusion of the idea of cosmic "sympathy." First came the study of the mysterious and miraculous powers of natural objects, powers which could be used in medicine and in magic. The most famous example of an object moved by "sympathy" is the iron which the magnet draws to itself, but there were many others. Such examples were often collected in the Hellenistic age, especially in the work (c. 200 B. C.) of Bolos of Mendes, the treatise called *Natural Powers* or *On Sympathies and Antipathies*. In the first century B. C. this work was more widely read than Aristotle or Theophrastus, and its popular influence was greater than theirs. [3] The theory of "sympathy" was also prominent among astrologers, who used it to explain the influence of the stars on the earth. Geminus [4] admits the influence of sun and moon on the earth but denies that of the fixed stars. He shares this opinion with the Stoic Panaetius. [5] On the other hand, Cleomedes, [6] probably following Posidonius, argues only that the moon has greater "sympathy" for the earth because it is closer to the earth than the other stars.

In the Stoic philosopher Posidonius the theory of "sympathy" becomes the key to the workings of the universe, [7] and "sympathy" is naturally a prominent feature of his idea of nature. Cleomedes (Posidonius) argues that nature must control whatever exists, and he tries to prove nature's administration of the universe by five proofs.

---

[1] Sext. Emp., *Adv. math.* ix. 81; cf. K. Reinhardt, *Kosmos und Sympathie* (Munich, 1926), 108. [2] Cf. Leisegang, *op. cit.* 1156. [3] M. Wellmann, *Die Physika des Bolos Demokritos und der Magier Anaxilaos aus Larissa, Abh. d. preuss. Akad.* 1928, philos.-hist. Kl. 7. [4] *Elem,* xvii. 15–17. [5] Cic. *Div.* ii. 91. [6] *Mot. circ.* ii. 3, 180 Ziegler. [7] Reinhardt, *op. cit.* 52–54.

(1) There is order in the various parts of the universe, (2) there is order in the things which come into being, (3) there is "sympathy" among the various parts of the universe, (4) each part was made for some purpose, and (5) everything in the universe is useful and advantageous. [1] The extent to which Cleomedes personifies nature may be seen from his statement that it is necessary for the temperate regions of the earth to be inhabited, for "nature loves animate being", and wherever possible its rational principle chooses for every part of the earth to be filled with animals both rational and irrational. [2]

While Posidonius had a lively interest in science and wrote many books on the subject (see c. 6), it is obvious that his doctrine of cosmic sympathy was hardly scientific and was in fact destined to support astrology rather than astronomy. Posidonius himself accepted astrology as a genuine science.

In Stoicism God and nature were often identified. We already find in Cicero [3] the ascription to Zeno of the belief that the universe is God. The Roman Stoics reiterate this belief. Seneca [4] asks, "What is nature but God and the divine reason inserted within the whole universe and its parts?" He states that it makes no difference whether God (nature) is called fate or not, for fate is the series of causes while God is the first cause from which the others are dependent. Here he is blending Aristotelian and Stoic language. He adds that nature does not exist without God, nor does God exist without nature; they are the same, although their functions are different. Again, Pliny argues that the universe is the equivalent of a divine being, since it is eternal, immeasurable, never coming into being or ever to perish. [5] The power of nature is what we call God. [6] As Marcus Aurelius expresses the same idea, "the oldest of the gods" is nature. [7]

This theological treatment of the idea of nature meant that the study of natural science, at least among such highly influential writers, was subordinated to theology. Instead of treating nature as at least relatively autonomous and trying to find out how it worked, many later writers were content to argue from general principles and describe the way it ought to work. At the same time, since the order

---

[1] *Mot. circ.* i. 1, 2 : 15–4 : 4.   [2] P. 28 : 6.   [3] *N. D.* ii. 21.   [4] *Ben.* iv. 7–8.
[5] *N. H.* ii. 1, perhaps ultimately (through Manilius? see p. 37) from Posidonius.
[6] *N. H.* ii. 27.   [7] *Medit.* ix. 1. Compare the views of Galen discussed below.

of nature was immutable, prayer to the gods was useless. [1] The combination of science with theology benefited neither.

If we turn from philosophers to medical writers we shall find a somewhat greater interest in the question of "nature." Among the writers of the Hippocratic corpus "nature" had already been regarded as the norm of healthful existence. [2] The word was also used in the sense of that which actually exists: precise knowledge of "nature", by means of medicine, was absolutely essential. [3] These writers also discussed the relation of the natural to the divine. To this question three answers were given. (1) Events which appear spontaneous are divine; everything else is natural. (2) Some events originate in nature; others have a human cause; still others have a divine cause. (3) There is no difference between divine and human. [4]

> Nothing is more divine or more human than anything else, but all are alike and all are divine. Each of them has its own cause and nothing takes place without a natural cause.

The author of the treatise *On the Sacred Disease* explicitly denies that there is such a thing as a sacred disease (epilepsy) and holds that it is impious to think that divine power can be controlled by mortals. [5]

Medicine and philosophy were always closely related, and the later Hellenistic debates among physicians were not unlike those among philosophers. The "dogmatists", close to Stoicism but somewhat eclectic, insisted that the physician ought to have not only experience but a reasoned knowledge of human bodies and of "nature" —the way in which natural forces work. [6] On the other hand, the more sceptical "empiricists" thought that the study of obscure causes and of "natural actions" was unnecessary—"because nature is not comprehensible". [7] Such an "obscure cause" was chance, which they believed themselves able to contrast with "nature". [8] Some ailments were "natural", for their cause was inside the body; others took place by chance, since their cause was external. [9] They criticized the "physiologists" (dogmatists) for believing that all the products of nature were rationally moved. [10]

[1] Sen. *Ep.* 77 : 12, *Ben.* vi. 23, *N. Q.* ii. 35. 1–2, 36 (H. Schmidt, *Veteres philosophi quomodo iudicaverint de precibus* [Giessen, 1908], 34). [2] Heinimann, *op. cit.*, 96–97. [3] *De med. ant.* 20; cf. Nestle, *op. cit.*, 243. [4] *De aere*, etc. 22. [5] Nestle, *op. cit.*, 226–31; on the relation of medicine to "general culture" cf. W. Jaeger, *Paideia* III (New York, 1945), 3–45. [6] Celsus, *Med.* prooem. 12, 3 : 12 Daremberg. [7] *Ibid.* 27, 5 : 21. [8] K. Deichgräber, *Die griechische Empiriker-schule* (Berlin, 1930), 44 : 18, 95 : 10. [9] P. 123 : 15. [10] P. 174 : 15.

A third school, the "methodical", included the Roman physician Soranus, of whose *Gynaecia* some parts survive. Soranus vigorously criticizes his predecessors, sometimes in discussing the subject of "nature". He has no use for the popular ideas of sympathy and antipathy. Because of these ideas some people hold that the best time for conception is at the full moon or in the spring. The evidence of phenomena is against them. [1] For the same reason they apply magnets to hemorrhages; the only value of this is psychological. [2] Soranus also distinguishes what is healthful from what is natural. Conception is natural but not conducive to health. [3] Perpetual virginity, on the other hand, is healthful but opposed to "the common rational principle of nature", which requires the perpetuation of the species. [4]

Another medical writer of great importance is the physician Galen, who lived at Rome toward the end of the second century. His significance for our purpose lies chiefly in two facts. In the first place, he constantly attacked contemporary medical writers and physicians for their adherence to theories rather than to observed facts. [5] In the second place, he was a convinced teleologist greatly influenced by the *Timaeus*, on which he wrote a commentary. He believed that divine purpose could be seen clearly in all nature but especially in the parts of the human body, to whose use he devoted the lengthy treatise *De usu partium*. This work was written between A. D. 169 and 176 at Rome. [6] Throughout its seventeen books we constantly encounter such expressions as "the marvelous art of nature", "the marvelous wisdom of the demiurge," and "the providential work of nature". The reader is urged to "marvel at the art of nature".

The work begins with an elaborate description of the wonders of the hand, the part of the body which distinguishes man from all other animals. Naturally Galen rejects the opinion of Anaxagoras that man's wisdom is due to the fact of his having hands, and defends the view of Aristotle that because he was wise he was given hands. He proves this point from the fact that newborn animals try to move before their parts are ready to support them. Therefore both instinct and reason are prior to the parts which they use. [7] Hands are suitable

[1] Pp. 205–6 Rose.  [2] P. 138 : 7–12; such beliefs were common, cf. Wellmann, *op. cit.*, 43.  [3] P. 207 Rose.  [4] P. 196 : 10.  [5] R. Walzer, *Galen on Jews and Christians* (Oxford, 1949), 37–42.  [6] *Ibid.*, 11.  [7] *U.P.* i. 3.

13

instruments for the "wise animal", man. He stands erect because
he has hands. [1] Some (Platonists) may argue that man is the only
erect animal because he wants to contemplate the heavens. But
this is not the case, for man has to bend his neck to look at the heavens
—the true observer of the heavens is the fish "ouranoscope"—and
man is also the only sitting animal. The reason for his standing and
sitting is his need to use his hands. [2] Two apparent objections to this
praise of man are rejected. The monkey has hands, but it is only a
"ridiculous imitation" of man. [3] And there is no such thing as a
Centaur except in the imagination of poets who do not recognize
the generative and digestive problems involved. [4]

Galen occasionally speaks of the wonders of the body which have
to be seen to be believed, and argues that the study of the human
body from the teleological point of view is not inferior to being
initiated in the Eleusinian or Samothracian mysteries. [5] The mysteries
of nature are the "truest mysteries"; the description of them is a
"sacred discourse". [6] Nothing among the products of nature is due
to chance; everything is due to providence and art. [7] Galen severely
criticizes atomists, especially the physician Asclepiades, because they
do not understand the four causes of Aristotle (or perhaps five, if
with Middle Platonists we include the Platonic ideas [see p. 30]).
Asclepiades overlooks both the first cause, the providence of the
demiurge, and the second material cause. [8]

Galen also attacks the opinions of "Moses", according to which
God is not bound by the orderly processes of nature and could make
men out of stones or a horse or bull out of ashes (see chapter 9,
p. 129). [9] He criticizes the Jewish conception of God's irrational will
as compared with the rational choices of the God of nature. [10] The
regularity of natural processes is the real proof of divine providence.
The stories of miraculous conceptions are not true, and although
some birds reproduce parthenogenetically, there has never been a case
of a woman who became pregnant without a man. [11]

His opponents point to the various monstrosities which sometimes
occur in nature. They can see only the one case of a man with six
fingers out of the millions of cases where men have five. Galen's

[1] *U.P.* iii. 1.   [2] *U.P.* iii. 1–3.   [3] *U.P.* i. 22, xiii. 11.   [4] *U.P.* iii 1.   [5] *U.P.* vii.
15, xv. 6.   [6] *U.P.* vii. 14, xii. 6, xvii. 1.   [7] *U.P.* iii. 10, 174 : 6 Helmreich.
[8] *U.P.* i. 21, iii. 10, xi. 7–8, xiv. 4, etc.   [9] *U.P.* vi. 13.   [10] *U.P.* xi. 14; cf. Walzer,
*op. cit.*, 23ff.   [11] Cf. *U.P.* xiv. 9, 313 : 16.   [12] *U.P.* xiv. 7.

answer to their objection is on Aristotelian lines. He compares nature to an artist and argues that the artist's errors do not prove that there is no art. The occasional errors of nature simply remind us of the general goodness, wisdom and power of the demiurge. [1]

It is obvious that when Galen speaks of the demiurge he does not mean the traditional gods of mythology or even the God of Jews and Christians. His demiurge, like the Stoic god, is nature, not something standing outside nature. For Galen nature has the religious meaning that the gods formerly had. [2]

In the early Roman empire there is nothing new in philosophical treatments of nature. Rhetoricians and philosophers repeat the phrases, especially the Stoic phrases, of earlier periods. We may add a few examples to Leisegang's collection. [3] Epictetus [4] defines the nature of the universe as "such as it was, it is and will be". It is "not such that things coming into existence will come into existence differently from the way they now do". This perpetualuniformity applies not only to the life of men and animals but even to the four elements. Thus the Stoic principle of "life according to nature" is reinforced. Similarly Plutarch [5] defines nature in words taken from Aristotle. "What is according to nature has been ordained and defined, for nature is order or a work of order. Disorder, like Pindar's sand, escapes counting, and what is contrary to nature is clearly indefinable and limitless." And the Peripatetic Alexander [6] defends Aristotle's definition of nature as the first principle of order. He also argues that nature, which he identifies with fate, is the measure of the possible and the impossible. [7]

This attitude toward the order of nature was also religious. Marcus Aurelius, the friend of Galen, addresses Nature with a prayer of thanksgiving. [8] "Everything is fruitful for me, o Nature, which thy hours bring; from thee are all things, in thee are all, for thee are all." There is one universe out of all things, and one God through all

---

[1] *U.P.* xvii. 1.    [2] Elsewhere Galen severely criticizes the followers of Erasistratus for not sharing the view of the followers of Aristotle and of Hippocrates that nature is artificent and works teleologically (XV 306–12 Kühn). The philosophical definitions of nature in the *History of Philosophy* (XIX 246; Diels, *Dox.* 611 : 17) and the *Medical Definitions* (XIX 371; cf. Mewaldt in *RE* VII 590) are not Galen's; both works were written after his time.    [3] Leisegang, *op. cit.*, 1157–58.    [4] Fr. 134 Schweighäuser.    [5] *Quaest. conv.* viii. 9. 3; Aristotle, *Phys.* 252 a 11.    [6] *Quaest.* ii. 18, 62 Bruns.    [7] *Fat.* 27, 197 : 31.    [8] *Medit.* iv. 23.

things; one essence and one law. [1] Individuals within nature may come into being and perish; nature itself remains. [2]

The difficulty with the Greek and Roman idea of nature is that it included so many meanings within one word, and that philosophers preferred to argue about these meanings (or simply to take them for granted) rather than to look at "nature" itself. The Hippocratic writers and Aristotle provide only partial exceptions to this general rule. Most writers preferred meditation on the order of the universe to critical examination of the order they assumed to exist. It is a sad commentary on Graeco-Roman thought to observe that the ideas of sympathy and antipathy were far more popular than the biological treatises of Aristotle or the Peripatetics. It cannot be denied that they were more popular, and that in late antiquity the scientific study of nature was practically dead.

When we turn to the examination of Hellenistic Jewish and Christian writers we find no significant differences from this general picture. Philo of Alexandria uses the word "nature" in most of the senses we have already discussed. [3] His usage is close to that of the Stoics, although we must observe (against Leisegang) that he does not identify God with nature. He speaks of nature as a vital force, a creative power (in this sense he can speak of Mother Nature [4]), the universe, the "nature" of things—i.e. their quality or substance—, or uses the word to denote a creature or animal or a species. The expression "according to nature" or "by nature" refers to the orderly processes of nature, especially in reference to morals.

The apostle Paul derives his presuppositions from the Old Testament and contemporary Judaism, but especially in his letters to the Corinthians he is dealing with readers largely Greek and he tries to speak their language. Thus he can ask them whether "nature" itself does not teach us that for men to have long hair and women short is disgraceful. [5] He uses the words "by nature," "natural", "according to nature", and "contrary to nature," in regard to moral behavior, almost in Stoic fashion. [6] Elsewhere in the New Testament the idea of nature does not often appear. In James 3 : 3 the plural *physeis* means "species" as it does in Greek writers. In Jude 10 (cf. 2 Peter 2 : 12) the irrational animals are described as possessing

---

[1] *Medit.* vii. 9.   [2] *Medit.* vii. 23; cf. 25.   [3] H. Leisegang, *Index Philonis* 836–45. [4] *Exsecr.* 155, *Dec.* 41, *Post.* 162, etc.   [5] 1 Cor. 11 : 14; cf. Dio Chrys. *Or.* XXXV. 10–12.   [6] Rom. 1–2 *passim*.

knowledge "naturally". In this sense the word means "by instinct", as it does in Stoic writers and in Philo. [1]

In a fragment of Clement of Alexandria *physis* is carefully defined. [2] It means (1) the truth of matters or their essence, (2) the genesis of things which come into existence, and (3) the providence of God, effecting existence and the mode of existence in things which come to be. The definitions are probably derived from a doxographical collection, for parallels to all three are to be found in the *Placita* of Aëtius. [3] The first is a grammatical definition, while the latter two reflect Aristotelianism and its teleological understanding of nature. The doxography ascribes them to Stoic sources, and this ascription shows the extent to which eclecticism flourished in philosophy.

Origen [4] follows Aristotle and the Stoa in making a distinction between "nature", which he regards as the expression of the reason and will of God, and "what is considered the ordinary ⟨ course of ⟩ nature". Some things take place which go beyond the latter, but they are not "contrary to nature." In his treatise *On Prayer* he gives an example of something for which it would be foolish to pray. This would be for the sun's course to be changed from the summer tropic to that of springtime. [5] "It is probable that God not only foreknows the future but also foreordains it, and that nothing takes place contrary to his foreordinances." [6] Origen does not identify God with the ordinary course of nature, but he holds that it expresses God's reason and will. [7]

On the other hand, Tertullian criticizes the "dialecticians" (presumably Aristotle, or Christians influenced by Aristotle) for confusing the whole distinction between the natural and the unnatural, so that their followers could vindicate for nature even what they really regarded as unnatural. [8] Tertullian himself prefers to distinguish sharply between the natural and what is "contrary to nature", for he believes that God works primarily through the unnatural. [9] He believes in the importance of the incredible, as we shall later see.

A little later in the third century we find an entire treatise *On Nature* written by Dionysius of Alexandria. It is primarily an attack on the atomism of Epicurus and Democritus and a defence of pro-

---

[1] Sen. *Ep.* 121 : 23; G. Tappe, *De Philonis libro qui inscribitur* Ἀλέξανδρος (Göttingen, 1912), 38–54. [2] *De prov.*, iii. 219 Stählin. [3] *Plac.* i. 27–28, pp. 322–23 Diels. [4] *C. Cels.* v. 23. [5] *Orat.* v. 3. [6] Cf. Max. Tyr. *Diss.* xi. [7] We shall find this true when he deals with miracle (chapter 12). [8] *An.* 43 : 6. [9] Cf. *Marc.* iii. 13.

vidence from the Stoic point of view. [1] In Dionysius' opinion the atomic theory does not really explain the workings of nature. How can disorder lead to order? This criticism reflects the argument of Aristotle, long since utilized by other schools, that the "necessity" of Democritus fails to explain the final cause of the natural process. [2] A similar charge was often made against Epicurus. [3] The natural process cannot be due to chance. Again, Dionysius asks how from one first principle the variety of nature can result. Man's life is short (Job 14 : 1), but there are long-lived birds (eagles, crows, phoenixes), land animals (deer, elephants, dragons), sea-monsters and plants (palms, oaks, and perseae). Dionysius ridicules the "marvelous democracy" of the atoms, and argues that on the contrary the wonders of the human body, described after Panaetius, [4] prove the existence of providence. Finally he accuses Epicurus of atheism and repeats the Stoic charge that he "drew shadows of the gods" in order to deceive the Athenian people and avoid the fate of Socrates. [5] Evidently for Dionysius "nature" means primarily the natural process, the way in which things come into existence, and he identifies this with the providence of God.

In later Christian writings we find nothing new. Most writers insist with Origen and with Neoplatonists that God works effects beyond nature; others occasionally say that he can produce results contrary to nature, but the expression "contrary to nature" is usually reserved for human actions contrary to the moral law. [6] Discussions of the relation of God to nature are most frequently found in Christian writers when they are discussing creation or the possibility of resurrection. We shall see (chapter 2) that Basil of Caesarea often speaks of the laws of nature in his homilies on the Hexaemeron, and we may note that in his treatise on the Hexaemeron Gregory of Nyssa treats the mutability of nature in some detail, pointing out that although we can recognize the transmutation of the elements we cannot explain it. [7] A thoroughly theological treatment of nature is found in the writings of Augustine, but since he is primarily concerned with its miraculousness we shall discuss his analysis at a later point. [8]

---

[1] Eus. *Praep.* xiv. 23–27; cf. M. Pohlenz, *Die Stoa* (Göttingen, 1948) I 431. [2] *Gen. anim.* 789 b 22. [3] Cic. *Fin.* i. 19. [4] Cic. *N. D.* ii. 136–51; Pohlenz, *op. cit.*, II 99. [5] Cic. *N.D.* i. 85; other refs. in Mayor. [6] H. de Lubac, *Surnaturel* (Paris, 1946), 355–73. [7] PG 44, 108A, 109C–D. [8] Chapter 2, p. 27; chapter 13, p. 215.

The Greek idea of nature developed gradually over a long period of time. By the time Christianity arose, the idea had become somewhat stereotyped and was employed by philosophers whose contact with the study of nature was minimal. By many philosophers nature was identified with God. For Christians such an identification was impossible, and they therefore at least initiated a new approach to nature. Fresh observations and a thoroughly fresh approach, however, are not to be found in antiquity.

# LAWS OF NATURE

In pre-Socratic philosophy "nature" and "law" were ordinarily contrasted, and we therefore do not find the expression "laws of nature" among these writers. Heraclitus speaks of the "law of God" on which human laws depend (B 114) but not of natural law. The equivalent apparently used by Heraclitus was "necessity," in accordance with which everything takes place. [1] On the other hand, according to other doxographical information, Anaxagoras (along with Democritus and the Stoics) contrasted events which took place "by necessity" with those caused by fate, choice, chance, and spontaneity. [2] This analysis seems to reflect the influence of Aristotle rather than the thought of Anaxagoras.

Among the atomists we find the belief that the coming into being of the universe took place "according to a certain necessity", but as the doxography copied by Hippolytus states, Leucippus did not define "necessity". [3] Democritus held that the motion of the atoms takes place "according to necessity and by the (cosmic) whirl". [4] The "whirl" is said to come "from spontaneity and chance", [5] and Aristotle tells us that since Democritus was opposed to the idea of chance he introduced the idea of the "whirl". [6]

In the late fifth century we begin to hear of the "necessity of nature" even among the poets (e.g. Euripides, *Troad.* 886), who reflect the popular sophistic treatment of the results of the study of nature. [7] In the plays of Euripides we also find the old antithesis *nomos-physis* transcended, for he closely associates "law" and "nature" in two passages. [8] In Thucydides, too, we find the idea of a law, the eternal law of the right of might, which is derived from "necessary nature". [9] Thus the way is being prepared for the idea of the "law of nature".

[1] Diels–Kranz, *Vorsokr.* Heraclitus A 8; cf. A 5.  [2] Anaxagoras A 66.  [3] Leucippus A 1; A 10; cf. B 2.  [4] Democritus A 83 etc.  [5] *Ibid.* A 67.  [6] *Ibid.* A 68.  [7] Heinimann, *op. cit.*, 125–31.  [8] *Ibid.* 166–67 (*Bacch.* 890ff., *Ion* 642ff.).  [9] *Ibid.* 167 n. 7 (Thuc. v. 105. 2).

The earliest actual occurrence of the expression "law of nature" is ascribed to the sophist Callicles in the *Gorgias* of Plato, although we may observe that Gorgias himself distinguished events which took place "by the decrees of necessity" from those which happened "by the plans of chance" or "by the plans of the gods". [1] Plato is evidently aware of the strangeness of the expression, for he qualifies it by adding a particle (*kata nomon ge ton tēs physeōs*). It is a paradoxical phrase. Here, as in the passage from Thucydides we have already mentioned, it refers to the right of the stronger, a right which Plato elsewhere contrasts with nature and derives from human law. [2] In the *Timaeus* he uses the expression again; disease is "contrary to the laws of nature". [3] At this point he means by "laws of nature" the normal working of the body. In his writings, therefore, the term does not mean "law of nature" in the modern sense, or even in the later Hellenistic sense. It is simply a term used in the place of "nature." [4]

Similarly Aristotle seems to allude to laws of nature only once, when he states that Pythagoreans regard numerical relations as "laws" received from nature itself (*De caelo* i. 1, 268 a 13). He prefers "nature". But he criticizes the "physicists" for their explanation of events as due to "necessity"; they fail to understand the element of purpose in nature; they deal primarily with the material cause and do not realize that there are four causes, the material, formal, efficient, and final. [5]

Similarly Epicurus, who ordinarily rejects mythology, tells us that

> it would be better to follow the myth about the gods than to be a slave of the Fate of natural philosophers; for the myth gives some hope for one's relief through worship of the gods, but Fate contains inevitable necessity. [6]

In order to preserve human freedom Epicurus introduced the idea of a "swerve" into the atomic system. Necessity brought about the motions and meetings of atoms, but chance caused them to fall into the positions which create our world. [7] Unfortunately, as the Academic sceptic Carneades later pointed out, there is no evidence for the existence of this "swerve". [8] Epicurus also tried to avoid determinism by insisting on the multiplicity of causes of celestial phenomena.

[1] *Gorg.* 483 e; Diels–Kranz, *Vorsokr.* Gorgias B 17 (ii. 289 : 21). [2] *Protag.* 337 c–d. [3] *Tim.* 83 e. [4] Cf. A. E. Taylor, *A Commentary on Plato's Timaeus* (Oxford, 1928), 596; F. M. Cornford, *Plato's Cosmology* (London, 1937), 339. [5] *Phys.* ii. 7–9, 198 a 14–200 b 8. [6] D. L. x. 134 (see chapter 11). [7] C. Bailey, *Epicurus* (Oxford, 1926), 341. [8] Cic. *Fat.* 23.

No single explanation is necessarily correct; therefore we cannot be sure that there is such a thing as fate. [1]

On the other hand, the Peripatetic Strato rejected the atomic system and at the same time denied the teleological explanation of nature. He accepted only material causation and taught that the world originated spontaneously and now operates "in accordance with nature" by "natural weights and motions" (fr. 35, 32 Wehrli).

Strato's materialism, as we have said before, influenced only scientists, and a far more popular school was that founded by Zeno and continued by Cleanthes and Chrysippus. It is often said that the early Stoics created the conception of the "law of nature", but a careful examination of the evidence shows that this is not true. For the idea of the endless chain of causation, the "motor power of matter", Zeno and his followers used the word "fate". Sometimes they called this "nature" or "the common rational principle of nature". [2] They did not call it the "law of nature". When the Christian apologist Minucius Felix tells us that Zeno sometimes regarded the "natural law" as the first principle of everything, we must remember that he is simply transcribing a passage in which Cicero says that Zeno regarded the natural law as divine and as having power to command right actions and to forbid their opposites. [3] This is the only fragment of the early Stoics in which we find the expression "natural law". It is also the only example of the expression in Cicero's philosophical writings; he ordinarily uses the term "law of nature", always in the moral sense.

Thus in Zeno "natural law" is used not of the workings of physical nature but of the moral law. Does he actually use the expression or is it due to Cicero? We may doubt that Zeno actually used it because in the Stoic definition of law (SVF III 323) we find it called "a rational principle (*logos*) of nature, ordaining the things to be done and forbidding the things not to be done". [4] Cicero translates the beginning of this definition by the words *ratio insita in natura*. [5] We may suspect that this is the correct translation of Zeno's words.

In Cleanthes we do not find the expression "law of nature", although at the beginning of his famous hymn he addresses Zeus as

---

[1] D. L. x. 78–80, 87ff.  [2] SVF I 176, cf. II 945, 937.  [3] Min. Fel. *Oct.* 19: 10; Cic. *N. D.* i. 36 (SVF I 162) cf. Diels, *Dox.* 542.  [4] We may note that the first Christian use of this expression is in Ptolemaeus (G. Quispel, *Ptolémée Lettre à Flora* [Paris, 1949], 87–88).  [5] *Leg.* i. 18.

"leader of nature, governing all things by law" (SVF I 537). This comes close to the idea of the physical law of nature, although in the Hellenistic period the expression "law of nature" was employed almost exclusively in the moral sense. We find it in Theophrastus and Ocellus Lucanus, as well as in Dionysius of Halicarnassus and Dio Chrysostom. [1] Seneca twice inserts the expression into a paraphrase of Epicurean teaching, although what seems to be a more original text makes no mention of it. [2]

Since the moral law of nature was regarded as governing everything in the universe, we might expect to find the physical laws of nature called by this name; but, as we have said, the Stoics preferred to use the word "fate" or to speak of "nature" or "the common rational principle of nature." Following Aristotle, Chrysippus taught that nothing at all takes place contrary to "universal nature" or its rational principle (SVF II 937). And it was the common teaching of Stoics and Academics that "things which are contrary to nature do not take place but seem to take place" (938).

A difficult fragment of Posidonius tells us that "first is Zeus, second is nature, third is fate". [3] Cicero elaborates this to some extent by saying that the whole power and rational principle of divination is to be sought "first from God, . . . then from fate, then from nature". [4] According to Reinhardt, the fragment means that "Zeus (or providence) and Physis serve him as two categories for the expression of the same original principle". [5] For Posidonius the identity of the world and God is expressed as the identity of nature and spirit, primal cause and will. [6]

Other commentators, including Reinhardt himself in his later *Kosmos und Sympathie*, regard the passage as showing that Posidonius regards Zeus as superior to nature. [7]

We should probably conclude that Posidonius himself regarded God as the ground of nature and the physical law of nature, which as a Stoic he called fate. [8] God is omnipotent (chapter 9) because fate is omnipotent, not because God is really above nature. After all, Posidonius said that "the being of God is the whole cosmos", [9] and

[1] Theophr. fr. 152 Wimmer; Ocellus Lucanus 49, 23 : 8 Harder; Dion. Hal. iii. 11. 3; Dio Chrys. *Or.* lxxx. 5. [2] Sen. *Ep.* 4 : 10, 27 : 9 (fr. 477 Usener; cf. fr. 200). [3] Diels, *Dox.* 324 a 4. [4] Cic. *Div.* i. 125. [5] K. Reinhardt, *Poseidonios* (Munich, 1921), 124–25. [6] *Ibid.*, 125 n. 1. [7] L. Edelstein in *AJP* 57 (1936), 304–5. [8] Cf. A. Schmekel, *Die Philosophie der mittleren Stoa* (Berlin, 1892), 244. [9] D. L. vii. 148.

defined God as "an intelligent fiery spirit, having no form but changing into whatever it wishes and assimilated to everything." [1] This doctrine does not really express transcendence.

On the other hand, later writers who separated God from nature could interpret Posidonius as if for him God and nature were quite distinct, and they were thus enabled to use his ideas to confirm their own.

The earliest examples of "laws of nature" in the physical sense seem to occur in the writings of Philo of Alexandria. Most of the "laws of nature" to which he refers are moral laws which have their primary source in God who is the creator of nature. In a certain sense all Philo's exegetical work is an attempt to prove that the law given to Moses is the highest expression of the universal law of nature. Thus he tells us that God's command to "increase and multiply" is a "law of nature" (*Praem.* 108). So is the requirement to worship God (*Post.* 185). Whatever is "suitable" is in accordance with the law of nature (*Sobr.* 25).

Pythagorean mathematics is also related to this law, for "according to the law of nature" the number six is the most noble of numbers (*Opif.* 13). Similarly disorder in the universe is "contrary to nature" (*Aet.* 32). The kind of physical disorder which Philo discusses is biological. By the law of nature only similar animals can be united (*Spec.* iv. 204). The coming into being of such an animal as the Minotaur was thus "contrary to nature" (*Spec.* iii. 47)—if there was such an animal. The story of the Myrmidons, created from seeds cast in the earth, is a mythical fiction, for the laws of nature, immovable bonds, do not permit anything to be produced full grown (*Aet.* 57—59). [2] The order of the world is not only mundane but also cosmic. Everything in heaven and earth is governed by immutable laws, whose existence Philo proves by the order of the universe (*Spec.* iv. 232). [3] At the same time he denies that fate and necessity are the causes of all events (*Heres* 300–1). [4] The God of the Old Testament has reserved freedom for himself, and can miraculously intervene in the course of nature. [5] Here Philo may find philosophical support in the thought of Posidonius. The few explanations of miracles Philo gives, as we shall later see, seem to reflect the ideas of this Stoic philosopher.

[1] Diels, *Dox.* 302 b 22.  [2] Aristotle (*Phys.* ii. 8, 199 b 7) had criticized a similar theory of Empedocles in the same way.  [3] Cf. W. Quandt, *Orphei hymni* (Berlin, 1941), 45 (hymn 64 : 3–4).  [4] H. A. Wolfson, *Philo* I 325–47.  [5] *Ibid.*, 348.

In early Christian writers the "law of nature" is exclusively moral. Justin speaks of sexual immorality as "contrary to the law of nature"; similarly Athenagoras uses the expression to describe the natural morality of animals. [1] Clement of Alexandria describes the law of nature as derived from God, and at one point argues that Chrysippus' definition of natural law comes from the Old Testament. [2] On the other hand, when Christian writers touch upon physical "laws of nature" they are exceedingly sceptical. With the sceptical rhetorician Lucian, Tatian asks how he can believe anyone who calls the sun a mass and the moon an earth. [3] To make such an affirmation would be to "legislate one's own dogmas". Similarly Tertullian militantly attacks philosophers who preserve nothing for divine freedom but make their opinions "laws of nature". [4] His attack is like that of Alexander of Aphrodisias, who criticizes the Stoics' definition of chance as due to the peculiar signification they give the word by "legislating." [5] These writers retain the old mistrust of *nomos* as contrasted with *physis*, or of philosophers' self-assurance.

An exception to the general rule is found in the *Octavius* of Minucius Felix. This apology, largely based on the treatise of Cicero *De natura deorum*, first sets forth a sceptical pagan attack on Christianity and then presents a philosophical defence. The idea of natural law is stressed in the attack but the same idea is expressed in the defence. We must assume either that the idea means so much to Minucius that he must express it throughout his work, or that it is a convention of rhetorical opposition to providence and defence of it. [6] The latter assumption is more probable.

What Minucius (or rather his Stoic rhetorical sources) means by "law of nature" is order or the rational principle of order in the universe (17 : 7, 9). Such a law makes the shore confine the sea (17 : 9). According to the pagan opponent of Christian eschatology, it is impossible for "the eternal order established by the divine laws of nature" to be overturned, or for "the compact of all the elements" to be dissolved (11 : 1). Minucius seems to be expressing the idea of the eternity of the natural order from two points of view, the Stoic and the Epicurean (as in 34 : 2–3). The idea that the natural law

---

[1] Just. *Ap.* ii. 2. 4; Ath. *Leg.* 3 : 1.    [2] Clem. *Str.* i. 182. 1, iii. 72. 3, i. 166. 5 (Pohlenz, *Die Stoa* I 418).    [3] Tat. *Or.* 27; Luc. *Icaromen.* 7.    [4] *An.* ii. 2; he contrasts divine power with „natural laws" (*Res. carn.* 42).    [5] *Fat.* 8, p. 174 : 3.
[6] Cf. G. Quispel in *Latomus* 10 (1951), 163–69.

is eternal and divine is his own interpretation of the philosophy of Zeno, as we have seen. The "compact of all the elements" is his phrasing of the Epicurean "compact of nature." [1]

When he argues from a Christian viewpoint (34), Minucius opposes other natural laws to the law of order. Every philosopher knows that what has a beginning must have an end. The Stoics themselves hold that there will be a cosmic conflagration; so do the Epicureans; and Plato teaches that if the "creator" of the world wishes, he can let it be destroyed. Similarly the order of days, seasons and years shows that there can be a resurrection. Here Minucius has simply taken over the Stoic examples which favor a cosmic renewal and has applied them to the Christian hope to show how natural it is (see chapter 15). It is in conformity with the order of nature or—he could have said—natural law.

In later times most of the "laws of nature" are moral laws. Epictetus speaks of the "law of nature and of God" that the better is always superior to the worse. [2] He also mentions the "measures and rules of nature" which provide men with knowledge of the truth, which is the moral law. [3]

Where the Stoics had identified natural and divine law, as they identified nature and God, the Neoplatonists separated God from nature and therefore distinguished the law of God from the law of nature.

In the philosophy of Plotinus there are three causes which bring about events. They are (1) the will of the gods, (2) "natural necessity", and (3) human additions to these causes. [4] The highest law is composed of seminal principles which are the causes of all beings. Some men live in accordance with this law, "which embraces all beings", while others submit to fate or natural necessity. [5] The difference between the work of nature and that of man lies in the fact that nature uses matter and gives form to it, while men use levers and other mechanisms. [6]

For Plotinus, then, the law of nature and the law of the gods are not the same; the law of the gods is above that of nature, for events contrary to the seminal principles in nature can take place. [7]

Plotinus' disciple Porphyry discusses the same subject in his *Letter to Marcella*. [8] He informs his wife that there are three kinds of laws:

---

[1] Lucr. i. 586 (cf. v. 57).   [2] *Diss.* i. 29. 19.   [3] *Ibid.*, ii. 20. 21.   [4] *Enn.* iv. 4. 39.   [5] *Ibid.*, iv. 3. 15.   [6] *Ibid.*, iii. 8. 2.   [7] *Ibid.*, iv. 4. 39.   [8] *Marcell.* 25–27; cf. *Abst.* i. 28, 106 : 20 Nauck.

(1) the law of God, (2) the law of "mortal nature", and (3) the legislation of nations and cities. Like earlier Greek writers he regards the third as conventional. The most important kinds are the first two, both of which were ordained by God. The difference between them is that the law of God cannot be broken, for there is no power above it, while the law of nature, which animals obey, [1] can be broken by "love of the body". This law defines the measures of the body's needs and while showing what needs are necessary condemns what is vainly and uselessly pursued. [2] This idea of natural law, as Usener has pointed out, [3] is Epicurean. To it Porphyry adds the idea that one must pass from the law of nature to the law of God. [4]

Similarly Porphyry's follower Iamblichus tells us that God is greater than nature and independent of it. [5] The mass of mankind is governed by nature and fate, but the few who use the power of mind separate themselves from nature and become more powerful than the powers of nature. [6] They are able to perform miracles by powers which are in no respect human. [7]

Sharply contrasting with the Neoplatonic separation of God from nature and its laws is the more Stoic idea found in Basil of Caesarea. In his homilies on the Hexaemeron Basil states that since the voice of God created nature, he provided in it a law of nature which is also the law of God. [8] The several unwritten laws of nature are universal and apply to men as well as to animals and to inanimate nature. [9] Divorce, for example, is impossible because marriage is a "bond of nature". Basil explains his identification of a biblical command with natural law when he deals with Paul's injunction, "Parents, do not anger your children" (Eph. 4 : 6). He alludes to 1 Corinthians 11 : 14 ("does not nature itself teach . . .?") and concludes that "Paul proclaims nothing new, but confirms the bonds of nature". [10] Here natural law has become of primary importance, and it is not only moral but physical as well.

At the one point where Basil considers the problem of something "outside nature"—the virginal conception—he first speaks of the "foolishness of the preaching" (1 Cor. 1 : 21) but next adds that God

---

[1] *Abst.* iii. 15, 204 : 19. [2] *Marcell.* 25, 190 : 1. [3] H. Usener, *Epicurea* (Leipzig, 1887), lviii–lx. [4] *Marcell.* 27, 291 : 12. [5] *Myster.* iii. 17, 142 Parthey. [6] *Ibid.*, v. 18, 223. [7] *Ibid.*, iii. 4, 110; the example given is walking on burning coals; cf. T. Hopfner, *Über die Geheimlehren des Jamblichus* (Leipzig, 1922), 210. [8] *Hex.* iv. 2; cf. Epictetus, cited above. [9] *Hex.* viii. 4, vii. 5. [10] *Hex.* vii. 5, ix. 4.

has given many examples from nature to prove the credibility of miracles. [1] These examples are presumably in accordance with natural law, although Basil does not explicitly say so. Here we find Christian motives mixed with the older Stoic idea of the moral law of nature. The structure of Basil's thought at this point is Stoic. Only the examples are Christian.

A more Neoplatonic treatment of the relation of the law of God to that of nature is found in the fourth-century *Commentary on the Timaeus* by the Platonist Chalcidius, to some extent influenced by Christianity but more directly relying on Middle Platonic sources. [2] Chalcidius differentiates the works of God from those of nature and those of man who imitates nature. [3] He calls fate a "divine law", [4] but holds that "the beginning of the divine law, i.e. fate, is providence", [5] which in turn is the will of God. [6] In summarizing his doctrine he says that the highest and ineffable God is the origin of everything; then there is a second God, his providence, which gives the law; finally there is a third God, the "second mind and intelligence" of God, which is the custodian of the eternal law. Beneath these gods are the ministering powers, nature, fortune, chance, and the demons. [7]

In Chalcidius, as in the Neoplatonists, the law of God is not the same as the law of nature, although it is God who gives both laws. The works of nature are produced from seeds, as in the cases of plants and animals; similarly the works of God are produced from causes which are clear to divine providence though not to human understanding. [8] The teaching of Chalcidius helps prepare the way for Augustine's treatment of miracles in their relation to nature.

We shall discuss Augustine's idea of natural law in somewhat more detail when we consider his thought on the subject of miracles (chapter 13), for to him nature is itself miraculous. Here, however, we must point out the stress which he lays on physical laws of nature in his commentary *De Genesi ad litteram*. He is arguing that miracles are not really contrary to nature, for all nature is the work of God. In the creation God inserted "causal principles," which govern all

---

[1] *Hex.* viii. 6; the example he gives is parthenogenesis in vultures, which comes from Origen. See chapter 12. [2] Cf. W. Theiler, *Die Vorbereitung des Neoplatonismus* (Berlin, 1930), 49–50; A. Gercke in *Rhein. Mus.* 41 (1886), 270–81, compares Ps.–Plut. *Fat.* [3] *Comm.* 23. [4] *Ibid.*, 149, 175, 178. [5] *Ibid.*, 149. [6] *Ibid.*, 174. [7] *Ibid.*, 186; cf. Numenius, Test. 24 Leemans; also the gnostic Basilides: cf. G. Quispel in *Eranos–Jahrbuch* 16 (1948), 101–10. [8] *Ibid.*, 23.

subsequent events, whether miraculous to us or not. [1] The whole ordinary course of nature is governed by "natural laws"; the elements have definite forces and qualities which determine what can or cannot take place. [2] Within himself, however, God has further hidden causes, which result in miracles when he desires to produce them. [3]

Here Augustine is combining the Stoic view that *seminales rationes* are contained within nature and govern its course with the Neoplatonic teaching that these *rationes* are not in matter but in the soul of the universe. For Plotinus these causes did not lead to novelty but maintained the order of the world. For Augustine, on the other hand, they explain the relation of an omnipotent creator to his creation in which both order and miracle are found.[4] He cannot entirely follow the Stoics, for in their thought God was identified with the world and did not transcend it. [5]

For Christian writers generally, "natural law" means *Naturrecht* rather than *Naturgesetz*. We have seen, however, that Hellenistic Jewish and Christian theologians accepted and developed the idea of physical laws of nature, always insisting at the same time on the freedom of God. The laws they accept have philosophical rather than scientific meaning, and were taken by theologians from philosophers. There was a considerable distance from "laws of nature" to scientific study of nature.

---

[1] *Gen. ad litt.* vi. 14, 18.  [2] *Ibid.*, ix. 17.  [3] *Ibid.*, ix. 18.  [4] J. Wytzes in *ZNW* 39 (1940), 150–51.  [5] *Gen. ad litt.* vi. 15–16.

# MATTER AND MOTION

In previous chapters we have discussed the idea of nature and natural laws. We turn now to examine some of the ways in which nature was regarded as working. This problem involves the question of causation and its analysis in Greek philosophy. How many causes are there? How do they operate? After we have discussed this question we shall turn to the "material cause" and ask the question whether the universe had any origin. Did matter come into existence?

For Greek philosophers the order of the universe was maintained by laws of nature, whether or not they were called laws. The principle of order is what some of the pre-Socratics called "necessity". In Plato there are two "causes", God and necessity (*Tim.* 68 e); in a certain sense necessity is opposed to the good (*Theaet.* 176 a) and is related to the disordered mythical "matter" shaped by the Demiurge in the *Timaeus.* Plato criticized such a physicist as Anaxagoras for his emphasis on physical causes (*Phaedo* 97 c). Since Plato sharply contrasts "being" with "becoming" he has little interest in the processes of nature. Soul is the cause of all change and motion (*Leg.* 896 b). [1]

On the other hand, Aristotle develops the thought of the earlier teleologist Diogenes of Apollonia [2] and finds purpose in nature. He ascribes to nature the characteristics of Plato's world-soul, [3] and says that "nature does nothing without purpose" or that "God and nature do nothing without purpose". [4] Nature "makes what is best out of the things which are possible". [5] Like Plato he argues that the physicist must not explain natural processes only by physical causes. [6] The difference between Plato and Aristotle is that Plato did not extensively analyze the question of causation, while Aristotle care-

---

[1] Cf. J. B. Skemp, *The Theory of Motion in Plato's Later Dialogues* (Cambridge, 1942), 108–15.  [2] W. Theiler, *Zur Geschichte der teleologischen Naturbetrachtung bis auf Aristoteles* (Zürich, 1924), 7ff.  [3] *Ibid.* 84ff.  [4] *Gen. anim.* 739 b 20, 741 b 4, etc.; *Cael,* 271 a 33.  [5] *Cael.* 288 a 2, *Part. anim.* 687 a 16.  [6] *Phys.* 198 a 21, cf. 200 a 30.

fully differentiated four "causes". These were the material, the efficient, the formal, and the final cause. Without a material cause nothing can be made. The efficient cause brings the thing into being. The "form" is that which makes the thing distinctively itself. And the final cause is the purpose for which it comes into being.

At a later date in the eclectic Middle Academy the four causes of Aristotle were combined with the ideal patterns of Plato, and a scheme of five causes was developed. This scheme, which Theiler [1] calls a "Metaphysik der Präpositionen", is reflected in Seneca, who lists the causes as *id ex quo, id a quo, id in quo, id ad quod,* and *id propter quod.* [2] We are not concerned so much with these developments, however, as with the questions of matter and teleology, the material and the final causes.

The necessity of a material cause was not in Aristotle's day a novel idea. He tells us himself that all the physicists held the doctrine that "nothing can come into existence out of what does not exist". [3] The axiom had been formulated by Parmenides (B 8–9), whose pupil Melissus reiterated it (B 1) and added that the universe is always the same; what was originally, is and will be. [4] Epicurus repeats both statements. Nothing comes into existence out of the non-existent; [5] and "nothing new happens in the universe, if you consider the infinite time past". [6] The cyclical theory of history of the older Stoics involved the exact repetition of previous events. [7] Other Greek philosophers argue that for the universe either to come into being or to decay would result in a contradiction, for it would imply either that something could come into existence out of nothing or that something could come into non-existence from existence. [8] Plutarch criticizes Epicurus' idea of an atomic "swerve" by calling it "causeless motion out of the non-existent". [9] While the Stoics did not regard matter as a cause, they followed Aristotle in stressing its importance. Matter exists eternally as a passive substance on which the one cause, the

---

[1] W. Theiler, *Die Vorbereitung des Neuplatonismus* (Berlin, 1930), 33; from Antiochus 37–38; from Arius Didymus, R. E. Witt, *Albinus and the History of Middle Platonism* (Cambridge, 1937), 75–76. [2] Sen. *Ep.* 65 : 8; cf. Galen, p. 13. [3] *Phys.* 18 a 27, *Metaph.* 984 a 31, etc. [4] Diels–Kranz (i. 276) reject this fragment but v. Blumenthal (*RE* XVIII 2, 2455) refutes their argument. [5] D. L. x. 38 (Lucr. i. 150). [6] Fr. 266 Usener (cf. Lucr. iii. 856). [7] SVF II 625–27. [8] E. g., Metrodorus of Chios in Plut. *Str.* 11, p. 582 : 18 Diels; Boethus (SVF III, p. 265); Ocellus Lucanus 12, p. 13 : 21 Harder. [9] *An. procr.* 6, 1015 c.

efficient, works. [1] They criticized Peripatetics and Platonists for introducing a "multitude of causes". [2]

The extent to which ancient writers regarded matter as essential may be seen in the fact that the mythical disordered "secondary matter" of the *Timaeus* was generally taken to be the material with which the Platonic demiurge worked. [3]

The existence or non-existence of a final cause was a matter of much more controversy. Theophrastus, who agrees with his teacher Aristotle that "nature does nothing without purpose" [4], actually gives examples of apparently purposeless natural phenomena. [5] Theophrastus' successor Strato absolutely rejects teleology. When he says that "the universe is not an animal", [6] he is suggesting that Aristotle took a principle of biology and made it the key to the physical universe. He himself holds with the older physicists that everything takes place "by natural weights and motions". [7] He refuses to accept Aristotle's formal or final causes. [8] Strato's views, however, were not widely accepted. In the second century of our era the Peripatetic Alexander of Aphrodisias tells us that the teleological principle is held by practically all philosophers. [9] We have already seen (chapter 1) the extent to which it is developed by Galen. Nothing is worse for a physicist, Cicero says, than to say that anything can happen without a cause. [10] The cause he has in mind is the final one.

Even the second-century sceptic Sextus Empiricus argues in favor of a teleological cause of some sort. If there were no cause, everything would be produced spontaneously and by chance. [11]

> Horses, for instance, might be born of flies, and elephants of ants; and there would have been severe rains in Egyptian Thebes, while the southern districts would have had no rain.

"Chance" is a cause which Hellenistic philosophers preferred not to discuss. It had been employed as a principle of explanation by the atomists, including Epicurus and Strato. Sometimes it had had religious overtones, and had been defined as "a cause unclear to human understanding, something divine and superhuman". Aristotle rejected this definition and spoke of it as "an incidental cause which interferes

---

[1] SVF II 299–301, 303–28, 336–56. [2] Sen. *Ep.* 65 : 11. [3] C. Bäumker, *Das Problem der Materie in der griechischen Philosophie* (Münster, 1890), 142–44. [4] *C. pl.* i. 1. [5] Theiler, *Geschichte* 102; Theophr. *Met.* 9, pp. 30–34 Ross–Fobes. [6] Fr. 35 Wehrli. [7] Fr. 32. [8] Fr. 72. [9] *De fato* 11 : SVF II 1140. [10] *Fin.* i. 19; parallels in Reid *ad loc.* [11] *Pyrrh.* iii. 18; cf. Lucr. i. 159–68.

with our willed actions". [1] The Stoics, on the other hand, simply dropped the religious meaning and held that it was "a cause unclear to human understanding". [2] In any event, as Greene notes, "chance is excluded from serious consideration". [3] Thus Sextus believes that the Epicurean "law of nature" (*seminibus certis quaeque creantur* [4]) is confirmed by empirical phenomena. Chance does not really exist.

We now have two "laws of nature" which were widely accepted in antiquity. The first is related to the material cause of Aristotle. Nothing comes into existence out of what does not exist. The second is an expression of his final cause. Nature does nothing without purpose. From the first was inferred the eternity of matter, which we shall presently discuss. From the second was inferred the regularity of natural processes. Along with a few simple maxims such as "like attracts like" or "unlike repels unlike" (sympathy and antipathy) they served as the base of popular scientific philosophy.

Let us look more closely at Sextus' example of the regularity of nature. It is old: Aristotle had spoken of the natural way in which a man reproduces a man while a bed does not reproduce a bed. [5] To be sure, monstrosities can come into existence, but they are not really contrary to nature. But what of spontaneous generation? Belief in this form of generation was universal in antiquity, [6] and Aristotle does not question its possibility. At one point he asserts that it can take place because matter is set in motion by itself. [7] To say this is to give up three out of the four causes, and also to accept the idea that matter is full of self-moved soul, an idea rejected in his treatise *De anima*. [8] At another point Aristotle says that

> animals and plants are formed in the earth and in the water because in earth water is present and in water *pneuma* is present, and in all *pneuma* soul-heat is present, so that in a way all things are full of soul. [9]

Again we seem to be contradicting the treatise *De anima*, where the only kind of soul which animals and plants have in common is "a kind of soul principle"—the vegetative soul. [10] How could this produce animals? What has happened to the formal and final causes?

We now turn back to Sextus. While he asserts that animals reproduce

---

[1] *Phys.* 196 b 5, 197 a 5.  [2] SVF II 965–67.  [3] *Moira* (Cambridge, 1944), 340. [4] Lucr. i. 169.  [5] *Phys.* 193 b 8, 11.  [6] E. S. McCartney in *TAPA* 51 (1920), 101–15.  [7] *Met.* 1034 b 15.  [8] *An.* 406 a 3.  [9] *Gen. anim.* 762 a 18.  [10] *An.* 411 b 28. We must admit that there is an unbroken sequence between plants and animals in *Part. anim.* 681 a 10.

only their own species he also accepts spontaneous generation. [1] Gnats come from putrid water, ants from sour wine, grasshoppers from earth, frogs from marsh, and worms from mud—not to mention bees from bulls and wasps from horses. We may ask why, if these things are so, horses cannot be born of flies and elephants of ants. Some Stoics (and others) believed that the earliest men came from "spermatic principles" in the ground. [2] Even Aristotle had suggested that *if* men were earthborn, they probably developed from larvae spontaneously generated. [3] Where is the scheme of four causes?

The only possibility of progress from this impasse lay in a principle mentioned but not stressed by Aristotle himself. [4] Speaking of the generation of bees, he says,

> The facts have not been sufficiently ascertained; and if at any future time they are ascertained, then credence must be given to the direct evidence of the senses more than to theories, — and to theories too, provided that the results which they show agree with what is observed.

Such stress on empirical observation was relatively rare in antiquity, partly because of the lack of interest in techniques and in mechanical aids to observation. As scholars have often pointed out, the ancients possessed neither the telescope nor the microscope. Moreover, the logical problems created by inferences from examples seemed insurmountable. The study of anatomy was not advanced by the alliance of medicine with philosophy. And Bickermann notes the great objection to observation brought forward in the late Hellenistic age. [5] "The empirical and positivistic approach led at best to a rather uncertain probability . . . . Mathematics alone offered reliable and certain knowledge." It was simpler to argue on general principles than to examine the evidence.

We now turn back to the question of the eternity of matter, for it was a problem which greatly concerned both Greek philosophers and Christian theologians. In discussing the subject, Stoic philosophers looked back to Homer for justification of their theories; but in Homer, we find no doctrine of the origin of the universe. Isolated passages were sometimes quoted to show that Homer did set forth such a doctrine; actually the question does not seem to have entered his mind. It was claimed, with a very slight degree of probability, that

[1] *Pyrrh.* i. 41.  [2] SVF II 739.  [3] *Gen. anim.* 762 b 28.  [4] *Gen. anim.* 760 b 0.3
[5] *AJP* 68 (1947), 447.

3

he taught Thales the doctrine of water as primal substance; did he not speak of "Ocean, origin of the gods" (*Iliad* xiv. 201)?

Stoic writers used allegorical interpretation in order to extract their views from Homer. Thus in the *Quaestiones homericae* of a certain Heraclitus we find two passages used to explain the origin of the universe. The first is Homer's description of the shield of Achilles (*Iliad* xviii. 473). Hephaestus, who made it, is fire; the gold and silver of the spherical shield mean ether and air (*Q. H.* 43). The second is the story of Proteus (*Odyss.* iv. 384). His transformations mean that formless matter turns into ether, then earth, then air, then water. His daughter Eidothea is really Providence. She derives her name from the forms (*eidè*) which she gave to matter (*Q. H.* 65–67).

All these interpretations reflect the problems of later philosophers and have nothing to do with Homer himself. The question of the origin of matter simply did not arise in his time. He was no philosopher or theologian, even though writers in the Hellenistic age thought he was. [1]

Similarly Hesiod fails to raise the question which so greatly interested later writers. He describes the gradual development of the universe. "First Chaos came to be, then Earth . . ." (*Theogony* 116). But he does not ask where Chaos came from (as early Christian writers and sceptics observed). [2]

Werner Jaeger points out that [3]

> Hesiod, who thinks in terms of genealogies, even Chaos came into being. He does not say, 'In the beginning was Chaos', but, 'First Chaos came to be, and then the earth', & c. Here the question arises whether there must not have been a beginning . . . of becoming — something that has not itself become. Hesiod leaves this question unanswered; indeed he never goes so far as to raise it.

The search of the Milesian naturalists for an "elemental principle" is an attempt to answer this question, but within the sphere of "nature" itself. For them there can be no "absolute initiative". Similarly, while Xenophanes speaks of God as omnipotent, he does not regard him as the creator ex nihilo. [4]

> But effortlessly he sets all things astir
> By the power of his mind alone.

[1] F. Wehrli, *Zur Geschichte der allegorischen Deutung Homers im Altertum* (Basel, 1928). [2] Theoph. *Ad Autol.* ii. 6; Sext. Emp. *Adv. math.* x. 18. [3] *The Theology of the Early Greek Philosophers* (Oxford, 1947), 14. [4] B. 25 (Jaeger, p. 45); cf. B. 29: „All things that come into being and grow are earth and water".

Similarly the Orphic theogony parodied by Aristophanes (*Aves* 696) mentions Chaos and Night as the origin of all coming-to-be; their own coming into existence is not mentioned. In the theogony of Epimenides Air and Night were "in the beginning". Both theogonies are based on Hesiod. In the sixth century, Pherecydes speaks of three primal forces. [1]

> Zeus and Chronos and Chthonié always existed.

As Jaeger points out, "this is a correction of Hesiod, who had said that even Chaos had come into being". [2] With this new correction we are prepared for Parmenides' stress on the eternity of the existent, and for Heraclitus' emphatic statement:

> This cosmos, the same for all, was made by neither a god nor a man; but it always has been and is and will be fire ever-living, kindling itself in measures, and quenching itself in measures.

This fragment is preserved for us by Clement of Alexandria. [3] The teaching contained in it was profoundly influential upon the minds of the founders of the Stoa. Cleanthes wrote four books of exegeses of Heraclitus (Diog. Laert. vii. 174), and Clement observes, after quoting this fragment, that the most notable Stoics held the same view of the place of fire in the universe (cf. SVF II 590) as Heraclitus.

Let us pass on to Plato. In the *Timaeus*, the cosmological handbook of all later antiquity, he gives us a picture of the work of God in fashioning the cosmos. It cannot be stated too emphatically that the material world had no beginning in time. This is the way in which Plato's successors understood him. Aristotle tells us [4] that in the Academy they stated that the universe did not ever really come into existence. And this is clearly implied by statements in the *Timaeus* itself.

> The god took over all that is visible—not at rest, but in discordant and unordered motion—and brought it from disorder into order, since he judged that order was in every way the better (*Tim.* 30 a, tr. Cornford).

God produced an intelligible and unchanging model for "creation",

---

[1] D. L. i. 119; cf. Max. Tyr. *Diss.* iv. 4, 45 : 5 Hobein.   [2] Jaeger, *op. cit.*, 67.
[3] *Strom.* v. 104. 2.   [4] *De caelo* 279 b 33; F. M. Cornford, *Plato's Cosmology* (London, 1937), 26. According to Plutarch (*Anim. procr. in Tim.* 1013 b), Xenocrates, Crantor and others held that Plato knew that the world was uncreated but described it as created for didactic purposes.

and impressed a copy of this model on a "receptacle". The receptacle is the mass of plastic material, or rather something comparable to a mass of plastic material—for Plato is using mythological language—on which the ideas were impressed. The chaotic state of the receptacle "before" it was brought into order is described in *Timaeus* 52 d–53 c. It was watery and fiery and received the characters of earth and air, but was "everywhere swayed unevenly and shaken". The work of God was to bring order out of disorder, not to create.

The obscurities of Plato's language were dissipated by his pupil Aristotle. According to Cicero, in the third book *On Philosophy* he upsets many things in his dissent from Plato, for he sometimes ascribes divinity entirely to the mind, and sometimes declares that the world is God. [1] As Jaeger suggests, this doctrine and the disturbance caused by it must be primarily Aristotle's teaching on the eternity of the world. [2] We find it reflected more clearly in another fragment: [3]

> The world is uncreated and eternal; Aristotle imputes terrible atheism to those who disagree, who suppose that so great a visible God is no better than works made with hands. (The cosmos is) a pantheon including sun and moon and the rest of the planets and fixed stars. He says that formerly he feared for his house, lest it collapse through strong winds or violent storms or old age or careless construction, but now a greater danger was impending, if we believed those who destroyed the whole universe in their statements.

Jaeger observes that he is mild in his criticism of Plato's works "made with hands", but that he spares none of his physicist opponents in his attack on them. Nevertheless, he certainly does not accept Plato's vague account of the origin of the cosmos. It is eternal and never came into existence. The doxographers testify to this doctrine as one of the fundamental elements of Aristotle's thought. [4] We find it clearly expressed in another fragment of the *De philosophia*, [5] where it is stated that the universe never came into existence, because no new plan was ever devised for its beginning, and that it will never grow old and die. According to Aristotle's disciple Theophrastus, Plato did not mean to say that the world came into existence, but simply used the expression for the purpose of explaining his teaching, just as

[1] Cicero, *N. D.* i. 33 = R. Walzer, *Aristotelis dialogorum fragmenta* (Florence, 1934), 92, no. 26. [2] W. Jaeger, *Aristotle* (Oxford, 1934), 140. [3] [Pseudo?] Philo, *De aeternitate mundi* 10 = Walzer 81, no. 18. [4] Aëtius, *Plac.* ii. 5. 1 (p. 332 Diels); Hippolytus (*ibid.* 570 : 34). [5] Cic. *Luc.* 119 = Walzer 83, no. 20. Cf. *De caelo* 279 b 12ff.; 301 b 31.

one may use diagrams in teaching. [1] We have already seen that this was the view of the Platonic Academy.

Among the Stoics the eternity of matter was also upheld. According to the second-century Peripatetic Aristocles, Zeno derived his doctrine of two first principles, matter and God, from Plato. [2] In giving exegesis of the cosmogony of Hesiod, he held that the "chaos" of Hesiod was water, while the active principle Eros was fire. [3] But for him as for his predecessors and followers there was no real beginning in time. God is an eternal active principle; matter is an eternal passive principle. [4] Matter never increases or diminishes. [5] Exactly the same view of the subject is held by Cleanthes and Chrysippus. The "substance" of God is the cosmos, the matter which before all time he has shaped, according to Zeno, Chrysippus, and Posidonius. [6] Minority opinions among the Stoics made his substance of air or placed it in the sphere of the fixed stars; but these opinions did not contradict the eternity of matter. Panaetius seems to have denied that the cosmos ever came into being, and he certainly denied that it would ever perish. [7]

Therefore when we read in the *Placita* of Aëtius that "Pythagoras and Plato and the Stoics say that the cosmos was created (*geneton*) by God", [8] we must be careful not to read any doctrine of creation *ex nihilo* into the statement. The matter out of which the cosmos was formed never came into existence. Even Posidonius, who laid great stress on divine power (chapter 9), explicitly denied the possibility of *ex nihilo* creation. [9] For all the Stoics God is inseparable from matter. [10]

The Roman astrological poet Manilius was strongly influenced by Posidonius, and after asking the question whether the universe has always existed and always will exist, or whether there was a primeval chaos which gradually developed into a cosmos, he concludes that this will always remain a matter of debate. [11] His own opinion, however, is that the universe remains eternal, divine, and of similar form; it had no beginning and will have no end. [12]

A fragment of Cicero's third book on the nature of the gods [13]

---

[1] *Phys. opin.* fr. 11, p. 485 : 20 Diels.   [2] SVF I 98 (Eus. *Praep.* xv. 14. 1).   [3] SVF I 103–4.   [4] SVF I 85.   [5] SVF I 87.   [6] D. L. vii. 148.   [7] M. van Straaten, *Panétius* (Amsterdam, 1946), 69–72.   [8] *Plac.* ii. 4. 1 (p. 330 Diels) : SVF II 575.   [9] Ar. Did. *Epit.* 27, p. 462 : 14 Diels.   [10] SVF II 307–10.   [11] *Astron.* i. 122–26, 145.   [12] *Astron.* i. 211.   [13] Fr. 2: Lact. *Div. inst.* ii. 8. 10–11.

probably represents the attitude of the Middle Academy on this question. In it we read that it is probable that matter has a certain power of its own. Just as a carpenter does not make his own materials and an image-maker uses already existing wax, so divine providence must have had matter available for its use. Therefore matter was not made by God. We may compare a statement made by Antiochus, according to which there is a certain power in matter itself. Matter can be changed and receive qualities or lose them, but it is eternal. This power can be called God. [1]

Similar ideas are found in Plutarch. He quotes Heraclitus' statement that the universe was made neither by a god nor by a man, and explains it as an attempt to avoid the supposition, by those who did not know God, that some man made it. This is strange exegesis, but Plutarch is mentioning Heraclitus only to contrast his teaching with the superior wisdom of Plato, who "said and sang" that the universe was made by God. Nevertheless the substance and matter which he used to make the cosmos always existed. Plutarch emphatically states that the "creation" was not out of something non-existent, and compares it with the work of one who makes a house or cloak or statue. [2] Elsewhere he says that the cosmos consists of two first principles, a body and a soul. God did not make the body but shaped and formed it. [3] God could not make the corporeal out of the incorporeal. [4] Ex nihilo creation is contrary to the laws of the universe because it lacks a cause.[5]

Proof of the wide diffusion of this axiom is given by two lines of the satirist Persius: [6]

aegroti veteris meditantes somnia, gigni
de nihilo nihilum, in nihilum nil posse reverti.

In the Middle Platonism of the second century we find further exegesis of Plato. Like earlier Platonists, but unlike Plutarch, Albinus tells us that "when Plato speaks of the world as created, it is not to be thought that there was a time when the world did not exist". [7] On the other hand, in explaining the "receptacle" of the Timaeus he identifies it with matter, "moved in disorder and discord". [8] This

[1] Luc. 24–29; cf. Strato, fr. 33.  [2] An. procr. 1014 a–b.  [3] Quaest. plat. 1001 c.
[4] An. procr. 1014 b–c.  [5] Quaest. conv. viii. 9. 2; cf. P. Thévenaz, L'âme du monde, le devenir et la matière chez Plutarque (Neuchatel, 1938), 108–18.  [6] Sat. iii. 83–84.
[7] Eisag. 14, 169 : 26 Hermann.  [8] Ibid., 167 : 12; cf. Tim. 30 a.

would suggest that the world came into being in time. We know that in the Middle Academy there was a considerable measure of disagreement on this point. [1]

In the theological philosophy of the Neopythagorean Numenius matter is regarded as eternal; it was not created but since it was originally indeterminate it was limited by God. [2] For Plotinus matter has no real existence. In so far as it does exist, it has always been ordered, and the universe is therefore eternal. [3] Both Porphyry and Iamblichus reject the story of "creation" in the *Timaeus* as mythology. [4] Iamblichus speaks of a "pure and divine matter which comes into existence from the Father and Demiurge". [5] Finally, the fifth-century Neoplatonist Hierocles adopts the idea of *ex nihilo* creation and ascribes it to Plato. If matter had been independent and eternal, God should not have interfered with it and would have been wrong in altering it. [6] We know that Hierocles was closely related to such Christian philosophers as Aeneas of Gaza, and his adoption of *ex nihilo* creation must reflect their teaching. No other Greek philosopher accepted it.

The *Commentary on the Timaeus* by Chalcidius indicates the way in which Greek and Christian ideas of creation could confront each other. In a collection of the opinions of various philosophers he states that the Hebrews regard matter as coming into existence (*generatam*), and cites the *Hexapla* of Origen to prove his point. [7] He argues that the true interpretation of Genesis is that "heaven" means incorporeal nature, while "earth" means matter. [8] After a long discussion of philosophical opinions, however, he decides that the correct Platonic view is that such elements as fire, earth, water, and air can come into existence; but because "nothing can come into existence out of nothing" [9] the primal matter of which Plato speaks, without quality or quantity, did not come into existence. [10]

Elsewhere, relying on Origen, he describes the arguments of Christians. [11]

> They prove that matter was made, and made in such a way that it exists although it did not previously exist, because the material prepared for mortal

[1] Thévenaz, *op. cit.*, 103.  [2] Test. 30, p. 91 Leemans.  [3] *Enn.* iv. 3. 9, ii. 1. 1.  [4] C. Bäumker, *Das Problem der Materie in der griechischen Philosophie* (Münster, 1890), 144.  [5] *De myst.* v. 23, 232 Parthey.  [6] Photius, *Bibl. cod.* 251; cf. C. M. Walsh, *The Doctrine of Creation* (London, 1910), 95 n. 1.  [7] *Comm.* 274.  [8] *Ibid.*, 276.  [9] *Ibid.*, 311.  [10] *Ibid.*, 314.  [11] *Ibid.*, 276.

craftsmen is supplied by other craftsmen, and supplied for them by nature, and to nature by God; but no one prepared it for God since nothing is older than God.

When he insists that the incorporeal matter is the origin of things, and that nothing is older than it, [1] he must be copying his Middle Platonic sources without Christianizing them.

From this sketch of the operation of the material and final causes, and from the Greek emphasis on the eternity of matter, we can see that most of the ancient ideas concerning the workings of the world were based on general principles. As Cornford points out in his pamphlet *The Laws of Motion in Ancient Thought*, they were taken over from common sense without critical analysis. From such common-sense notions as "nothing comes into being out of the non-existent" or anthropomorphisms like "nature does nothing without purpose", an elaborate superstructure of theories was developed. Against these theories there was a fairly steady current of scepticism, but the basic notions were unquestioned.

The example of spontaneous generation, which we have already discussed, shows the way in which uncritical acceptance of authority led to further confusion. Only empirical observation could have led away from the tyranny of what were thought to be laws of nature, and toward laws of nature based on probabilities. But probability as a philosophical method was found only with Carneades and his immediate successors, and in the later Middle Academy it was supplanted by obedience to authority, especially that of Plato.

[1] *Ibid.*, 317.

# 4

## CREDIBILITY

The problem which confronted Greek scientists who considered spontaneous generation was one which other Greeks also had to face. This is the question of evidence and the credibility of evidence. The credulity of the Greeks and Romans has often been exaggerated in modern times, and we shall see that credulity not only varies from person to person and from group to group, but also has a cyclical history of its own like the fever chart of a sick man. Credulity in antiquity varied inversely with the health of science and directly with the vigor of religion. After the Ionian philosophies of nature reached Athens and were popularized by the sophists, credulity declined, increasing again with the collapse of the Athenian empire. It is at this point that we find Plato advocating compulsory belief. With the appearance of Aristotle and the rise of the Hellenistic kingdoms comes renewed criticism of mythology and emphasis on science and historical writing. When Greek philosophy reached Rome its critical spirit strongly affected intelligent Romans. Perhaps the least credulous period of antiquity was the late Hellenistic age. At the end of the first century B. C., however, the tide had already turned. Roman writers in the next century who are interested in science and critical of mythology are somewhat old-fashioned. Under the guidance of Platonists and Neoplatonists absolute credulity came into vogue. The first four centuries of our era are marked by stagnation in science, complete traditionalism in education, subjectivism in philosophy, and the gradual decay of the Roman empire. The only sciences which flourished outside Christianity were astrology and magic.

Let us begin at the beginning. There are miracles in Homer.[1] The gods constantly intervene in human affairs. Of Homer Ehnmark writes:[2]

> The supernatural was interwoven with the natural to such an extent that it appeared to him as a single context.

[1] Cf. E. Ehnmark, *Anthropomorphism and Miracle*, Uppsala Univ. Årsskr. 1939, no. 12; W. den Boer, „Het wonder bij Homeros", *Hermeneus* 16 (1944), 81–87.
[2] Ehnmark, *op. cit.*, 58.

The gods are described anthropomorphically, but the heroes are described theomorphically. The dividing line between gods and men is hard to fix.

In most cases in Homer there is no description of the way in which a miracle takes place; it simply happens and the result is noted. Sometimes, however, various magical devices are employed by the gods, and sometimes an intangible or subjective result is described in concrete terms. Again, in some cases the gods act in a perfectly natural way, although exercising power which is greater than that of men. But there is no trace of rationalism in Homer. As Ehnmark says, the "mixture of natural and supernatural elements makes it impossible to regard Homer as a rationalist". [1]

The only way to prove that Homer did not believe in the miracles he relates is to argue that the divine apparatus is a later addition to a story of events regarded originally as entirely natural. But for such additions there is no evidence, and it is difficult to imagine a setting in which a non-religious poem would have been written or would have found an audience. Ehnmark points out the way in which stories in the Old Testament similarly combine natural and supernatural factors. [2] "Occurrences in themselves natural are interpreted as the result of divine intervention."

At the same time, it must be admitted that the power of the gods is limited. We read in the *Odyssey* (x. 306) that the gods are able to do anything, but as Otto points out, this statement is not to be taken literally. [3] Over against the gods there stands the power of nature, which even the gods must respect (*Odyss.* iii. 228). This power expresses itself above all in death, which the gods cannot overcome.

With the rise of the Ionian philosophy of nature there comes implicit criticism of mythology. When Thales uses Babylonian methods in order to predict an eclipse in 585 B. C., the idea that the gods are directly responsible for such phenomena tends to be shaken. [4] Later in the sixth century Xenophanes explicitly criticizes mythology. In his thought, as Jaeger says, "the critical side of the new philosophical theology becomes fully conscious". [5] According to Xenophanes, Homer and Hesiod are responsible for the common errors

[1] *Ibid.*, 47.  [2] *Ibid.*, 59: Deut. 8 : 17–18, Ps. 44 : 3, Judges 7 : 22. Cf. chapter 9.
[3] W. F. Otto, *Die Götter Griechenlands* (Bonn, 1929), 339–40; cf. W. Nestle, *Vom Mythos zum Logos* 26; see chapter 9.  [4] Nestle, *op. cit.*, 83.  [5] W. Jaeger, *The Theology of the Early Greek Philosophers* (Oxford, 1947), 46.

of mythology. The gods as they described them are immoral. He also attacks stories of Titans, Giants, and Centaurs as "fictions" (B 1, 11, 12). He denies that gods can be born. Finally he explains the myths of anthropomorphic gods as invented by men in their own image. If cattle and horses had hands, they would make images of cattle-gods and horse-gods (B 14, 15). God is not anthropomorphic: "in neither his form nor his thought is he like mortals" (B 23). [1]

Such criticism was widespread in the sixth century; we find it expressed by both Heraclitus (B 104, 57) and Pythagoras, [2] as well as implied by other writers. It apparently did not have much effect on the thought of ordinary Greeks, for we do not hear of reactions against the criticism or the critics. On the other hand, in the fifth century the popularization of scientific ideas through the Sophists led to the decree of Diopeithes at Athens in 433–32. This decree forbade disbelief in the gods or teaching concerning the heavenly bodies. [3] It was directed against Anaxagoras, a member of the circle around Pericles, who not only had explained the cause of eclipses to his friend but also had taught that the sun was a red-hot stone. [4] Anaxagoras was probably fined and banished from Athens. He fled to Lampsacus, where he was greatly revered. There he died several years later. [5]

Within a few years Diogenes of Apollonia was probably in danger of arrest, but the case did not come to court. [6] On the other hand, about 416 the Sophist Protagoras was tried for disbelief in the gods and teaching on meteorology. He escaped in a small boat bound for Sicily but was drowned before reaching his refuge. At Athens his books were burned. [7] Within two years the poet and philosopher Diagoras was accused of atheism and of divulging the Eleusinian mysteries. He was fortunate enough to escape to Pellene, a city allied with Sparta, just before war broke out between Athens and Sparta. The Athenians placed a price on his head: one talent for his corpse, two talents if he were alive. [8] In 399 Socrates was put to death for disbelief in the gods and for his earlier scientific teaching. [9] Later in the fourth century accusations were brought against Demades, who

[1] Note that these fragments are preserved by Clement of Alexandria (*Str.* v. 109). [2] Nestle, *op. cit.*, 97f., 108. [3] Plut. *Per.* 32. [4] D. L. ii. 12. [5] E. Derenne, *Les procès d'impiété intentés aux philosophes à Athènes aux Vme et IVme siècles avant J.-C.* (Paris, 1930), 41. [6] *Ibid.*, 42–43. [7] *Ibid.*, 45–55; D. L. ix. 55, 52. [8] *Ibid.*, 57–70. [9] *Ibid.*, 71–184.

had favored the deification of Alexander, as well as against Aristotle, Theophrastus, Stilpon, and Theodore of Cyrene. Demades was fined; Aristotle escaped to Chalcis; Theophrastus was acquitted; and Stilpon and Theodore were banished. Finally the law of Sophocles in 307 forbade philosophical teaching by anyone not licensed by the state, but a year later the law was repealed. There had been more than a century of religious tyranny at Athens. After this time only the Stoic Cleanthes could imagine invoking legal prosecution against philosophical opinions with which he disagreed. [1]

We must observe that there are two significant aspects to such trials. In the first place, they did nothing to suppress the opinions against which they were directed. In the second place, there were many writers who were never accused although their views were strikingly similar to those of the martyrs. The second fact suggests that the working of the law was somewhat capricious and that political considerations (especially in the case of Anaxagoras) were important. Outside Athens early in the fifth century the historian Hecataeus of Miletus begins his *Genealogies* with the avowal that

> I write these as they seem to me to be true, for the stories of the Greeks are many and ridiculous, I think. [2]

Hecataeus therefore proceeds to rationalize the stories of mythology. [3] Was Cerberus brought up from Hades? On the contrary, he may have been a large snake in Boeotia which by killing men compelled them to go down to Hades. [4] Did Heracles go to the end of the world? He probably visited the west coast of Greece. [5]

Similarly the Sophists and their disciples developed theories to explain (away) the stories of the gods. Prodicus tells us that the ancients regarded as a god anything which was useful to man; thus they called wine Dionysus, bread Demeter, water Poseidon, and fire Hephaestus. [6] The philosopher Democritus teaches that unusual natural phenomena aroused belief in the gods. [7] The tyrant Critias argues that the gods were invented by a wise man to ensure the stability of the state. [8] Apparently only those who investigated the

---

[1] Aristarchus of Samos; Plut. *Fac.* 923 a.   [2] Fr. la Jacoby.   [3] Cf. F. Wipprecht, *Zur Entwicklung der rationalistischen Mythendeutung bei den Griechen* (Tübingen, 1902–8); P. Decharme, *La critique des traditions religieuses chez les grecs* (Paris, 1904).   [4] Fr. 27. [5] Fr. 26.   [6] B 5; cf. Jaeger, *op. cit.*, 172–90.   [7] A 75.   [8] B 25; cf. Nestle, *op. cit.*, 413–20.

heavenly bodies were themaelves "investigated"; others could teach without being disturbed.

The sceptical rationalistic view is also reflected in some of the ideas of Plato, although he is torn between rejection of mythology because of its falsity and acceptance of it because of its social utility. The Platonic Socrates is represented (*Phaedrus* 229 d) as regarding rationalistic explanations without enthusiasm.

> I think that these explanations are pleasant, but they are the task of a clever and laborious and not very fortunate man, who will have to go on to rectify the form of Centaurs and of the Chimaera; and there will flow in a crowd of Gorgons and Pegasuses and other impossible beings, and many other incredible marvels. If he does not believe them and tries to make each one probable, using some kind of crude wisdom, he will need much leisure time.

The simplest way to deal with mythology is to exclude it from the education of the élite. It is harmful to the young, for it brings in false ideas of the gods and of ethical behavior (*Rep.* 377 a–395 e).

At the same time Plato believes with the legislators of fifth-century Athens (although without the faith they probably had) that the rulers of the state may tell lies for the public good (*Rep.* 389 b). He gives as an example of a "royal lie" an old Phoenician tale which could not, perhaps, be made credible in more modern times (*Rep.* 414 b–c). What is this story? Plato tells it in the second book of the *Laws* (663 e), where he is discussing the way in which the legislator can make the young believe anything. It is the story of the Sidonian Cadmus and the armed men who sprang up after he had sown teeth in the ground. If this very improbable story is believed, it is certain that the legislator can make use of a "useful lie".

Plato's ambivalent attitude toward mythology is reflected in two further statements in the *Laws*. On the one hand, he rejects mythological stories, for they are ancient but neither useful nor true (886 b–e). On the other hand, he "hates and abhors" impious men who will not believe the myths which they have heard from their youth up (887 d). By the time Plato writes the *Laws* he is so devoted to the good of the state—which for him means government by the élite—that he wishes to enforce with heavy penalties belief in a mythology he himself rejects. [1]

[1] Cf. B. Farrington, *Science and Politics in the Ancient World* (London, 1946), 87–106. We need not here discuss Plato's own myths, on which cf. L. Edelstein in *Journ. Hist. Ideas* 10 (1949), 463–81; J. Bidez, *Eos ou Platon et l'orient* (Brussels, 1945).

The attitude of Aristotle is also ambiguous. Reiterating the idea of Plato that the beginning of philosophy is found in an attitude of wonder,[1] he says that in a certain way the lover of myth is a lover of wisdom (philosopher). Myth is full of things which arouse wonder; the person who wonders thinks he is ignorant; he who thinks he is ignorant desires knowledge; therefore the lover of myth is a lover of knowledge.[2] In so far as Aristotle accepts mythology, he does so on the ground that it preserves primitive traditions of primeval man, preserved only in tribal tradition. This theory too is Platonic, but Aristotle utilizes it to such an extent that, as Jaeger points out, "in the *Meteorologica* he argues from the mythical tradition to the prehistorical existence of the hypothesis of ether, which as a matter of fact was invented by himself".[3] He criticizes such myths as those of Cadmus and the Myrmidons as biologically impossible.[4] At the end of his life a pathetic fragment of a letter states that the more he is alone the more fond of myths (*philomythoteros*) he becomes.[5] This does not represent his attitude during the vigorous scientific researches of his maturity.

In his school we also find the rationalization of myths. Clearchus states in his *Erotica* that Helen was thought to be born from an egg because the upper part of a house used to be called an egg.[6] In his treatise *On Proverbs* he says that Cecrops, who instituted marriage at Athens, was called "two-sexed" because in the previous situation of indiscriminate mating men did not know who their fathers were.[7] Theophrastus also rationalizes myths. Prometheus gave philosophy to men—hence the myth about fire.[8]

Epicurus also rejected the stories of mythology, calling them "mythical fictions".[9] He explicitly criticized popular beliefs about the gods, as well as their mythological foundation in the writings of the poets.[10] By means of a knowledge of nature the philosopher can avoid mythology.[11] At the same time, as we have seen (chapter 2), Epicurus prefers even mythology to the "necessity" of Plato's astral theosophy. He recognizes that mythology can preserve human freedom in the face of a deterministic science.

Normally, however, Epicurus prefers the study of nature to mytho-

[1] *Theaet.* 155 d. [2] *Met.* 982 b 17. [3] W. Jaeger, *Aristotle* (Oxford, 1934), 137 (*Meteor.* 339 b 20). [4] *Phys.* 199 b 7. [5] Fr. 1582 b 14. [6] Fr. 35 Wehrli. [7] Fr. 73. [8] Fr. 50 Wimmer. [9] Fr. 391 Usener (Orig. *C. Cels.* viii. 45). [10] D. L. x. 123; Plut. *Mor.* 1087 a. [11] D. L. x. 87.

logy or marvel. He relied on the "clarity" of sense perception. [1]
Similarly in the early Stoa "clarity" was important. Zeno's disciple
Aristo is said to have argued with Arcesilaus, the founder of the
Middle Academy, who "withheld assent because of the contra-
dictions of arguments". [2] When Aristo saw a remarkable bull (or
cow) which was both male and female, he is said to have exclaimed,
"Alas! Arcesilaus has been given an argument against 'clarity' ".
Evidently "clarity" implies a faith in the regularity of natural pheno-
mena and disbelief in marvels.

Thus far we have discussed philosophical and scientific objections
to the stories of mythology. Similar, and more influential because
more widely diffused, objections are found in rhetoric. Aristotle
distinguishes between events which take place and those which might
take place and are merely probable. The probable is that which
generally takes place. It is the proper subject matter of poetry because
of its universality. For this reason poetry is more philosophical than
history, which deals with details of facts. [3] A metrical version of
Herodotus would still not be poetry. On the other hand, the incredible and the absurd should be excluded from poetry. [4] Later
grammarians, whom we shall later discuss, systematized Aristotle's
ideas and held that there were three kinds of content in poetry:
fiction (the probable), myth (the improbable), and history (the true).

A combination of rhetoric and a modicum of scientific information
is found in a popular text book of antiquity under the name of
Palaephatus. This little treatise, apparently influenced by Peripatetic
ideas, gives the substance of forty-five mythological stories and
explains them away as misunderstandings of historical events. [5]

Palaephatus begins with the case of Centaurs, which he rejects on
the grounds that the "natures" of horse and man cannot be united;
they do not eat similar foods, and the food of a horse cannot pass
through the mouth and throat of a man. Moreover, there are no
Centaurs nowadays. He criticizes the story of Pasiphae and the bull
on zoological grounds. If the story of Cadmus' sowing snakes' teeth
were true, men would do the same thing today. There is no such

[1] Cf. C. Bailey, *The Greek Atomists and Epicurus* (Oxford, 1928), 240; A.–J.
Festugière, *Épicure et ses dieux* (Paris, 1946), 86–88. [2] SVF I 346; D. L. vii. 162.
[3] *Poet.* ix. 1450 b 31; A. Rostagni, *Arte poetica di Orazio* (Turin, 1930), xlvii–xlix.
[4] Rostagni, *op. cit.*, lvi. [5] Cf. v. Blumenthal in *RE* XVIII 2, 2451–55; Nestle,
*op. cit.*, 148–52.

thing as a Sphinx with a body of a dog, the head and face of a girl, the wings of a bird, and the voice of a man. It is said that a fox ate the men Cadmus produced, but no other land animal can drag men away, and besides the fox is small and weak. Actaeon cannot have been eaten by his dogs, for the dog loves his master. Some say that Artemis changed him into a stag and the dogs killed the stag. To be sure, Artemis is able to do whatever she wishes (here we see a theological principle or, more probably, an ironical concession), but it is not true that a man turns into a stag or vice versa. The horses of Diomede did not eat men, for this animal eats grass and hay. These examples are all based primarily on the observations of natural history.

Other stories are rejected on the ground that they are self-contradictory, or that what they describe is impracticable, or impossible, or "silly". The resurrection of Glaucus, son of Minos, is denied because the story says Polyidos discovered the plant which raised Glaucus by watching snakes use it. It is impossible for a dead man or snake to be raised when no other animal is raised. The return of Alcestis is rejected because no one who dies can live again.

A large number of Palaephatus' criticisms is based simply on assertion. The man of experience will know without any demonstration that the story is false. He will be aware that things do not change, that he lives in a closed system whose limits are well known. If Hesiod says that the first men came from ash trees, the intelligent man will know that men do not come into existence from wood. Someone might argue that this first race of men has perished, and that at the present time the situation is different. Palaephatus replies that such an argument is nonsense. There never were iron or bronze ages. "Everything is always the same".

The method of Palaephatus is not new, but his work is important because it was so widely read and thus influenced later treatments of mythology. We find it reflected in Diodorus Siculus, whom we shall presently discuss, and we know that it was recommended by the first-century rhetorician Theon. It was also employed by some Christian opponents of mythology. [1]

Another and older method of treating the stories of mythology

---

[1] Julius Africanus, fr. 22, 28 Routh; Lact. *Div. inst.* i. 9. 8–9, 17–23; Jerome, *Chron.* pp. 50, 52, 53, 55, 56, 57, 62 Helm; Aug. *Civ. dei* xviii. 8, 13; Orosius, *Hist.* i. 12. 7, 13. 4 (from Jerome).

flourished in the Hellenistic age, especially among the Stoics. This is the method of allegorization, which presupposes the wisdom of the ancients and implies that when they wrote things which seem wrong to us they really meant to write down the opinions which we hold. If the stories about the gods in Homer are not allegories, Homer must be accused of impiety. Homer must not be accused of impiety. Therefore the stories are allegories. [1] Stoic writers therefore found natural science in the *Iliad* and ethical teaching in the *Odyssey*. Their starting point was their belief that the gods are not anthropomorphic.

The allegorical method has a long history, perhaps beginning in Orphism [2] but certainly expressed in the sixth century by Theagenes of Rhegium and reiterated in the fifth century by Anaxagoras' pupil Metrodorus of Lampsacus. [3] At first it was used to make sense of Homer's stories, but later it was used for finding ethics. Its flowering, as we have said, comes with Zeno, Cleanthes and Chrysippus, and in the later manuals such as those of Heraclitus and Cornutus. From philosophy it passed into rhetoric. Later it was employed lavishly by Philo and the Christian Alexandrians, as well as by Neoplatonist and gnostic writers.

The allegorical method is not an explicit criticism of wonder stories. It is possible, though rather difficult, to allegorize a story and at the same time believe its literal truth. The method can be used to express such criticism, however, and among those ancient writers who use it, it often does reflect disbelief in incredible tales.

On the other hand, one more method of dealing with stories of the gods clearly reflects scepticism. This is called Euhemerism after its pioneer Euhemerus, who wrote his *Sacred Scripture* at the end of the fourth century. He was in the service of one of the successors of Alexander, and was well acquainted with the deification of the Hellenistic kings. In his book he describes a journey which he made to the mythical island of Panchaea in the Indian Sea. A golden column in the temple of Zeus there revealed that the gods had been men who were great kings and conquerors, worshipped in gratitude for their benefactions. Naturally Euhemerus also rejected the "fictitious myths" of Homer, Hesiod, and Orpheus. His simple theory was sligthly developed by his younger contemporaries Mnaseas of Lycia and Leon of Pella (who wrote a letter supposed to be from the divine

---

[1] Pseudo-Heraclitus, *Quaest. Homer.* 1–2.    [2] Nestle, *op. cit.*, 129.    [3] K. Müller in *RE* Suppl. IV 16–20; J. H. Waszink in *RAC* I 283–93.

Alexander to his mother), and Euhemerus' own work was translated into Latin by the poet Ennius. [1] In Rome it was widely accepted, [2] and a large number of Christian writers later used the method to attack mythology. [3]

The attitude of Hellenistic historians toward wonder stories is even more subjective than the methods of analysis we have discussed. We must agree with Wilamowitz's remark: [4] "The ancients were even further from a genuine science of history than from a genuine science of nature". It was almost a convention of Greek historical writing to claim that one's predecessors (who are often one's sources) are uncritical and credulous, while one's own work is based on reliable reports. Here are some examples. The historian Theopompus wrote his *Philippica* in the fourth century B. C., including in the eighth book a collection of wonder stories. [5] Polybius in the second century regards him as credulous; so do Cicero, Strabo, and even Aelian. [6] On the other hand the rhetorical historian Dionysius of Halicarnassus praises his collection. [7] Again, the third-century historian Timaeus attacks the earlier Heraclides of Pontus for telling "paradoxical stories"; Heraclides even says that a man fell from the moon. [8] In turn Polybius criticizes Timaeus, saying that his writings are full of "low superstition and womanish marvel-telling". [9]

In the treatise *De mari erythraeo* of the second-century geographer Agatharchides we find a long digression on the subject of mythology. [10] In the course of it Agatharchides rejects as untrue stories, told by poets who prefer edification to truth, nearly all the ordinary stories of Greek mythology, beginning with Centaurs and going on to the story of Atlas and the foolish narratives about the gods. In only a few cases does he explain why the stories should be rejected; evidently he believes that any intelligent reader will spontaneously deny their truth. The exceptions are based on biology. Pasiphae would not have united with a bull, nor Tyro with a river. Leda would not have laid

---

[1] Fragments in Jacoby, *FGrHist* I 300–13; cf. *RE* VI 952–72. [2] T. S. Brown in *HTR* 39 (1946), 259–74. [3] Athenagoras, Theophilus, Minucius Felix, Tertullian, Arnobius, Lactantius, etc.; cf. the Hermetic *Asclepius* 37 (p. 247 Nock–Festugière). [4] *Greek Historical Writing* 4, cited by H. J. Cadbury, *The Making of Luke-Acts* (New York, 1927), 319. [5] Jacoby, *FGrHist* 115, F 64–76. [6] F 343, 381, T 26. [7] T 20, p. 530 : 27. [8] D. L. viii. 72. [9] Polyb. *Hist.* xii. 24. 5. [10] *Geog. gr. min.* i. 113–17; Agatharchides also criticized Jewish „superstition" (Josephus, *C. Ap.* i. 205–12). On his empiricism cf. E. Schwartz in *RE* I 739–41.

an egg. Men are not, "contrary to nature", born from the earth. And Atlas could not have held up the world and begotten daughters at the same time. The method and the content of Agatharchides is very similar to that of Palaephatus, but he does not give Palaephatus' explanations of the original meaning of the stories. His digression probably reflects the opinion of an ordinary intelligent man of the second century B. C.

In the second century the writing of history passed under the influence of Stoicism, which had just won the support of the Roman aristocracy. The Stoic teacher who achieved what Pohlenz calls the Hellenization of the Stoa was Panaetius of Rhodes. [1] His ideas of credibility not only reflect the attitude of the Roman circles in which he was prominent, but in turn influence historians who belong to these circles or admire them.

Panaetius either was agnostic on the subject of divination or actively rejected belief in it, and Cicero tells us that he was sceptical of the truth of responses of augurs, auspices, oracles, dreams, and the predictions of seers. [2] A late collection of philosophical opinions [3] says that he rejected the stories of the gods and called theology nonsense. This statement may be an exaggeration, but we probably possesss a proof of his rejection of mythology in a passage of Sextus Empiricus. [4] This passage states that the later Stoics (second-first centuries B. C.) could not regard the criterion of knowledge as simply an assured sense-impression; it had to be a sense-impression to which no objection could be made. These Stoics gave two examples from mythology. When Alcestis was brought back from the earth, her husband Admetus saw her; he had an assured sense-impression; but he did not believe. The reason for his disbelief was that she had died and he knew that a dead man does not rise again. Again, when Menelaus, returning from Troy with an imaginary Helen in his ship, saw the true Helen with Proteus, he did not believe this sense-impression because he already had the impression that he had left Helen in the ship. This was the objection. It is obvious that when we analyze mythology in this way we are well on our way toward scepticism.

In the same circle of the Roman aristocracy we find another Greek, the historian Polybius, who reflects and helps form their

[1] M. Pohlenz, *Die Stoa* (Göttingen, 1948), I 207; on Panaetius cf. M. van Straaten, *Panétius* (Amsterdam, 1946). [2] Van Straaten, *op. cit.*, 78–87. [3] Diels, *Dox.* 593 : 7. [4] *Adv. math.* vii. 253–57.

scepticism. He severely criticizes his predecessors. They are credulous.

> Those persons who from dulness or lack of experience or idleness can never take a clear view of the occasions or causes or connections of events are likely to give the gods and chance the credit for what is really effected by sagacity and far-seeing calculation (x. 5. 8).

On the other hand, Polybius admits that if we cannot possibly find out genuine causes of events or natural phenomena we may assign them to the gods (xxxvii. 9). Presumably some day the causes will be discovered. Polybius has a firm faith in science (see chapter 6, p. 83). Because of the progress of knowledge Polybius can be quite scornful on the subject of credulity. It is said that there are statues on which snow and rain never fall. The historian is "strongly opposed to such stories . . . which go not only beyond the observation of intelligent people but also beyond what is possible" (xvi. 12. 5–6). When Theopompus ventures to tell of bodies which cast no shadow even in bright light, Polybius says that his tale is characteristic of a distempered soul. To be sure, these stories help preserve the piety of the masses, and *somebody* must tell them; but Theopompus is too extravagant (xvi. 12. 7, 9). Polybius' ideal of genuine history entirely excludes gods and heroes.

Unfortunately he was so sceptical that, as his admirer Strabo observes (c. 24), he wholeheartedly accepted the theory of Euhemerus. On the other hand he denied the truth of the travel narrative of Pytheas of Marseilles, who had sailed to Britain and beyond. [1] And his theology is at base simply a substitution of chance for the old gods.

Panaetius' pupil Posidonius continued Polybius' history into the first century B. C. He also wrote on geographical and meteorological subjects, and was distinguished, as Strabo points out (c. 104), for his "Aristotelian" interest in explaining causes. The most famous example of this interest is his visit to Cadiz in order to observe the effect of the moon on the tides. [2] He was so convinced of the existence of cosmic "sympathy" that he accepted the astrology which was gaining favor in his day. [3]

His wide travels led him to a considerable measure of scepticism in regard to his predecessors in the writings of geography. Several of

[1] Cf. J. O. Thomson, *History of Ancient Geography* (Cambridge, 1948), 143–51. On Polybius' history cf. W. Siegfried, *Studien zur geschichtlichen Anschauung des Polybios* (Leipzig, 1928); I. Heinemann, *Poseidonios' metaphysische Schriften* I (Breslau, 1921), 18–26. [2] Strabo, c. 138. [3] Cicero in Aug. *Civ. dei* v. 2.

the fragments preserved by Strabo report his criticisms of Herodotus, Heraclides of Pontus, and even of Polybius. His own work was remarkably influential, and long sections from it are quoted, often withous acknowledgement, by Greek and Roman writers in the three centuriet after his death.

Long passages from Posidonius, and from many other writers, are preserved in the forty books of world history compiled by Diodorus Siculus in the middle of the first century B. C. He follows literary convention in contrasting mythology with history. Myths should be preserved, for even the fictional stories of Hades can lead men to piety and justice; but history, the prophetess of truth, the "mother city" of all philosophy, is even more valuable (i. 2. 2). He criticizes earlier historians for omitting myths, for great deeds were accomplished by the heroes and demigods and many other good men (iv. 1. 3–4). This idea is closely related to the extensive quotations from Euhemerus which he gives in his sixth book. In parts of the fourth book, [1] on the other hand, his sources employ the method of interpretation associated with Palaephatus. The myths are due to misunderstood events.

A clear statement on the credibility of mythology is given in the fourth book (iv. 8), where Diodorus is following the rhetorician Matris. Many people disbelieve the myths because of their antiquity and paradoxical character. When they compare the power ascribed to Heracles with the weakness of their contemporaries they do not believe what is written, because of the excessive greatness of his deeds. These readers wrongly seek an accuracy in mythology equal to that of history. In mythological histories we should not seek the truth too harshly. When we go to the theatre we expect mythological histories, even though we do not believe that there are such things as Centaurs composed of heterogeneous bodies or a triple-bodied Geryon.

Diodorus' scepticism about remarkable animals has its limits. In other words, he is employing several sources whose attitudes vary. In writing about Ethiopia in his third book he insists that one should not marvel at or disbelieve his stories about the country, since there are many more remarkable things which have taken place throughout the world and have been handed down "through true history". Again,

---

[1] Diod. Sic. iv. 47. 2–3, 70. 1, 76. 2, 77. 1–4. He states that because Asclepius performed marvelous cures he seemed to make the dead come back to life (iv. 71). Cf. E. Schwartz in *RE* V 674–75.

some people say they have seen snakes a hundred feet long; but one really should not question their stories when a snake thirty feet long was in the zoological collection of Ptolemy II. [1]

The principal value of Diodorus' anthology is the proof it provides in regard to a widespread attitude in the first century B. C. Almost everything in Diodorus comes from someone else, but it is he who has made the selection, and the result shows that it was customary in his time to question the reliability of strange stories of divine or semi-divine power. The value of the stories lies in their effect on the masses.

Another first-century writer who owes much to Posidonius is the geographer Strabo. He firmly rejects mythology and stories of miracles. In the introduction to his work (c. 19), perhaps following Posidonius directly, [2] he sets forth the theory of the political origin of mythology.

> Poets were not alone in giving currency to myths. Long before the poets, cities and their lawgivers had sanctioned them as a useful expedient. They had some insight into the emotional nature of the rational animal. Illiterate and uneducated men, they argued, are no better than children, and, like them, are fond of stories. When, through descriptive narratives or other forms of representational art, they learn how terrible are divine punishments and threats, they are deterred from their evil courses. No philosopher by means of a reasoned exhortation can move a crowd of women or any random mob to reverence, piety and faith. He needs to play upon their superstition also, and this cannot be done without myths and marvels. It was, then, as bugbears to scare the simple-minded that founders of states gave their sanction to these things. This is the function of mythology and it accordingly came to have its recognized place in the ancient plan of civil society as well as in the explanation of the nature of reality. [3]

Thus Strabo often explains mythological stories as based upon the misunderstanding of natural phenomena, and criticizes Homer's geography as well as Eratosthenes' attempts to vindicate its accuracy. [4] Homer, as the Stoics taught, wrote allegory rather than history. At the same time his geographical knowledge leads him to reject not only the history but also the theory of Euhemerus. There is no such island as Panchaea, where Euhemerus said he had found the inscriptions on which his theory was based. [5]

---

[1] Diod. Sic. iii. 36. 1, 37. 9.   [2] I. Heinemann, *Poseidonios' metaphysische Schriften* II (Breslau, 1928), 53–84.   [3] Tr. B. Farrington, *Greek Science* 2 (Penguin, 1949), 113–14.   [4] P. Decharme, *La critique des traditions religieuses chez les grecs* (Paris, 1904), 397–98.   [5] Strabo, c. 47.

While in Strabo we find natural science and a sceptical attitude toward mythology, his contemporary Dionysius of Halicarnassus was no scientist but a rhetorician. His ideal is beauty of style rather than exactness of fact, and his *Roman Antiquities* is essentially a work in praise of Rome. His abandonment of critical historiography is illustrated by the often repeated expression, "Let each person judge these matters as it pleases him". [1] He cannot, however, refrain from making some judgments, and he tries to steer a middle course between piety and scepticism. On the one hand, the masses are surely wrong when they take Greek myths literally and thus either despise the unfortunate gods or imitate their immorality. Romulus should be praised for rejecting Greek mythology. [2] On the other hand, Epicurean rejection of myth is too extreme, especially when applied to stories of the gods' favor toward Rome. [3]

> Those who profess atheist philosophies (if we must call them philosophies) ridicule all the epiphanies of the gods which have taken place among Greeks and barbarians, and arouse much laughter over the stories by ascribing them to human imposture, on the ground that none of the gods cares for any man. But those who do not reject divine concern for human affairs, but have studied much history and have concluded that they are favorable to the good and unfavorable to the wicked, will not suppose that these epiphanies are incredible.

Here we see a rhetorician recoiling from the ideal of "genuine history" as outlined in the school of Polybius and Posidonius and insisting on the importance of theological presuppositions. He claims that the presuppositions are in turn based on historical study. Ultimately his concern is not with theology but with the importance of divine guidance in Roman affairs. [4] He is trying to prove to his fellow Greeks that Roman power is not due to chance but to virtue, which the gods reward.

We cannot say that his concern for theological principles amounts to much when he actually investigates or rather retells stories from Roman history. He knows that Rhea Silvia became the mother of Romulus and Remus after bathing in the grove of Mars. He also knows three explanations of the fact. First, one of the girl's suitors was overcome with passion for her. Second, her uncle Amulius

[1] *Ant.* i. 48. 4, ii. 40. 3, 70. 5, iii. 35. 5; Josephus (p. 183) takes the phrase from him.
[2] *Ant.* ii. 18. 3–2. 1. [3] *Ant.* ii. 68. 2; cf. viii. 56. 1. [4] He accepts divination primarily because it is favored by Romans (ii. 6).

56

disguised himself as Mars. Third, an apparition of the god took place, accompanied by many portents such as thick darkness, and was shown to be divine when it predicted the birth of twins and disappeared upward in a cloud. Dionysius cannot quite accept the third explanation, but he cannot deny that a demon may have appeared to Rhea Silvia (i. 77). In describing the death of Romulus he clearly rejects the story of his ascension, and compares the portents said to accompany his death with those said to accompany his conception—"whether by some man or by a god" (ii. 56). He is very cautious in relating the story of Numa and the nymph Egeria, and after mentioning those who regard it as derived from similar Greek stories, protests briefly against overscrupulous investigation of such matters and passes on (ii. 60–61). He cannot really accept such stories.

When we turn from the Greeks to the Romans they so much admired, we find the writers of the first century B. C. exceedingly sceptical of wonder stories. In his scientific poem *De rerum natura*, Lucretius praises his master Epicurus for saving mankind from superstition, for he finally discovered what could come into existence and what could not (i. 75). Mortals need fear the gods no longer, for everything has its natural cause or causes. The gods do not dwell anywhere on earth, but are far removed from mankind and its troubles. In his sixth book Lucretius gives physical explanations of all sorts of phenomena in which divine power was thought to be active. The plague at Athens, with which the poem concludes, was not due to the gods but to nature. Lucretius' poem is the high water mark of the tide of scientific scepticism which was soon to recede, although even in the fourth century the Christian apologist Lactantius believed it needed refutation.

Cicero, who is said to have edited the poem of Lucretius, [1] can hardly be discovered apart from his sources. In his works on religion he relies largely on Panaetius, Posidonius, and the Academic Clitomachus. He represents the *pontifex maximus* as an Academic sceptic who denies the rationality of religion but insists on its value as tradition. The defender of Stoicism asserts that with the passage of time the untrue myths are fading away. No one believes in the Centaur or the Chimaera or in the stories of the underworld. [2] On the other hand, we must admit with van den Bruwaene that Cicero's

[1] Jerome, *Chron.* 149 Helm.  [2] *N. D.* ii. 5.

own religion may not be fully represented in his formal writings. It was a genuine, if somewhat anemic, piety. [1]

His contemporary Caesar speaks of fortune rather than of the gods and we find no wonder stories in his writings. [2] On the other hand, early in the first century of the empire the historian Livy includes so many miracles in his books that in the fourth century he was the principal source for the *Book of Prodigies* of Julius Obsequens. He accepts stories of portents because when he reads of them he is impressed by the wisdom of the ancients, who thought them worthy of attention (xliii. 13). Nevertheless, he is sufficiently influenced by the Polybian approach to history, to say nothing of the attitude of his cultivated readers, to assign the ascension of Romulus to the imagination of Proculus (i. 16. 5–8) and to regard the nymph of Numa as fiction (i. 19. 5).

The court poets of Augustus present us with a variety of attitudes. Vergil is devoted to the Augustan religious revival and represents the gods as actively participating in human affairs. The Fourth Eclogue depicts in glowing colors the return of the golden age, when peace and harmony will reign among men and animals. On the other hand, Ovid, whose poems are full of mythological allusions, does not really believe any of the stories he relates. In his *Tristia* (iv. 7. 11–20) he makes clear the fact that he rejects all the fabulous monsters of mythology. [3] Again, Horace seems to combine a scepticism tinged with Epicureanism with an enthusiasm for rural piety. All three poets, as well as Propertius, have been influenced by Lucretius, and all reflect an interest—a minor interest, to be sure—in questions of natural science. [4] This interest does not take them far into questions of credibility.

Roman poets also employed the literary device known as "the impossible" (*adynaton*) to an even greater extent than Greek poets had used it. They were accustomed to use it to show that something else was impossible, or to insist that something (usually love) would last as long as something else regarded as unchanging and un-

---

[1] *La théologie de Cicéron* (Louvain, 1937), 46–53.    [2] R. Lembert, *Der Wunderglaube bei Römern und Griechen* (Augsburg, 1905), 47–49.    [3] E. Dutoit, *Le thème de l'adynaton dans la poésie antique* (Paris, 1936), 108.    [4] Vergil, *Georg.* ii. 477ff., *Aen.* i. 742–46; Horace, *Ep.* i. 12. 15–20; Ovid, *Met.* xv. 69–74; Propertius, *Eleg.* iii. 5. 23–48. In the contemporary *Aetna* the fallacious inventions of poets are rejected (29–93) and a physical explanation of the volcano's activities is undertaken.

changeable. Canter and Dutoit [1] have listed these "impossibilities", which clearly reflect the idea of the unalterability of nature. The stars are always above the earth, and always shine; night always follows day, and the sun never changes its course; the seasons never vary in their order. Rivers never flow upstream, nor do they alter their courses which run to the sea. The characteristics of plants and animals always remain the same. Trees are not in the sea, nor are fish on land. No one can count drops of water or grains of sand, and no one can change the past.

A similar list is given in the *Metamorphoses* (i. 3) of Apuleius. Rivers cannot reverse their courses; the sea cannot be bound so that it is immovable; winds cannot expire; the course of the sun cannot be checked; the moon cannot drop foam on the earth; the stars cannot be pulled down; the day cannot be darkened; and the night cannot be held back.

The importance of such *adynata* lies in the fact that they reflect the semi-scientific common sense which conflicts with both religion and magic. We shall see when we discuss omnipotence (chapter 9) that these *adynata* are precisely the achievements ascribed either to God or to magicians. They are used by philosophical theologians like Porphyry to provide examples of what God cannot do.

It is worth pointing out with Lembert [2] that while Roman writers often speak of divine epiphanies and of meteorological and zoological "prodigies", there are no stories of wonder-workers in pre-Christian Rome. The one exception to this general statement is Tacitus' story [3] of Vespasian's healings at Alexandria, which, as Lembert says, is a "Greek-oriental" tale and is not pre-Christian.

Among the Roman historians of imperial times Suetonius is conspicuous for his tales of marvels related to the emperors; Tacitus is generally quite sceptical, but occasionally tells stories of miracles which he regards as genuine. The minor Roman historians, including the *scriptores historiae Augustae* in the fourth century, are almost completely uncritical.

When we turn from historians and poets to rhetoricians we find that literary analysis looks more scientific than simple opinion but actually is not. In general, rhetoricians classified narratives in

[1] H. V. Canter in *AJP* 51 (1930), 32–41; Dutoit, *op. cit.*, 167–73.  [2] R. Lembert, *Der Wunderglaube bei Römern und Griechen* (Augsburg, 1905), 40.  [3] *Hist.* iv. 81; cf. Suetonius, *Vesp.* 7.

three ways,—as myth (fable), fiction, or history. Myth is an account of events which did not and could not happen. Fiction is an account of events which could have happened but did not. And history is an account of events which in fact did happen. [1] In classifying a narrative, the rhetorician applied the method of refutation. This method is described by the Greek rhetorician Theon and by the Roman Quintilian. [2] Both writers observe that myth, fiction, and history are to be treated in the same way. The best example of the method in practice is Theon's discussion of Medea's murder of her children. [3] One can prove that the story is improbable (fiction) by using a six-barreled argument. (1) The *person* involved makes it unlikely: a mother would not harm her children. (2) The *action* is improbable: she would not kill. (3) The *place* is unsuitable: it was the city where the children's father lived. (4) The *time* is wrong: her former husband's power was much greater at Corinth than hers. (5) The *manner* in which she acted is questionable: she would have tried to conceal the act, and would not have used a sword since she was skilled in pharmacy. (6) The *cause* ascribed to the action is incredible: she would not kill her children when she was angry with her husband. The flatness and weakness of these six arguments is obvious, and the popularity of Euripidean psychology in antiquity [4] suggests that they were largely disregarded. Theon's appeal to Palaephatus [5] does not commend his judgement in matters of credibility.

Another rhetorician, Hermogenes, writing in the second century, discusses the use of myths in political addresses, and devotes a page to examples which show what myths are. [6] In the first place, they are stories of the gods which ascribe human passions to them. These stories tell of the gods' actions in regard to one another and to men, as well as of their loves, wars, friendships, begettings of offspring, meals, and other similar activities. In the second place, myths are paradoxical narratives about men or other animals. These myths include such stories as metamorphoses from human into animal form or from men into women or vice versa. They describe the existence of winged men and synthetic animals such as Centaurs. In the third

---

[1] R. Reitzenstein, *Hellenistische Wundererzählungen* (Leipzig, 1906), 90–94; A. Rostagni, *Arte poetica di Orazio* (Torino, (1930), lvi–lvii; P. de Lacy in *AJP* 69 (1948), 267–69. See the section on Origen, p. 198. [2] *Progym.* 6, 93–96 Spengel; *Inst.* ii. 4. 18–19. [3] P. 94 Spengel. [4] See p. 92 *infra.* [5] P. 96 Spengel. [6] *Rhet. de ideis* ii. 10, p. 407 Spengel, 391–92 Rabe.

place, there are myths which "exceed human nature". These are wonder stories about heroes which ascribe superhuman strength to them. Finally there are other impossible and incredible myths which depict inanimate objects as endowed with sense-perception and obeying the gods. Purely mythical are the stories which describe horses or other animals as speaking with human voices.

There is nothing new about Hermogenes' analysis, but it reflects the kind of teaching which the student of rhetoric received, a common-sense approach to mythology which would lead him to reject the miraculous as impossible or incredible. In defining myth, Hermogenes discusses only the animal fables of Aesop. [1] His attitude toward them determines what his attitude toward mythology in general is to be.

A significant passage from the second-century sceptic Sextus Empiricus deserves quotation because it reflects so adequately the feeling of futility resulting from grammatical studies of probability. [2]

> Since there exists no art which deals with things false and unreal, and the legends and fictions, which form the main subjects of the historical part with which grammar is concerned, are false and unreal, it will follow that there exists no art which deals with the historical part of grammar. Hence they deserve to be laughed at who assert that even if the subject-matter of history lacks method, yet the judging of it will be a matter of art, by means of which we ascertain what is falsely related and what truly. For, firstly, the Grammarians have not furnished us with a criterion of true history, so that we might determine when it is true and when false. In the next place, as the Grammarians have no history that is true, the criterion of truth is also non-existent; for when one man says that Odysseus was killed in ignorance by his son Telegonus, [3] and another that he breathed his last when a sea-gull dropped on his head the spike of a roach, [4] and yet another that he was transformed into a horse, [5] surely it is a hard task to try to discover the truth in such incoherent accounts. For we must establish first which of these dissentient narrators is telling the truth, and then inquire as to the facts; but when all relate what is improbable and false no opening is given for a technical criterion.

The difficulty of making historical judgments is still more apparent when Sextus himself gives an example of "things which are true and have happened" (*Adv. math.* i. 263). His example of a fact is "that Alexander died at Babylon through having been poisoned by plotters". But earlier in the second century Arrian (*Anab.* vii. 27) had rejected the story of Alexander's poisoning as false. [6]

[1] *Progymn.* 1, p. 3.   [2] *Adv. math.* i. 265–68 (tr. R. G. Bury).   [3] Cf. Hyginus, *Fab.* cxxvii. 2, p. 94 Rose.   [4] Cf. *Odyss.* xi. 134, the prediction of Tiresias.   [5] Cf. *Adv. math.* i. 264.   [6] Cf. J. H. Waszink on Tert. *An.* 50 : 3 (p. 522).

# 5
## CREDULITY

In the first century B. C. the foundations for the later revival of credulity were being laid. Perhaps one factor in this process was the concentration of power at Rome, combined with a decline in individual initiative as the republic gradually developed into the empire. In any event, we see in the first century an increase in interest in astrology, magic, and a credulous Pythagoreanism.

One prominent figure was the Neopythagorean Nigidius Figulus, who was devoted to astrology and to the occult. In his "scientific" works he paid special attention to the strange and paradoxical. Another was the Pythagorean magical writer Anaxilaus of Larissa, who was expelled from Rome in B. C. 28. He strongly influenced Pliny and is his source for much magical information. [1] At a later date his book on chemical magic was used by Christian writers to explain gnostic miracles.

The philosophical and scientific problems created by astrology could be solved by a judicious use of the principle of "sympathy" (see chapter 1). Magic was somewhat more difficult. It is defined by a rhetorical writer as "an art which goes against nature". [2] But Stoics agreed with Academics that what was contrary to nature merely seemed to take place, and they added that all magical art was excluded by this principle. [3] The Christian writer Minucius Felix reflects their views when he describes magical miracles as making the unreal seem to be and the real seem to disappear. He calls these miracles tricks. [4]

On the other hand, magicians were not troubled by criticism and continued to claim that they could control natural phenomena. They could do "whatever they wished". [5] Magicians were especially

[1] M. Wellmann, *Die Physika des Bolos Demokritos und der Magier Anaxilaos aus Larissa*, Abh. Berl. 1928, phil.-hist. Kl. nr. 7. [2] Pseudo-Quintilian, *Decl.* x. 15; T. Hopfner, *Griechisch-ägyptischer Offenbarungszauber* II (Leipzig, 1924), § 2. [3] SVF II 938. [4] *Oct.* 26 : 10; cf. Tert. *An.* 57. [5] A. S. Pease, *Publi Virgili Maronis Aeneidos IV* (Cambridge, 1935), 371, 401–3.

skilled in performing "impossibilities". The omnipotence which was being ascribed to the gods in this period was at the disposal of the magician (see chapter 9).

Among the Neopythagoreans there was a marked interest in the marvelous. In the first century B. C. we find Alexander Polyhistor writing not only a *Collection of Marvels* but also a treatise *On Pythagorean Symbols*. In the following century there are the wonderworker Apollonius of Tyana, later the subject of Philostratus' romance, and the romance of Antonius Diogenes, *Incredible Things Beyond Thule*, full of erroneous geography and miracles, including even a trip to the moon. We need not, as Chassang observes, suppose that Antonius Diogenes took his own work seriously; [1] but it is significant that the Neoplatonist Porphyry did so. [2] In the Neopythagorean communities the legendary figure of Pythagoras was revered and his magical-miraculous works were remembered. It was thought that a river spoke to him, that he was with his disciples both in Italy and in Sicily on the same day, that he moved a ship by remote control. He performed thousands of miracles "still more marvelous and more divine". He could predict earthquakes, drive away famines, check violent winds and the waves of rivers and seas. From him his disciples received these powers. [3]

Tales about Pythagoras' disciples are almost a stock feature of the popular literary form called paradoxography, a form which was especially prominent in the early imperial period. The earlier examples are relatively restrained, since they are based largely on Aristotle. [4] But interest in the marvelous could not be satisfied by stories of natural phenomena. [5]

As early as the second century B. C. a certain Apollonius devotes the first six chapters of his *Marvelous Stories* to the miraculous feats of divine men, although the rest of his materials as usual come from the Peripatetic school. In the second century of our era we find the stories more remarkable than ever. Phlegon's work *On Marvels* includes ghost stories, examples of hermaphrodites, stories of the discovery of huge bones, tales of monsters (human and other) and of quintuplets, myths about those who had fifty sons or daughters,

---

[1] A. Chassang, *Histoire du roman* (ed. 2, Paris, 1862), 380.  [2] *Pyth.* 13.  [3] Porph. *Pyth.* 27–29; Iamblichus, *Pyth.* 134–36.  [4] E.g. Pseudo-Aristotle, *On Marvelous Things Heard*; Antigonus of Carystus, *Paradoxical Narratives.*  [5] Cf. A. Westermann, *Paradoxographi* (Brunswick, 1839); K. Ziegler in *RE* XVIII 3, 1137–66.

stories of premature senescence, and finally narratives of Centaurs at Saune in Arabia. On a high mountain near Saune in Arabia the local king found a Centaur and sent it with other gifts to Egypt for the Roman emperor. Phlegon solves the problem of its diet by stating that it ate meat. Unfortunately it died because of the change of climate, and the prefect of Egypt had it embalmed and sent it to Rome, where it was on exhibit. It did not exactly resemble the Centaurs of the poets, but it was almost the same. If anyone doubts this story he can still see the embalmed Centaur in Rome. [1]

How were these stories taken by their readers?

Something of an answer to our question is provided by the second-century anthologist Aulus Gellius. [2] He was coming back from Greece to Italy, and when he landed at Brundisium he happened to see some books for sale. They were all Greek books full of marvels and myths, remarkable and incredible events, composed by ancient authors of no slight authority. Because they had been left outdoors and were in bad condition they were very cheap, and Gellius bought them at once. He then spent the next two nights going through them and making excerpts to use in his anthology. He found them full of stories of one-eyed men, dogheaded men, and other strange peoples in the distant east; but when he was transcribing such stories he became wearied by the task because there was nothing in them which was of value for ordinary life. However, he goes on to quote a tale about hermaphrodites from Pliny, for Pliny not only had reliable sources but witnessed a metamorphosis from female to male. [3] Gellius does not question the accuracy of the wonder-books but their moral value.

Elsewhere [4] Gellius criticizes Pliny for ascribing to Democritus a story about the chaemeleon, which can catch birds with ease and can produce lightning and thunder if burned. He is doubtful about the mechanical flying bird which the Pythagorean Archytas is said to have made; but since the philosopher Favorinus relates the story he feels that it ought to be accepted. Clearly his only principle of criticism is the authority of the story-teller.

Another second-century writer who apparently used such wonder-

---

[1] Pliny saw the same Centaur, preserved in honey (*N. H.* vii. 35). But according to the emperor Claudius it was born in Thessaly, not Arabia. For Stoics the Centaur was the stock example of the non-existent (A. S. Pease on Cic. *Div.* ii. 49). [2] *Noct. att.* ix. 4. [3] *N. H.* vii. 36, 34; note, however, that Gellius does not refer to c. 35, where the existence of the Centaur is attested. [4] *Noct. att.* x. 12.

books is Celsus, the opponent of Christianity, who compared some of these stories with the gospel narratives about Jesus. [1] Unfortunately we cannot tell whether he really considered them true or not. Origen argues that he did, but this argument is probably intended simply to discredit Celsus' questioning of the gospels. Origen himself regards the stories as fictitious.

In the *Natural History* of the elder Pliny (who was killed while trying to observe the eruption of Vesuvius in A. D. 79) we find a confusion between rational principles and credulous practice. His rational principles include his determination to accept only items on which his authorities agree (xxviii. 1); and although both Cicero and Varro had heard of a man who could see ships 135 miles away he rejects the story (vii. 85). Only Greek credulity, he says, could accept the story of men who became wolves for nine or ten years (viii. 34). But he himself argues in favor of miracles in Ethiopia and India (vii. 6-9, 21).

> Who believed in Ethiopians before seeing them? What is not miraculous when it first comes to our notice? How many things are judged impossible before they take place! The power and majesty of nature lacks credence at every point if you consider only its parts and not the whole.

On the other hand he himself does not accept all these stories, as he says (vii. 8).

Sometimes Pliny gives a rational explanation of what seems irrational. An Ethiopian tribe called "four-eyed" derives its name from its accurate aim with arrows (vi. 194). But Pliny's very next section tells of a king who had one eye on his forehead and of a tribe of dog-headed men. The lack of clarity in Augustine's view of nature owes much to Pliny. Aulus Gellius (*Noct. att.* ix. 4. 13) rightly compares him with the paradoxographi—even though Pliny tells us (praef. 12) that he intends to omit marvelous happenings. [2]

A century later the *Metamorphoses* of Apuleius, itself almost entirely fiction, discusses the question of credibility. Aristomenes (presumably named for the legendary figure) tells a story to which his companion objects: "Nothing is more fabulous than this fable, more absurd than this lie". Aristomenes replies that he thinks nothing impossible, that many ordinary events would be incredible to an ignorant hearer, and that stories have the power to amuse their audience (i. 20).

---

[1] Orig. *C. Cels.* iii. 26–33; Celsus, p. 90 Bader. [2] On Pliny's attitude cf. L. Thorndike, *A History of Magic and Experimental Science* I (New York, 1923), 50f.

Apuleius was accused of being a magician, and Abt has shown that there were good grounds for the charge. [1]

In the latter part of the first century we find the essayist and biographer Plutarch discussing many of the themes with which we are concerned. Plutarch is always moderate. His thought is rarely incisive. Moreover, his attitude toward theological problems changed over a period of time. His early work *On superstition* is in part derived from customary themes of the Epicurean school. [2] Later works attack both Epicureanism and Stoicism. The constant element in all his works is his enthusiasm for a course between two extremes.

In the treatise *On superstition* Plutarch distinguishes between the impious man who does not believe what he ought and the superstitious one who accepts a harmful opinion. Atheism is false opinion, while superstition is an emotion arising from error. [3] If any harm befalls the superstitious man, he ascribes its cause not to a human being or to fortune or to the occasion or to himself, but to God. The atheist does not believe in the existence of gods; the superstitious man does not wish to believe, but does so against his will because he is afraid to disbelieve. Plutarch recommends the course between atheism and superstition.

The same caution is expressed in his work *On the failure of oracles*, where he observes that all oracles are inspired and all religious rites favorably regarded by the gods. On the other hand, we should not suppose that God moves among these things or is present or takes part in them. [4] As we should expect, there is nothing original about this compromise; Cicero [5] expresses almost exactly the same thought. When Plutarch encounters unpleasant facts he glosses over them. He has to admit, in his comparison of Nicias and Crassus (v. 2), that both Nicias and Crassus perished, even though Nicias was devoted to divination while Crassus wholly neglected it. But he can offer a moralizing conclusion. "Failure from caution, going hand in hand with ancient and prevalent opinion, is more reasonable than lawlessness and obstinacy."

The same cautious opinion is elsewhere [6] used as a ground for accepting a story from Livy about an image which talked to the Roman

---

[1] A. Abt, *Die Apologie des Apuleius von Madaura and die antike Zauberei* (Giessen, 1908). [2] A. J. Festugière, *Épicure et ses dieux* (Paris, 1946), 77–80. [3] *Superst.* 2, 165 c; cf. P. J. Koets, *Deisidaimonia* (Purmerend, 1929), 68–83. [4] *Def. orac.* 13, 417 a. [5] *Harusp. resp.* 62; cf. Xen. *Mem.* iv. 3. 13· [6] *Camill.* vi. 3.

general Camillus. Livy himself had argued that some of the bystanders had spoken for the goddess Juno; others said that she herself had spoken. Other writers contended that the miracle actually happened and tried to prove it by parallel stories of sweating statues and the like. Here Plutarch argues that immoderate credulity leads to superstition and thence to neglect of the gods and contempt for religion. "Nothing too much."

As a follower of the Academic school, Plutarch does not actually believe in talking statues. In his *Life of Coriolanus* he says that a story about an image which spoke on two occasions "would have us believe what is difficult of belief and probably never happened". Statues can seem to sweat or to exude blood; this phenomenon could be caused by mold, and the divinity could use it for a sign. [1] Statues can seem to utter a sound; this could be caused by internal rupture. But articulate speech from an image is absolutely impracticable, for neither the human soul nor God can speak without a body. Suppose such a story is well attested. In this case, presumably "a feeling unlike sense-perception, arising in the imaginative part of the soul, gives rise to the impression as it does in dreams". [2]

Unfortunately Plutarch then proceeds to contradict himself. He begins by speaking of those who out of excessive love and friendship for God cannot reject stories of this sort, and hold that the marvel is a great aid to faith since God's power is greater than ours. He then adds his own opinion, confirmed by a quotation from Heraclitus, to the effect that God is unlike man in respect of his nature, movement, ability, and strength. Therefore his working of something we cannot achieve is not irrational. But Plutarch had just said that it *was* irrational, at least in the case of talking statues.

In his *Life of Pericles* Plutarch attempts to solve the problem by separating the spheres of science and religion. [3] After describing the way in which the philosopher Anaxagoras raised Pericles above superstition by explaining the physical causes of events such as eclipses, he goes on to point out that both the philosopher of nature and the seer can be right in their analyses. His distinction is based on Plato, as he elsewhere [4] states. "Plato found fault with old Anaxa-

---

[1] *Coriol.* xxxviii. 1–4; cf. Cic. *Div.* ii. 58.    [2] A similar theory is set forth by Athenagoras, *Leg.* 27.    [3] *Per.* vi. 3–4.    [4] *Def. orac.* 47–48; Plato, *Phaedo* 97 c. According to Plutarch, Plato combined the two sets of causes „first of the philosophers or more than any of them" because he ascribed the final and efficient causes to God and the material and formal to matter. „All becoming has two causes". Cf. *Timaeus* 68 e.

goras because he attached himself too much to physical causes and because . . . he dismissed the better causes or principles, the final and the efficient." Plutarch wishes to allow the event to be explained in both ways. The "naturalist" deals with the cause from which the event arose and the way in which it arose. The seer deals with its end or purpose and with its significance. Theologians may argue that to discover the cause of the event takes away its significance. To them Plutarch replies that such an argument denies meaning to all signs. Ringing gongs, fire signals, and shadows on sundials can be explained naturally, but the natural explanation does not take away their meaning in terms of purpose. [1]

We might find this argument relatively persuasive were it not for the problem it is intended to solve. A one-horned ram had been brought to Pericles, and the seer Lampon had explained to him that it meant that he would become master of Athens. Anaxagoras, on the other hand, had the skull cut in two and showed that the brain had not filled out its position, but had drawn together to a point like an egg at that particular spot in the entire cavity where the root of the horn began. A little later, however, Pericles did become master of Athens. Therefore Plutarch feels that he must argue that both the naturalist and the seer were right. Following the Aristotelian classification of causes (which had been taken over by Platonists in Plutarch's time [2]), he describes the causal relation between the one-horned ram and the career of Pericles. His analysis depends on the prior assumption that in matters of divination such a relation is causal; and not every school would have accepted this assumption. To many it would seem that Plutarch had confused cause with sign. [3]

We may compare Plutarch's analysis of this relation with the statement made by Posidonius, who was also interested in the relation between science and philosophy. Posidonius [4] contrasts the work of the "physicist" (the philosopher of nature) with that of the "astrologer" (the mathematical astronomer). The first deals with the question of causes while the second does not deal with causes sufficiently. The "physicist" must lay down the basic principles for the "astro-

[1] A similar statement is made by Basil of Caesarea, Hex. 1. 10, 10 D.   [2] Cf. R. E. Witt, Albinus and the History of Middle Platonism (Cambridge, 1937), 73–75.   [3] Cf. Cic. Div. i. 29, with Pease's note.   [4] Simplicius on Aristotle's Physics, Comm. graeca ed. Diels IX (1882), 291 : 21–292 : 31; text and commentary in L. Edelstein, AJP 57 (1936), 319–21. The statement is based on Arist. Phys. i i. 2, 193 b 22–194 a 12.

loger" to follow. When we compare this analysis with that of Plutarch we find that Plutarch has almost reversed Posidonius' view while claiming as usual to be doing justice to both sides. He wants to separate the spheres of science and religion, of theory and action, of physical causes and teleology, and ends by confusing them.

In Plutarch we find no solution for the problem of miracle. His caution in such matters does not reflect a naive piety but a genuine unwillingness to think through his difficulties. His middle ground, "nothing too much", is an indication that he cannot face the real contradiction between traditional religion and natural science and philosophy. He solves the contradiction for himself by disregarding it.

A similar attitude of caution is reflected in the *Anabasis of Alexander* by the second-century historian Arrian, a pupil of Epictetus. In his preface Arrian states that when his two principal sources agree, the result is "absolutely true"; when they disagree, he will give the account which seems more credible to him and more worth the telling. He omits paradoxical stories about India, reserving them for a separate work, [1] but relates the various fictions about Alexander's death for the sake of completeness. [2] He argues that Alexander's claim of divine origin was not a great fault unless he used it as a mere device in order to win support. [3]

His analysis of stories about gods or heroes who visited India shows the ambiguity of his attitude. Did Heracles reach India?

> I cannot state confidently; I rather incline to think that he did not, but rather that whatever difficulties men meet, they exaggerate so far as to relate a legend (μυθεύειν) that Heracles himself could not have overcome them.

Heracles is mentioned in the legend only to commend the story. [4] On the other hand, if one were to hold that Dionysus founded the city of Nysa, one would have to hold that he visited India. Such a visit is very dubious.

> Still, one must not be a precise critic of ancient legends about the divine. For things which are incredible to one who judges according to probabilities do not seem absolutely incredible when one introduces the divine element into the story. [5]

Such stories, we must conclude, are not really true, but they must be rejected with discretion.

[1] *Anab.* v. 4. 3.  [2] *Ibid.*, vii. 27.  [3] *Ibid.*, vii. 29. 3; cf. iv. 10. 2.  [4] *Ibid.*, iv. 28. 2.
[5] *Ibid.*, v. 1. 2.

A later Middle Platonist, Maximus of Tyre (c. 180), is equally confused. On the one hand, he expresses his belief in divine omnipotence and proves it by the story that Zeus once tripled the length of a night. [1] He states that in his own time Asclepius is working cures, and tells of sailors who heard and saw the god Dionysus, although other sailors only heard him. He himself has seen the Dioscuri, as well as Asclepius, "not in a dream", and Heracles, "a real appearance". [2] He believes firmly in the activity of demons. [3] On the other hand, the Dioscuri whom he saw were shining stars (this makes his testimony difficult to evaluate), and he rejects the poets' pictures of the gods, which are "credible because of their charm, but incredible because of their paradoxical nature". [4] Other stories from the paradoxographical literature are "difficult to believe", and therefore contain an allegorical meaning. [5]

The second-century rhetorician Aelius Aristides is even more religious. He lays much stress on the marvelous character of the cures which Asclepius worked for him. They are marvelous and divine largely because they contradict the prescriptions of doctors. Who, asks Aristides, could discover the reason for the commands of the god? For instance, he required the patient to jump into a river in midwinter. The author's conclusion is purely anti-rational. "Can one hesitate between obedience to a god and respect for human knowledge?" [6] He knows that the god Heracles is active in his own day. Great marvels are worked around Cadiz, and in Messene in Sicily there are cures of diseases and rescues from shipwreck. [7] His allegorization of the birth of Athena [8] is due to theological rather than critical interest.

Again, two second-century papyri reflect the vigor of miracle stories. The earlier, P. Oxy. xi. 1381, tells us that the author is recording miracles because of cures worked for him. He states that "the healing power of the god has spread to every place" (Aelius Aristides expresses a similar sentiment) [9] and adds that he is "going to proclaim his miracles, the great epiphanies of his power and the gifts of his benefactions" (lines 215-222). The later fragment, P. Oxy. xi. 1382,

---

[1] *Diss.* xxxviii. 6–7, 444–48 Hobein.  [2] *Diss.* ix. 7, 109–10.  [3] *Diss.* vii–ix.
[4] *Diss.* iv. 6, 46.  [5] *Diss.* x. 1, 111; xxxviii. 3, 440.  [6] *Or.* xlvii. 63, 391 Keil; cf. A. Boulanger, *Aelius Aristide et la sophistique dans la province d'Asie au ii⁰ siècle de notre ère* (Paris, 1923), 204–5; also C. Bonner in *HTR* 30 (1937), 124–31.  [7] *Or.* xl. 12, 327.  [8] *Or.* xxxvii. 2, 304.  [9] *Or.* xlii. 4, 335.

gives us the end of a miracle story "which is filed in the library of Mercurium"—perhaps a quarter of Alexandria—and concludes with the rubric, "Those who are present are to say, 'One Zeus Sarapis' ". Last of all comes the title: "The miracle of the great Zeus Helios Sarapis concerning the pilot Syrion". We know from Strabo (c. 801) that such stories of miracles were collected for the Serapeum at Canopus. Presumably the "library of Mercurium" also had its wonder section. [1]

An interesting example of increasing credulity is to be found in the work of the traveler and mythographer Pausanias. He tells us about his "conversion".

> When I began this work I used to look on these Greek stories as little better than foolishness; but now that I have got as far as Arcadia my opinion about them is this: I believe that the Greeks who were accounted wise spoke of old in riddles and not straight out, and accordingly I conjecture that this story about Kronos is a bit of Greek philosophy. In matters of religion I will follow tradition (viii. 8. 3, tr. J. G. Frazer).

Thus in the earlier part of his work he regards the metamorphosis of a bird into a man as incredible (i. 30. 3). It is unlikely that Lynceus was really so sharp-sighted that he could see through the trunk of an oak (iv. 2. 7). Such stories are the inventions of poets. The many heads of the hydra are due to the poetic license of Pisander (ii. 37. 4). The poets say that Heracles brought Cerberus up from Hades through a cave at Taenarum, but there is no road there leading underground through a cave, and in any case it is difficult to believe that the gods live underground. Hecataeus of Miletus gives a probable explanation: a snake lived there (iii. 25. 5). [2]

Even in the more sceptical part of his book Pausanias accepts some strange stories. At Taenarum there is a spring which, people say, formerly showed harbors and ships to those who looked in the water. They no longer appear, for a woman once washed dirty clothes in the spring (iii. 25. 8). The testimony of various people at Elis is almost strong enough to make Pausanias believe that at the Dionysiac festival water changes into wine (vi. 26. 2). [3] And he holds that metamorphoses, admittedly impossible now, could take place in the old days. Wickedness is prevalent now, and men no longer become gods. He adds the rhetorical commonplace that ancient stories, while

[1] On libraries and aretalogy cf. E. Peterson, $ΕΙΣ ΘΕΟΣ$ (Göttingen, 1926), 217–20.
[2] See p. 44.  [3] On this story see p. 179.

possessing a foundation of fact, are generally discredited because of the fictions which lovers of the marvelous have added (viii. 2. 5-7). At this point his "conversion" seems to have left his mind unclear.

The closest he comes to any theory of the marvelous is in his statement that scepticism sometimes arises because of the rarity of a natural phenomenon; but he adds that he can readily accept stories of winged snakes without having seen any, on the ground that a Phrygian once brought to Ionia a scorpion with wings (ix. 21. 6). Again, he cites a certain Cleon who used to say that men are sceptical of marvels which exceed what they have happened to observe. Cleon believed that tradition was correct in telling of Tityus and other monsters. He had once been at Cadiz and put to sea at the command of Heracles. On his return he and his fellows found cast ashore a man of the sea, 500 feet long, burning because it had been struck by the god's lightning (x. 4. 6). We may accept Frazer's explanation that this was a wooden effigy of Heracles, burned annually at his feast, and somewhat exaggerated in length; but Cleon and Pausanias clearly had no such idea. To them it was convincing proof of divine activity.

We must also consider the historian Dio Cassius, who about 195 began his historical work with a book on the dreams and signs which encouraged Septimius Severus to hope for the throne (*Hist. rom.* lxxii. 23). Upon receiving an encouraging letter from the emperor he himself had a dream in which his *daimonion* instructed him to write a history of the reign of Commodus. A further divine call impelled him to compose a history of Rome from the beginnings. This personal experience explains his acceptance of some stories of wonders, although he holds that many stories are due to idle talk and fear (xiv. 57. 7). Thus stories multiply. "Once any of these is believed, immediately the others receive credence." From his sources he takes over a political explanation of several old miracle stories (cf. p. 54), and he criticizes Hadrian for believing that the soul of his favorite Antinous had become a star (lxix. 11. 4). It is evident that this historian offers us no clear grounds of credibility in regard to miracles.

The only important exception to the credulity of second-century writers is the satirist Lucian of Samosata. In his *Lover of Lies* Lucian vigorously attacks the "deceivers of antiquity"—Herodotus, Ctesias (the author of the fantastic *Persica*), and the poets, including Homer. They tell such stories as those of the castration of Uranus (such stories were often under attack [1]), the bonds of the giants, the meta-morphoses of Zeus, and so on. These are "dreadful and portentous myths". [2] In opposition to stories of divine healings Lucian claims that those who tell them and defend them are reasoning from false premises; they "drive in a nail with a nail"; they cannot prove the presence of divine activity. [3] To this objection his opponents reply that disbelief in their stories implies disbelief in the gods. Lucian answers that on the contrary he worships the gods and takes note of their healings, which are actually effected by medicines and by physicians. Asclepius himself healed men in the same way. [4]

The conventional reply of the believer in miracles is given through the person of the Peripatetic (!) Cleodemus. Formerly he was more incredulous than Lucian and thought these things quite impossible. [5] Then he saw a barbarian stranger from the Hyperboreans who flew through the air in broad daylight and walked on water—with "ordinary shoes"—and through fire. He could also raise corpses which were already mouldy. [6] A physician then adds the story of a man raised from the dead after being buried for three weeks. [7] To these examples Lucian replies with an appeal to "the truth" and to "right reason". [8]

In his *True Stories* Lucian parodies the miracle stories and the geographical romances of his time. Conventional historians claim to have seen the events they describe or to have used reliable sources, as Lucian himself reminds us. [9] Here he states that he is writing "of things which he neither saw nor experienced nor inquired about from others, and things which neither exist nor in the nature of things can exist". [10] Included in his narrative are a navigable river of wine, a trip to the moon, a journey in a great fish, and a visit to the Isle of the Blessed. We are reminded of the *Incredible Things Beyond Thule* (see p. 62).

From what standpoint does Lucian write? In his *Life of Peregrinus* [11] he states that when he meets an honest man he tells him the truth, but for imbeciles eager for the marvelous he adds some dramatic detail, such as the earthquake at the moment Peregrinus threw

---

[1] Cf. A. D. Nock, *Sallustius Concerning the Gods and the Universe* (Cambridge, 1926), xlvi–xlvii. [2] *Philops.* 2. [3] *Ibid.*, 9. [4] *Ibid.*, 10. [5] *Ibid.*, 13; cf. Gal. 4 : 12, Theoph. *Aut.* i. 14, Ps.-Just. *Orat.* 5. [6] Abaris the disciple of Pythagoras; cf. Iamblichus, *Pyth.* 136. [7] *Philops.* 26; cf. Heraclides Ponticus on Empedocles; D. L. viii. 61. [8] *Ibid.*, 40. [9] *Quom. hist. conscr.* 29. [10] *Ver. hist.* i. 4. [11] *Peregr.* 39.

himself on a pyre. In his treatise on historiography he sharply distinguishes between history and poetry; only in the latter can you yoke winged horses or walk on water or through fire. [1] Lucian's criticism of wonder stories is primarily based on rhetoric. It is reinforced, however, by enthusiasm for Epicureanism. Of Alexander the prophet he notes that a Democritus, Epicurus or Metrodorus was needed to expose his tricks. [2] Epicureans were always opposed to this charlatan, who in turn had the *Kyriai Doxai* of Epicurus burned in the market place because it is opposed to portents, visions, and wonders. [3] Lucian attacks the followers of Plato, Chrysippus, and Pythagoras, who enjoyed "deep peace" with Alexander. [4]

With Lucian's use of rhetoric and philosophy against miracle stories must be mentioned his own sceptical and ironical personality. Caster [5] has pointed out the significance of this point. We must add that in the second century, Lucian was essentially one born out of due time.

At the end of the second century we find credulity widespread. It is nothing new. In earlier periods there were many writers who accepted fantastic stories as literally true. The credulity of the late second century, however, is a kind of "neo-credulity" which is all the more striking because it comes after a time of criticism when it seemed possible to deny the reality of the incredible on scientific grounds.

In the third century such an attitude is reflected in the philosophy of Plotinus, whose physics, as Bréhier [6] has observed, is really based on the reality of marvels. Plotinus believes firmly in magic, and explains its operations as due to the working of cosmic sympathy. [7] His aesthetic theory, finally realized in the Christian art of the middle ages, turns away from objectivity to the vision of the inner eye of the soul. [8]

When his disciple Porphyry attacks the miracle stories of the Christians, his grounds for doing so are exceedingly weak. He finds it incredible that two thousand swine should have run into the sea and perished, especially in a Jewish country; [9] but he cannot criticize the

---

[1] *Quom. hist. conscr.* 8.   [2] *Alex.* 17; cf. Orig. *C. Cels.* viii. 45; p. 199.   [3] *Alex.* 47; K. D. i. (D. L. x. 139) denies the activity of the gods.   [4] *Ibid.*, 25.   [5] M. Caster, *Lucien et la pensée religieuse de son temps* (Paris, 1937), 332–34.   [6] *La philosophie de Plotin* (Paris, 1928), xiii–xvi, 56–57.   [7] *Enn.* iv. 4. 40–42.   [8] A. Grabar in *Cahiers archéologiques* 1 (1945), 15–34.   [9] Fr. 49 Harnack.

exorcism of demons. He ridicules the story of Jesus' walking on water only on the ground that what the gospel calls a "sea" is really a lake. [1] What he did with other stories is indicated by two chapter headings discovered by Mercati. [2] "How it was said by Jesus, The girl is not dead but asleep." "How Lazarus, dead for four days, was raised from the dead." He must have argued that the girl was really asleep and that the resurrection of Lazarus was impossible because the body has no value (see p. 235). On the other hand, he accepts miracle stories about Pythagoras. [3]

The *Life of Apollonius of Tyana*, written by Philostratus in the third century, is a strange mixture of rationality and credulity. He claims that his information comes largely from a certain Damis, one of Apollonius' disciples. Whether this be the case or not—Eduard Schwartz called Damis "pure fiction"— [4] there is a certain difference between the sayings of Apollonius, often somewhat sceptical of marvels, and the stories about him which recount his miracles. This difference can be explained without source-criticism, for one of the principal purposes of Philostratus' work is to acquit Apollonius of the charge of magic brought against him. If Apollonius is represented as somewhat sceptical, his miracles will seem all the more probable!

Examples of this sceptical attitude are found in Apollonius' refusal in India to learn about the fakirs' tricks, his rejection of the Sardian story that the trees are older than the earth, his incredulity concerning paradoxical animals, his natural explanation of what some of his audience thought miraculous, his doubts (later eradicated by the fact) of the existence of a three-headed boy, and his attack on the stories of mythology. [5] Philostratus himself asks whether Apollonius really raised a girl from the dead or found some spark of life in her. [6]

These mild expressions of scepticism leave Philostratus free to describe the levitation of the Brahmans and their miraculous covering from rain and sun, as well as their production of springs at will. [7] He can describe a talking elm tree in Egypt, and the sobering of a satyr demon in Ethiopia. [8] And he can tell how Apollonius vanished from his trial before Domitian and later the same day appeared to

[1] Fr. 55. [2] G. Mercati, *Nuove note di letteratura biblica e cristiana* (Rome, 1941), 66. [3] *Pyth.* 27–29; see p. 62. [4] *Fünf Vorträge über den Griechischen Roman* (Berlin. 1896), 126. [5] *Vit. Apoll.* v.12, vi. 37, iii. 45, iv. 3, v. 13, 14, 16. [6] *Ibid.*, iv. 45, [7] *Ibid.*, iii. 15. [8] *Ibid.*, vi. 10, 27.

his disciples in Puteoli, over a hundred miles away. He can even give Apollonius' explanation. [1]

> Imagine what you will, flying goat or wings of wax excepted, so long as you ascribe it to a divine escort.

Finally he can tell a story of Apollonius' assumption into heaven. [2]

In the fourth century the steady decline of rationality is centered in the Neoplatonic school, which strongly influenced many Christian theologians. [3] Its opposition to the reliability of sense-perception was centered on a slogan common since the time of Plato—a line of Epicharmus which declared that "the mind sees, the mind hears, but everything else is dumb and blind". [4] Iamblichus, head of the school after Porphyry, expressly states that sight and hearing contain no truth for men. [5] In view of this emphasis, we are not surprised to find him giving as a Pythagorean watchword the admonition [6]

> Doubt no marvel concerning the gods, nor any religious doctrines (cf. Pindar, *Pyth.* x. 49f.).

He explains this watchword as meaning that we are not to reject marvels as impracticable or impossible or contrary to nature. Knowledge of the gods results from the belief that all things are possible for them. Whittaker [7] claims that Iamblichus is not really superstitious, for the religious doctrines are Pythagorean teachings which can be proved by mathematical demonstration. And according to Eunapius, [8] Iamblichus denied the truth of a story of his own levitation and transfiguration. On the other hand, the second of his philosophical works convicts him of credulity.

In this treatise, his *Life of Pythagoras*, he includes a more detailed discussion of credibility (*Pyth.* 138—40). The Pythagoreans believe miracle stories because they have experienced miracles, and they tell stories which seem like myths because they "doubt nothing which is referred to the divine". Sophists say that some things are possible for the gods while others are impossible, but actually all things are possible for them, as the opening lines of the *Epoi* of Linus state. [9]

---

[1] *Ibid.*, viii. 10.  [2] *Ibid.*, viii. 30.  [3] Cf. P. Courcelle, *Recherches sur les Confessions de saint Augustin* (Paris 1950).  [4] *Rep.* iii. 411d, *Phaedr.* 270e, Cic. *Tusc.* i. 20, Plut. *Soll. an.* 3, Max. Tyr. *Diss.* xi. 10, Porph. *Abst.* iii. 21, *Pyth.* 46, Iamblichus, *Pyth.* 228; cf. Waszink on Tert. *An.* 18 : 1 (p. 256).  [5] *Protr.* 13, 62 Pistelli.  [6] *Protr.* 21, 110; also *Pyth.* 148.  [7] T.Whittaker, *The Neoplatonists* (ed. 2, Cambridge, 1918), 129f.  [8] *Vit. soph.*, 458 Boissonade.  [9] In passing he points out that this is a Pythagorean forgery.

Pythagoreans have faith in their presuppositions because they were given them not by a man but by a god—Pythagoras, whose miracles in turn prove him to be a god!

Late in the fourth century we find a measure of rationality in the legend of Iamblichus as reported by the sophist Eunapius. Eunapius even lists his authorities for Iamblichus' denial of his levitation. Aedesius, one of Iamblichus' chief disciples, told Chrysanthius, who told Eunapius. [1] Rationality soon disappears, however, when Eunapius hears a story from men who, though incredulous of other miracles, were converted by a certain event. By "men" Eunapius means Aedesius, who told the story solely from oral tradition; none of Iamblichus' disciples wrote it down. It relates how Iamblichus visited springs of water and made boys miraculously appear out of them. In consequence his disciples sought no further evidence, but because of the evident signs "believed everything". Eunapius claims that he has refrained from introducing "more paradoxical and marvelous stories" because he did not wish to include "spurious and fluid tradition in a stable and well-founded narrative". [2]

Later in his work we find another story about Iamblichus. The philosopher was present when an Egyptian invoked Apollo and produced an epiphany of the god. Iamblichus said to the astonished witnesses, "My friends, stop marveling; this is only the ghost of a gladiator". [3] Eunapius gives a revealing comment on the astuteness of the philosopher. [4]

> So great a difference does it make whether one beholds with the intelligence or with the deceitful eyes of the flesh.

Eunapius' standard of credibility is no higher than that of his hero.

The memory of Iamblichus was kept fresh in the Neoplatonic school, and his attitude toward the gods and miracles remained normative. Marinus' *Life of Proclus* includes a long section (29-33) on theurgy and divine epiphanies. One story portrays the gods' favor toward both Iamblichus and Proclus. Proclus was praying in Adrotta for a revelation to inform him what god or gods should be worshiped in the temple there. Some said it was Asclepius, for there were many signs of his presence; voices were heard, a table was dedicated to him, oracles on health were given, and miraculous

---

[1] *Vit. soph.* 458 Boissonade. [2] *Ibid.*, 459–60. [3] On exorcism and gladiators cf. Tert. *An.* 57, with Waszink's notes. [4] *Vit. Soph.* 473.

cures took place. Others held that the Dioscuri lived there because visions of two young men on horseback had inspired immediate belief. Proclus "doubted none of the stories" but asked for his own revelation. In a dream the god clearly appeared and said, "Did you not hear Iamblichus say who the two were, when he praised Machaon and Podalirius?" [1] Marinus recounts the natives' enthusiasm over this vision, and asks what greater proof could be given of Proclus' friendship with the gods, of his "sympathy" with them. We may recall that in the second century Platonists were already becoming credulous. [2] Neoplatonism goes far beyond the earlier school.

Damascius, the last head of the Neoplatonist school at Athens, explicitly writes "in order that the ancient and mythical accounts may no longer be incredible". [3] Photius describes one of his works which included 352 chapters "on paradoxical works", 52 on "paradoxical tales about demons", 63 on "paradoxical tales about souls appearing after death", and 105 on "paradoxical creatures". [4] Small wonder that in the year 532, three years after the Christian emperor Justinian closed the philosophical schools, Damascius and six companions left Athens for Persia. [5] Though they could endure the life of the mystic East for only a year and returned to Greece, there is a symbolical appropriateness about their brief exile. The end of Greek philosophy had come.

[1] Sons of Asclepius, according to *Iliad* ii. 731–32. [2] See p. 69 *supra*. [3] *Vita Isidori* 309. [4] Photius, *Bibl. cod.* 130, in A. Westermann, *Paradoxographi* (Brunswick, 1839), xxix. [5] Agathias, *Hist.* ii. 30, 231 Dindorf.

# 6

# EDUCATION

In the preceding chapter we have seen the ways in which ideas of credibility were diffused through grammatical and rhetorical education. We now turn to examine the ways in which Greeks and Romans in the late Hellenistic period would become acquainted with natural science and with the laws of nature. We should first point out that these two subjects are almost entirely divorced. Natural science was studied, when it was studied at all, as a part of the "encyclia" or general education which followed grammar and rhetoric; the principles of order in the universe belonged to the field of philosophy. Where Aristote had combined detailed studies of natural phenomena with the creation of a system, later writers (with the partial exception of Posidonius) wrote either on some special topic such as zoology or studied principles without much reference to facts. When "natural philosophy" was studied in the late Hellenistic age, it was subordinated either to rhetoric or to ethics. As we have seen (chapter 2 above), "natural law" usually implies moral rather than physical law.

Scientific studies, as Marrou has observed, gradually lost ground before the emphasis on literary disciplines. [1] He proves his case from the treatise of Theon of Smyrna, *Mathematical Knowledge Useful for the Study of Plato*, written early in the second century of our era. Theon states that many people who want to study Plato have not studied as much mathematics as they need, Even before this time Philo describes those who come late to the study of philosophy, feel the need of preliminary training, go back to the *encyclia* and never return to philosophy. [2] The problem of the value of the *encyclia*—including geometry, arithmetic, astronomy, and music—was widely discussed in antiquity. They were rejected by Zeno, Epicurus, and many others, [3] but supported by Chrysippus, Posidonius, Philo, and the Christian Alexandrians. [4]

---

[1] *Histoire de l'éducation dans l'antiquité* (Paris, 1950), 253–54.  [2] *Gig.* 13.  [3] D. L, vii. 32; Cic. *Fin.* i. 71–72.  [4] F. H. Colson in *JTS* 18 (1916–17), 151–62; E. Norden. *Die antike Kunstprosa* (Berlin, 1898), 670–87.

For use in encyclical instruction we find the creation of a whole new literature of introductory manuals. For example, there is the *Phaenomena* of Aratus, a didactic poem about astronomy, soon the object of much grammatical exegesis and later translated into Latin. We may mention also the treatise *On Circular Motion* by Cleomedes, the *Introduction to Phenomena* by Geminus, and the pseudo-Aristotelian treatise *On the Universe*. In Latin we have such a book as the *Physical Problems* of Seneca. None of these introductions does anything to advance knowledge, but all of them aid in its diffusion. [1] Similarly in zoology we find many treatises (mostly lost) on animals or on fish or on birds. These works are largely limited to the copying of earlier works. In medicine there is the treatise of A. Cornelius Celsus on medicine, the surviving section of an encyclopedia in six parts which dealt with agriculture, medicine, military arts, rhetoric, philosophy, and jurisprudence.

We must observe with Diels [2] that apart from medicine and warfare, technical science aroused very little interest in antiquity. Xerxes' bridge of boats was famous, but only in a papyrus fragment do we find the name of the Greek engineer who built it. Alexander's capture of Tyre was also well known, but we know the engineer who was responsible for it only from the same scrap. Strato of Lampsacus performed experiments with vacuums, but we hear of them only in the mechanical works of Alexandrian technicians.

This divorce between hand and head is ascribed by Diels to the aristocratic nature of ancient society and to the existence of slavery, which made machinery unnecessary. It led to the decline of science in a wave of subjectivism, for without a microscope or telescope the confirmation of scientific theories was impossible.

The student who read the introductory manuals, then, would have to assume that their authors knew what they were talking about. At the same time, he would be faced with the proof that on scientific and philosophical questions there was an enormous amount of disagreement. He would find this proof in the doxographical literature.

In 1879 Diels published his inclusive collection of the doxographical writers [3] and traced its origin back to Theophrastus, Aristotle's successor in the Peripatetic school. Theophrastus had compiled the Φυσικῶν Δόξαι, views of philosophers on physics. Later, in the

---

[1] A. J. Festugière, *La révélation d'Hermès Trismégiste* II (Paris, 1949), 345–50.
[2] *Antike Technik* (ed. 2, Leipzig, 1920), 29–33.  [3] *Doxographi Graeci* (reprinted 1929).

first century B. C., this collection was enlarged and slightly revised. It was used by Varro and included philosophers as late as Posidonius and Asclepiades. In the next century an epitome of this work was made by a certain Aëtius, whose treatise in turn was largely reproduced by Plutarch (*De placitis philosophorum*) [1] and by the fifth-century anthologist Stobaeus. The work of Aëtius is restored by Diels, who prints the collections of Plutarch and Stobaeus in parallel columns.

The collection is arranged under six main topics: first principles, the universe, meteorological phenomena, earthly phenomena, the soul, and the body. Under these topics various items are discussed. For example, the section on meteorological phenomena includes chapters on the Milky Way, on comets, on thunder, on clouds, on the rainbow, on winds, and on winter and summer. Each chapter gives a very brief statement of the opinions of various philosophers.

The obvious result of the study of such a compendium is complete scepticism, and some of the chapters, such as the one on the gods, seem to be arranged in order to lead to such a conclusion. In any event, our earliest witnesses to its use employ it for sceptical purposes. We find it reflected in the *Menippus* and *Icaromenippus* of Lucian and in the Christian writers Athenagoras, Theophilus, and Irenaeus. The case of Irenaeus is perhaps the most interesting because of the sceptical conclusion he explicitly draws. He is stressing the complete adequacy of scripture and the impiety of looking for solutions of problems not given there. While he admits that there are problems in scripture itself, he argues that they are no greater than the insoluble difficulties in science. [2] These scientific problems he takes from the chapter headings of the doxography of Plutarch.

No one knows the cause of the rise of the Nile, where the birds go in winter, the cause of the tides, what lies beyond the ocean, the cause of rain, lightning, thunder, clouds, fogs, winds, etc., the cause of snow, hail, etc., the cause of the phases of the moon, the cause of the difference between salt and fresh water, or the differences between metals, stones, etc. "In all these matters we shall not be loquacious in searching for their causes; God alone who made them is truthful."

Irenaeus' method is very simple: he takes the chapter headings, observes that the authorities cited disagree, and concludes that certain knowledge is impossible. There is considerable justification

[1] Perhaps „Pseudo-Plutarch", but a certain conclusion cannot be reached.
[2] *Adv. haer.* ii. 28. 1–2; cf. *HTR* 42 (1949), 44.

for his conclusion, however. The doxographical theories about the rise of the Nile are worthless. Only the method of the emperor Nero, whom Seneca calls "veritatis in primis amantissimus", could have brought satisfactory results; he sent two centurions to investigate the source of the Nile. [1] Aristotle, followed by Aelian, had known where storks and cranes went in the winter, but the naturalist Pliny does not know. He says that the place "has not yet been discovered", combining ignorance with optimism. [2] Posidonius had made a famous journey to Cadiz, where he investigated the cause of the tides and correctly concluded that they were related to the phases of the moon; but his theory had not been widely diffused. [3] Since no one had actually crossed the ocean, and since the voyages of Pytheas were generally regarded with suspicion, one could hardly state accurately what lies beyond it. Cleomedes, perhaps following Posidonius, had said that the ocean could not be crossed. [4] The lack of factual information naturally made the existence or non-existence of the Antipodes a favorite topic of discussion. Similarly meteorological phenomena could be discussed indefinitely in the absence of detailed observations. They were phenomena "in which the workings of nature showed some apparent element of caprice", [5] and Epicureans were accustomed to give several alternative explanations of them. The influence of this Epicurean refusal to assign a definite cause to these phenomena was reinforced by the Sceptics' refusal to come to any definite conclusion on such matters.

We see, therefore, that to a considerable extent a sceptical attitude toward the achievements of contemporary science was warranted. The method of these sceptics was wrong. As Posidonius argued, the fact that scientists disagree does not discredit science. [6] But their conclusion was correct. The actual information about the world which was taught in schools consisted of a few highly significant guesses along with a lofty superstructure of philosophical generalizations. And when the stress of scientific writers was laid on the diffusion of these materials rather than on fresh discovery, the decline of science was well under way.

In spite of a gradual decline in scientific interest at the end of

---

[1] Sen. *N. Q.* vi. 8. 3–4; cf. J. O. Thomson, *History of Ancient Geography* (Cambridge, 1948), 272. [2] *N. A.* 596 b 20; *N. A.* iii. 13; *N. H.* x. 61. [3] Strabo c. 173 c. [4] *De motu circ.* ii. 15; cf. 1 Clement 20 : 7. [5] C. Bailey, *Lucretius De Rerum Natura* (Oxford, 1947), 1551f. [6] D. L. vii. 129.

6

the Hellenistic age, we must observe that such a decline had been threatened for many centuries. Science had been under attack almost since its rise among the pre-Socratic naturalists, some of whom had been tried for impiety by the state. When it became popular, among the Sophists, it encountered a formidable opponent in the person of Socrates, whose final attitude was not inaccurately summarized in the later phrase, "The things above us have nothing to do with us". [1] Xenophon carefully separates the views of Socrates from those of the Sophists. [2] He was not interested in "the nature of the universe", or in the "necessities" by which the heavenly bodies move; it was clear to him that to discover such things was impossible. He said such studies were like magic, for he thought that if these "necessities" were discovered, their discoverers could produce winds and waters and times or whatever else they might need. He himself was interested only in moral problems. In the later Academy science was ridiculed, [3] and Socrates was praised as the one who called philosophy away from the study of occult matters, who "first summoned philosophy down from the sky". [4]

Both Plato and Aristotle [5] attack the older naturalists for their concentration of attention on the "material cause". At the same time, both Plato and Aristotle gradually came to appreciate the study of natural science, although for Plato it always remained subordinated to his interest in the good of the state. The uniformity of celestial motions was used by him to confirm the rule of absolute law among men. And while Aristotle produced scientific works on biology which were unequaled until modern times, he was known in the Hellenistic age as a religious philosopher. His scientific works were lost until the first century B. C.

The successors of Aristotle were interested in science. Theophrastus and Strato of Lampsacus continued scientific investigations. But very soon even among the Peripatetics the rising tide of interest in moral problems swept away enthusiasm for natural science. Strato was severely criticized, especially by Stoics, for his attempt to explain the universe without reference to divine power. [6] His pupil Aristarchus, who first expressed the theory that the earth revolves around the sun, was attacked by Cleanthes, head of the Stoic school. Cleanthes suggested that the old Athenian practice of trials for impiety should

[1] Min. Fel. *Oct.* 13 : 1.   [2] *Mem.* i. 1. 11, 13, 15.   [3] Cic. *Luc.* 55.   [4] Cic. *Ac.* i. 15, *Tusc.* v. 10.   [5] *Phaedo*, 97 c; *Phys.* 198 a 14–200 b 8.   [6] Fr. 32–37 Wehrli.

be revived for Aristarchus because he had "moved the hearth of the universe". [1]

The interest of Epicurus in science was largely due to his effort to introduce the principle of multiple causation and thus avoid the astral mysticism of Plato. If a man observes celestial phenomena and realizes that they take place by necessity and regular succession, he will know that they are not due to any being who controls and ordains or has ordained their movements. [2] The study of nature frees mankind from its fears. The same attitude is expressed in more detail in the great poem of Lucretius *De rerum natura*.

In the *Roman History* of the Roman Stoic Polybius we find an interest in science combined with great admiration for its achievements. "At the present time, when all seas are navigable and all lands open to exploration, it is no longer suitable to use the testimonies of poets and mythographers concerning unknown matters, as our predecessors generally did. As Heraclitus says, such testimonies in disputed matters offer only weak proof. Only through methodical investigation (*historia*) can we try to provide our readers with a trustworthy explanation." [3] This statement reflects the debates over the reliability of Homeric geography, and places Polybius on the side of science against poetry. Again, he lays emphasis on the contemporary progress of science. "Techniques and arts have advanced with us to such an extent that people who wish to learn can learn everything, if they undertake the study methodically." [4] And the means for this methodical study is available. "All branches of science have now made such progress with us that instruction in most of them has been systematized." [5] We have already seen (chapter 4) that because of the progress of science Polybius is strongly opposed to miracle stories and to those who relate them.

Among the Stoics, Posidonius was remarkable for his interest in science and his "Aristotelian" interest in causes (τὸ αἰτιολογικὸν . . . . Ἀριστοτελίζον), which most Stoics did not study because of their obscurity. [6] He wrote more than seventy books *On Meteorology* (strongly influencing Seneca), treatises on the size of the sun, on the ocean, and on the universe, a "treatise on nature" (*physikos logos*), and a commentary on the *Timaeus* of Plato. As Galen tells us, [7] he was

---

[1] Plut. *Facie* 923 a; the text should be emended with all editors except P. Raingeard (p. 69). [2] D. L. x. 76–77. [3] *Hist.* iv. 40. 2–3. [4] *Hist.* ix. 2. 5; Festugière, *op. cit.* II 347. [5] *Hist.* x. 47. 12. [6] Strabo c. 104. [7] *Scr. min.* ii. 77 : 18.

"the most learned of the Stoics". His influence on the study of natural science at the beginning of our era was very great. [1]

In the Stoicizing Academy under Antiochus there was a certain revival of interest in science. Even when the subject matter was very obscure, its study was regarded as providing considerable pleasure. The search for truth was itself a goal, whether any other goal was reached or not. [2] Elsewhere we find Antiochus arguing that the study of science is not only pleasant but useful. It not only makes a happy life happier but alleviates unhappiness. [3] Both these ideas are repeated by the eclectic Jewish philosopher Philo, who states at one point that the search for truth in scientific questions is its own reward, and elsewhere argues that the study of science is both pleasant and useful. [4] Antiochus speaks of Pythagoras, Plato, and Democritus, who because of their desire for learning traveled to the ends of the earth. He adds that those who do not understand this passion have never loved anything great or worth knowing. [5]

We have already mentioned the fact that Pliny speaks of the future progress of knowledge. The principal ancient witness to this belief is his contemporary Seneca, who says in his tragedy *Medea* (375-79) that eventually the ocean will be crossed and Thule will not be the limit of our knowledge. He believes firmly that sometime there will be a scientist who can explain meteorological phenomena, for later generations must make their contribution to learning. [6] Pliny and Seneca are not our only witnesses, however, for in the medical encyclopedia of Celsus [7] vivisection of criminals is defended on the ground that "by the torments of a few criminals remedies can be found for innocent people of all the ages". We may note that this argument comes from the Dogmatic school of physicians, which was, like Pliny and Seneca, essentially Stoic.

This optimistic faith in the future of science is expressed by Roman Stoics. They were Romans and therefore interested primarily in the practical aspects of science rather than in theory. Their belief that science would progress was not justified by any discoveries in their own day or in their own country. Moreover, the Stoicism with which

[1] M. Pohlenz, *Die Stoa* I 359-60.  [2] Cic. *Luc.* 127.  [3] Cic. *Fin.* v. 48-55.
[4] *Prov.* in Eus. *Praep.* viii. 14. 51; *Abr.* 65; cf. E. Bréhier, *Les idées philosophiques et religieuses de Philon d'Alexandrie* (ed. 2, Paris, 1925), 283 n. 4.  [5] Cic. *Fin.* v. 50.
[6] *N. Q.* vii. 25. 7 (and vii. *passim*); cf. *Ep.* 64 : 6-9.  [7] Cels. pr. 26, 5 : 16 Daremberg. On modern inventions cf. *Ep. Arist.* 137.

they were identified was sympathetic toward astrology and was about to disappear in the face of the subjective theurgy of Neoplatonism. The actual state of science is better represented by Plutarch in his dialogue *On the Face in the Orb of the Moon,* a hodge-podge of old science and new demonology, all subordinated to the needs of literary form. Many theories of the nature of the moon are discussed in much detail, but the climax of the dialogue is found in the idea that demons and souls are to be found in the moon, and that the moon itself generates souls. This mixture of science and theology obviously marks the decline of both.

In Lucian's *Icaromenippus* the increasingly sterile science of his time is ridiculed. Philosophers (scientists) claim to know the boundaries of heaven, to measure the sun, to visit the spheres beyond the moon, and to know how many cubits lie between the sun and the moon—though not how many *stadia* between Megara and Athens! They know the height of the air, the depth of the sea, the circumference of the earth, and the cubic content of the heaven. They make no hypothetical assertions, but state definitely that the sun is a mass, the moon inhabited, the stars drink water, and the sun draws up moisture from the sea with a rope and bucket, so to speak, and distributes the beverage to all of them in order. [1] In his *Sale of Lives* Lucian describes a Peripatetic philosopher who can tell his hearers "how long a gnat lives, how far down into the sea the sunlight reaches, and what the soul of an oyster is like". He can also tell about "sperm and conception and the shaping of the embryo in the womb, and how man is a creature that laughs, while asses do not laugh or build houses and sail boats". [2]

Such ridicule of science was eagerly utilized by Christian writers; we find it clearly reflected in Tatian and in the *Clementine Homilies.* Unfortunately there was much justification for it. Science had become philosophy or had become so severely technical and practical that it had lost touch with the half-educated public, always more easily amused than taught.

In the early Roman empire a person who knew anything of science would have read an introductory manual and a collection of philosophical opinions. He might have studied some special field like zoology, but if the surviving treatises on this subjects are any guide,

---

[1] *Icaromen.* 6–7.  [2] *Bion prasis* 26; cf. *Clem. hom.* i. 10.

he was left in a state of complete confusion. The general principles of Aristotle had been forgotten, and descriptive science had developed a taste for anecdote. If we consider the state of medicine we shall find it somewhat more satisfactory, but the close alliance of medical with philosophical schools had not increased medical learning. Celsus treats adherence to a particular school as a matter of faith rather than of knowledge. Galen, himself an exception to the general rule, constantly attacks his contemporaries who prefer theory to practice. [1] At the same time he is a convinced teleologist who does not hesitate to ignore opposing evidence in his search for teleology.

In short, the ordinary educated person knew almost nothing about science except as a subdivision of philosophy. If he was an adherent of Stoicism, he would know much more about natural law than about nature. His approach to science, no matter what his school, would be governed by the principles the founder of his school had laid down. He would be a dogmatist, possibly an eclectic dogmatist, but certainly a dogmatist. If he lost his faith in philosophy he would look for a new faith but not for new facts. For the discovery of such facts he would have neither the aptitude nor the ability.

[1] R. Walzer, *Galen on Jews and Christians* (Oxford, 1949), 38–39, 46. We find a similar attitude in Soranus.

# SCIENCE IN HELLENISTIC JUDAISM AND CHRISTIANITY

What A. D. White called "the warfare between science and theology" has a long history. In the life of Greece its high points are perhaps the series of trials for impiety at Athens in the fifth century B. C. and the attack on Aristarchus by the philosopher Cleanthes. These trials resulted in the expulsion from Athens of the philosophers Anaxagoras, Protagoras, and Diagoras, and in the execution of Socrates. In the fourth century Aristotle was similarly exiled, but from his time until the sixth century of the Christian era teaching at Athens remained free. At that point the Christian emperor Justinian closed the Platonic academy. [1] On the other hand, Cleanthes' attack on Aristarchus because he had "moved the hearth of the universe" by his heliocentric theory of the universe had no appreciable result. The conflict between the newer science and the older religion in Greece resulted in a steady process of reinterpretation of religion in terms of science. The allegorical interpretation is the most significant witness to this fact. When oriental religions entered the area of Roman paganism their myths also underwent the same process. Their rites might remain unchanged, but the interpretation of the rites was changed.

Only with the rise of credulity and of Neoplatonism in the third century do we find theological attacks on science. They are foreshadowed in the Hermetic *Asclepius*, with its depreciation of scientific knowledge in favor of religion, [2] and, as we shall see, in Christian attacks (often borrowed from sceptical rhetoricians) on the possibility of science. But in general the influence of science and of scientific philosophy upon religion was so strong that before this time the reconciliation of science and religion was an accomplished fact.

[1] Cf. W. Nestle, *Vom Mythos zum Logos* (ed. 2, Stuttgart, 1942), 479–83; E. Derenne, *Les procès d'impiété intentés aux philosophes à Athènes au Vme et IVme siècles avant J.-C.* (Paris, 1930). [2] *Asclepius* 13–14, pp. 311–12 Nock–Festugière (with n. 115 on p. 369).

A certain amount of astronomical knowledge is to be found in "the book of the courses of the luminaries of the heaven" which constitutes a part of the pseudepigraphical book of Enoch (72-82). This book, probably composed in the first or second century B. C., describes the "laws of the luminaries" which govern the sun, the moon, the twelve winds, and the stars which lead the seasons and months. Along with these laws we find descriptions of the four quarters of the world, with notes on the principal mountains, rivers, and islands, as well as the names of the sun and moon.

> Blessed are all those who sin not as the sinners in the reckoning of all their days in which the sun traverses the heaven, entering into and departing from the portals for thirty days (82 : 4).

The author's purpose is strictly theological.
He advocates a 364-day year (72 : 34) instead of the lunar year of the Pharisees. No one else seems to have thought that the solar year was 364 days long, [1] although according to Censorinus, [2] Philolaus taught that it was 364 $1/_2$ days. In general, the sources of the "book of the courses" seem to be Babylonian rather than Greek.

The oldest example we possess of the influence of Greek science upon Judaism is probably the Wisdom of Solomon from the first century B. C. The author's attitude toward science is ambivalent; as Fichtner points out, [3] he does not seem to have mastered his materials completely. He is combining Jewish apocalyptic and wisdom with a smattering of Greek philosophy. On the one hand, he criticizes philosophers for their inability to find God. "If they had power to know so much as to be able to form theories (stochasasthai) about the world, how did they not earlier find the Lord of these things?" (13 : 9). The idea that Greek learning is purely conjectural was destined for a long life in later apologetic. [4] On the other hand, he uses the Stoic theory of the transmutation of the elements in order to explain miracles (we shall discuss this use in chapter 9), and speaks with enthusiasm of the various kinds of learning which Wisdom brings (7 : 17-20). It teaches man to know the composition of the world and the working of the elements, the beginning and end and middle of times, the changes of solstices and the alteration of the

---

[1] Cf. Ginzel in *RE* IX 604–12.  [2] *De die natali* 19.  [3] *ZNW* 36 (1937), 120.
[4] Athenag. *Leg.* 7, p. 125 : 21 Geffcken (also p. 176 n. 4); Clem. *Str.* vi. 55. 4; Theoph. *Aut.* iii. 16; cf. ii. 8.

seasons, the cycles of years and the locations of the stars, the natures of animals and the rages of wild beasts, the powers of winds and the thoughts of men, the differences of plants and the powers of roots. This is a summary of the principal parts of a Greek encyclical education. [1] In discussing the formation of man, Wisdom not only mentions the idea of the pre-existence of the soul (8 : 19-20) but also makes use of Aristotelian embryology (7 : 2). [2]

A century later the Jewish Christian Epistle of James reflects a somewhat similar combination of Jewish moralism and Greek popular philosophy. [3] From popular philosophy come the diatribe illustrations in James 3 : 3-6. [4] Semi-scientific notions include the mention of "no variation in turning of the shadow" (1 : 17), the "wheel of becoming" (3 : 6, an Orphic expression not understood by the author of the epistle), the "natures" of beasts, birds, reptiles, and fish which are "tamed by human nature" (3 : 7), and the differences between sweet and bitter water. The author also knows, perhaps through the sayings of Jesus (Matthew 7 : 16) that fig trees do not bring forth olives nor do vines produce figs (3 : 12). These scientific ideas do not amount to much and most of them can be found in the curriculum outline provided by the book of Wisdom. We may add that the poetical illustrations the author gives in support of his attack on gossip are much like the collection we find in Plutarch's treatise *De garrulitate*. Like his scientific ideas, they are stock illustrations of a stock theme.

When we turn to the Jewish philosopher Philo of Alexandria we find the same kind of interest in science but on a higher level. Philo believes firmly in the necessity of an encyclical education. Such an education not only leads to virtue but provides the essential preliminary training for philosophy. "The soul descending from heaven, if it maintains its true nature amidst the constraints of the body, obtains from the encyclia provision for its heavenward return". [5] On the other hand, those who begin their studies late in life should not bother with the encyclia, as they might never get back to philosophy (*Gig.* 13). Moreover, Philo frequently attacks the sciences from the standpoint of the New Academy (see p. 82 above). In themselves

---

[1] Perhaps derived from Posidonius; cf. I. Heinemann, *Poseidonios' metaphysische Schriften* I (Breslau, 1921), 136–53.   [2] *Plac.* v. 6. 1, pp. 418–19 Diels.   [3] W. L. Knox, *JTS* 46 (1945), 10–17.   [4] J. H. Ropes, *The Epistle of St. James* (New York, 1916), 231.   [5] *Quis rer. div. heres* 272; F. H. Colson in *JTS* 18 (1916–17), 158.

they have no value whatever. They are to be studied only as preparation for true knowledge which is to be found in philosophy. [1]

Philo is not actually opposed to science. He actually was interested in many aspects of contemporary science, usually those which were curious or unusual. [2] In this respect he was a forerunner of Augustine, whose own mind is characterized by the *curiositas* which he too condemned. Philo was once on his way from Alexandria to Jerusalem when he passed through Ascalon and saw an enormous number of pigeons. He could not refrain from asking why there were so many, and he was informed that religious scruples forbade anyone's catching them. [3] This is only one example out of many which show his interest in scientific or semi-scientific details. As we have already seen (chapter 6) he takes over from Antiochus the idea that science is not only pleasant but useful. He follows the examples of Archimedes and Posidonius [4] in regarding the study of science as dearer than his native country. [5] Moreover, as we have seen in examining his ideas of the laws of nature (chapter 2), he greatly esteems such laws and believes that since they have their origin in God they are immutable, or at least generally immutable.

Philo's attitude toward science is thus marked by severe criticism and unstinted praise. Possibly these two characteristics reflect different sides of his personality. At the same time they also reflect the use of different kinds of sources. The attacks on science are derived from the attacks of the New Academy of Carneades and Clitomachus. The praise of science comes from Antiochus and ultimately from Posidonius.

When we consider the attitudes of Christian writers toward science we shall find the same contradiction, although Christian writers usually express one or the other idea rather than both at the same time. On the one hand, we find militant attacks upon science and philosophy, usually based on Academic scepticism and ringing no changes on the old themes. On the other hand, we find enthusiastic support for science which usually reflects Stoic philosophy.

We should add that we possess one "scientific" treatise from the hand of Philo, although it exists only in an Armenian translation. This is the work "Alexander, or on the question whether the irrational animals possess reason". The title itself reflects Philo's position:

[1] Bréhier, *op. cit.*, 289–91, 294–95.  [2] *Ibid.*, 283–84.  [3] *Prov.* in Eus. *Praep.*viii. 14. 64.  [4] Cic. *Fin.* v. 50; Galen, *Scr. min.* ii. 77 : 20–78 : 2.  [5] *Migr.* 217; Bréhier, *op. cit.*, 283 n. 4. On Philo and scientific themes cf. Festugière, *op. cit.*, II 528–33.

animals do not possess reason but know things by instinct. Naturally there is nothing new in Philo's theses. The first half of the book gives the stock arguments and the stock examples by which Carneades and his followers in the New Academy tried to prove that animals possessed both "external reason" and "internal reason", resulting in virtues and vices. The presence of "external reason" (expressed by the voice) is proved by the examples of the parrot and some other birds. The presence of "internal reason" is proved by ants, bees, monkeys, elephants, and many other animals. The second half of the book simply reiterates the Stoic position against Carneades. The societies of animals and their apparent virtues and vices do not prove that they use reason, and the parrot cannot clearly articulate words. Philo's arguments on both sides are taken solely from books, or in a few instances perhaps from contemporary reports. His work is simply a philosophical *thesis*, in which arguments on both sides are presented. [1]

When we come to examine Christian writers on the same subject we shall see the same method being used, except that Christian writers usually present only one side of the debate. The importance of the subject lies in its relevance to the place of man in the universe and the propriety of his definition as the rational animal. Jewish and Christian writers take their materials, however, not from scientific treatises but from philosophical works in which the materials are already digested. [2]

In the earliest days of Christianity we should not expect to find much material related to science or philosophy. The movement was essentially religious. It was also eschatological; it was facing toward the future and therefore the things of this transient age were largely irrelevant. Early Christianity was accompanied by miracles and signs of the power of God, not by reflective consideration of the nature of the world. The word "philosophy" occurs only once in the New Testament (Col. 2 : 8), and it is used as a term coordinate with "vain deceit". [3]

In the Christian community at Corinth, however, we find persons who have been influenced by the Stoic-Cynic ideal of the wise man, [4]

[1] On this work cf. G. Tappe, *De Philonis libro qui inscribitur* 'Αλέξανδρος (Göttingen, 1912).  [2] Josephus' acquaintance with such a science as medicine is very limited; cf. M. Neuburger, *Die Medizin im Flavius Josephus* (Bad Reichenhall, 1919). [3] Cf. M. Dibelius, *An die Kolosser* (ed. 2, Tübingen, 1927), 19.  [4] See my note in S. E. Johnson, *The Joy of Study* (New York, 1951); J. Dupont, *Gnosis* (Louvain, 1949), 374–77.

and when Paul writes against them and to them in 1 Corinthians he makes use of scientific and philosophical examples. To be sure, when he argues on the ground of natural law (1 Cor. 11 : 14) he is not regarding nature as an autonomous power; [1] but the Stoics, from whom he takes his example, also considered nature as the ground of the working of divine providence. We shall later discuss his use of scientific "proofs" of the resurrection (chapter 15). Here it will suffice to say that he has no clear idea of their meaning and presumably borrows them simply for the occasion. They are samples of the way in which he could become all things to all men (1 Cor. 9 : 22).

Another point at which Paul's form of expression seems to be due to philosophy is his description of the conflict within the human personality (Gal. 5 : 17, Rom. 7 : 15–23). Here his basic idea is presumably Jewish. It reflects the common rabbinic idea of the two *yetsers* within man, the "good impulse" and the "bad impulse". [2] His expression of it, however, is Greek and goes back to Posidonius. A very famous passage in the *Medea* of Euripides (1078–80) had portrayed Medea as knowing that what she was about to do was evil but realizing that passion was stronger than her own thoughts. [3] On this passage Posidonius based his interpretation of the passions as constituting a real power within man, an interpretation which we also find in the Middle Platonist Albinus. [4] Paul comes very close to Posidonius when he sees a law in his members warring against the law of his reason (Rom. 7 : 23). [5]

A fairly high level of literary culture along with a considerable interest in medicine is to be found in the two-volume work often called Luke-Acts. Its author gives more specific accounts of the cures of diseases than do the other synoptic evangelists, and it may have been this interest in healing which led to the identification of the author with the physician Luke of Colossians 4 : 14. The medical language (so-called) which he uses is not sufficiently technical, however, to prove that he was a physician. [6] Among his scientific

---

[1] M. Pohlenz in *ZNW* 42 (1949), 77.  [2] F. C. Porter in *Biblical and Semitic Studies* (New Haven, 1901), 93–156.  [3] Ovid, *Metam.* vii. 18–21 (*deteriora sequor*) is simply a translation.  [4] SVF III 473; M. Pohlenz, *Die Stoa* (Göttingen, 1948), I 224–26, II 112–13; Albinus, *Eisag.* 24, 176–77 Hermann.  [5] I cannot translate *nous* with Bultmann (*Theologie des Neuen Testaments* I, 208) as "das eigentliche Ich des Menschen."  [6] H. J. Cadbury, *The Style and Literary Method of Luke* (Cambridge, 1921).

interests are geography and navigation. After mentioning "every nation under heaven" in Acts 2 : 5, he proceeds to list these nations or at least a representative sample of them. The result possesses more value as rhetoric than as science. Again, he gives a detailed description of a shipwreck (Acts 27), which provides us with one of our principal sources for the study of ancient shipping. The author is also acquainted with philosophy, as we see from his Pythagoreanizing description of Christian life (Acts 4 : 32) and from the Stoicizing address ascribed to Paul on the Areopagus (Acts 17 : 22–31). [1] Probably when he explains the darkness over Palestine at the death of Jesus as caused by "the failure of the sun" (Luke 23 : 45) he knows that he is referring to an eclipse.

Elsewhere in the New Testament there is practically no interest in science or philosophy. The 153 fish of the appendix to the gospel of John are unrelated to ichthyology; they have more to do with theology. [2] Only in the epistle of Jude do we find a reflection of contemporary discussions. The author speaks of gnostics who "learn naturally as the irrational animals do" (Jude 10). As G. Quispel has observed, this is plainly derived from discussions of whether animals possess reason or not. [3] The author of Jude believes that animals know only by instinct, and is pointing out that the gnostics' "innate" knowledge is like theirs.

The New Testament, then, does not yield much evidence of the relation of early Christianity to natural science. We should not expect it to do so. The apostle Paul was probably not exaggerating when he said that not many "wise" persons were members of the Corinthian church, and this condition probably was common. Christianity with its apocalyptic message had no time to examine the things of this world. Only when Christians gradually became aware that the world was likely to last a long time did they make an effort to understand it.

The beginning of this change is found in the writings of two of the apostolic fathers, although it is only a beginning, and a feeble beginning at that. The first example is the letter to the Corinthians

[1] M. Pohlenz in *ZNW* 42 (1949), 82–98 ("ganze hellenische Gedankengänge"). [2] See my note in *HTR* 42 (1949), 273–75. We should perhaps compare the story about Pythagoras in which fishermen brought their catch to him to count; he made a rapid but accurate estimate (Porph. *Pyth.* 25; cf. L. Bieler, *ΘΕΙΟΣ* ANHP I [Vienna, 1935], 105–8). [3] See chapter 1, p. 15.

by Clement of Rome. It is sometimes said that this is a letter of the
Roman church as a whole. The relatively good style and the intelligent use of sources in 1 Clement does not reflect the work of a
community, however; it reflects a single author, Clement of Rome. [1]
But apart from his sources Clement is not interested in science. Only
in these sources, largely Stoic, do we find such an interest, and
science has already been made the handmaid of a rhetorical philosophy. Two examples will suffice. The first (1 Clem. 20) is his mention
of the ocean which men cannot cross, and the worlds (*kosmoi*) beyond
it. Here we may have a reflection of Posidonius' treatise *On the Ocean*,
for we find the same idea in a work based on Posidonius. [2] It is a
common theme in the first century; we find something like it in Strabo,
Seneca the elder, Seneca the younger, and Pseudo-Aristotle, *De
mundo*. [3] Clement is not interested in it for its own sake. It is simply
a rhetorical ornament for his theme, the harmony of the universe.
The scientific question itself is irrelevant.

Similarly the story of the phoenix (1 Clem. 25), which he uses to
illustrate the resurrection (see chapter 15), comes to him from writers
for whom it possesses rhetorical rather than philosophical or zoological
significance. [4] Clement is not really concerned with the existence
or non-existence of such birds; he takes over the rhetorical example
without questioning it.

Another of the apostolic fathers, "Barnabas", makes use of zoology
in order to bring out the moral significance of various animals. At
this point he is following a Hellenistic Jewish tradition exemplified
by the letter of Aristeas and by Philo. This tradition ultimately leads
to the treatise called the *Physiologus*, which we shall presently discuss.
"Barnabas" finds hidden moral meanings in the Mosaic dietary
legislation. [5] The immorality of the pig is shown by its greediness.
When it eats it does not know its master; when it is hungry it cries
out, and when it has received food it becomes silent again. Some
birds are so lazy that they do not hunt for their own food but steal it
from others. Three fish, the lamprey, polypus, and cuttlefish, do
not swim but simply lie on the bottom of the sea. To this group of

[1] Not from the second century, in spite of the attempt of C. Eggenberger, *Die
Quellen der politischen Ethik des 1. Klemensbriefes* (Zurich, 1951), 74–106, to prove his
use of Dio Chrysostom. [2] Cleomedes, *De motu circ.* ii. 15, 28 : 2 Ziegler. [3] Strabo
c. 65; Sen. rhet. *Suas.* i, 7 Kiessling; Sen. *Medea* 377–79; Ps.–Arist. *Mund.* 3,
392 b 23. [4] Cf. Sen. *Ep.* 42 : 1; Tac. *Ann.* vi. 28. [5] Barn. 10.

lazy animals "Barnabas" adds a collection of stories of animals given to sexual immorality. The stories, which are concerned with the hare, the hyena, and the weasel, are derived from the zoological folklore which we find collected in such writers as Pliny and Aelian. [1] Of the hyena, "Barnabas" says that it changes its sex annually. We shall see that Clement of Alexandria follows Aristotle in correcting this error.

The examples we have discussed constitute practically all the scientific information to be found in the New Testament and the apostolic fathers. Obviously there is not much. What there is seems to be derived primarily from rhetoric, in which such examples were employed. The examples have little influence on the thought of the authors who use them. They are merely ornaments to illustrate ideas already formed.

On the other hand, among the followers of Simon Magus, the first Christian gnostic, we find a strong interest in science, although the science in question is magic. Wellmann [2] has analyzed the examples of magic ascribed to Simon in the *Clementine Homilies* (ii. 32, iv. 4) and has shown that they are typical of the magical papyri and of the opponents of the satirist Lucian. Simon could make statues walk, could pass through fire without being burned, could fly through the air, could make bread from stones, and so on. Two of Simon's feats are paralleled in the fragments of the Pythagorean magician Anaxilaus, his breaking of iron and his creation of apparitions with all sorts of forms. Did the Simonians know Anaxilaus' book of magical tricks? The pseudo-Cyprianic treatise *De rebaptismate* (16) tells us that many people thought that when they made fire appear on the surface of water they were relying on Anaxilaus.

Another gnostic group which employed magic was that which followed the Valentinian Marcus in the second century. They could make mixed wine appear purple and red like blood, and they could also make a large vessel overflow by pouring into it the contents of a smaller one. Irenaeus, [3] who describes these practices, says that the Marcosians were combining the "tricks" of Anaxilaus with the craft of magicians.

More orthodox Christians rejected magic and ordinarily ascribed

---

[1] On the sources of Barnabas cf. H. Windisch, *Der Barnabasbrief* (Tübingen, 1920), 359–61. [2] *Die Physika des Bolos Demokritos und der Magier Anaxilaos aus Larissa* (*Abh. d. preuss. Akad.* 1928, philos.-hist. Kl. 7), 55–56. [3] *Adv. haer.* i. 13. 2.

its apparent successes either to trickery or to the work of demons. At the same time, critics of Christianity often claimed that Jesus had worked his miracles by magic. [1] The question of exact evidence was swallowed up by theological controversy.

Early in the second century we find some Christian contact with science in the *Apology* of Aristides. It is a science which has been mediated to Aristides through philosophical handbooks, but it is worth examining because of Aristides' antiquity. He is arguing against what he calls the Chaldaeans' worship of the heavenly bodies, and he claims that the heaven is moved with its luminaries "by necessity", that the sun is moved "by necessity" (it is much smaller than the heaven), and that the moon, which waxes and wanes and has eclipses, is also moved "by necessity". [2]

This is of course not Stoic, or even Christian; it actually seems to be derived from Epicurean criticism of the Stoa. Epicurus had denied that the movements of the heavenly bodies were due to any demiurge or to their own volition; they took place by "the necessity of regular succession". [3]

In order to oppose Stoic and other astrological doctrines, Aristides uses the weapons provided for him by Epicurus. We shall see the same use being made in Theophilus of Antioch. In general, however, Christian writers regarded Epicurus as one of their chief enemies.

In the middle of the second century Christian writers were addressing themselves to the literary public of the Graeco-Roman world, and we begin to find a greater number of themes of a scientific or semi-scientific nature.

Justin Martyr, who tells us himself that his education was sadly deficient, does know a little about geography. In listing the regions in the east to which Christianity has come he mentions the tribes of the Hamaxobioi, the Aoikoi, and the tent-dwelling herdsmen. [4] These are presumably the Scythians, the Nomads of India or Africa, and the tent-dwelling Arabs of Syria, described by Pliny. [5] Justin also knows that India is a land where strange animals dwell or are said to dwell. [6] This information does not come from geographical study, however; it is a stock example of Academic attacks upon Epicureans. The Academics insisted against Epicurean reliance on

---

[1] L. Blau, *Das altjüdische Zauberwesen* (Strassburg, 1898), 29.  [2] *Apol.* 4 : 2, 6 : 1–3.  [3] *Ep.* i. 77, 28 : 14 Usener.  [4] *Dial.* 117.  [5] *N. H.* iv. 80, vi. 55 (v. 22, vi. 189), v. 87.  [6] *Dial.* 3.

sense-perception that our not having seen the animals of India does not prove their non-existence. [1] Most of the rest of Justin's "scientific" ideas are really philosophical. His idea that man differs from the animals only because he stands erect [2] is, as Alfonsi has pointed out, derived from the Platonic-Aristotelian school tradition. [3] Justin himself speaks of his close relation to the Platonic tradition. [4]

What knowledge of philosophy he has is derived from the same area. His analysis of the history of philosophy [5] comes from Middle Platonic sources. He tells us that philosophy was "sent down" to men who at first investigated the truth. Their followers did not continue the investigation but simply admired the constancy and continence of their teachers and the strangeness of their words; they were content with a simple traditionalism. In precisely the same way Cicero [6] and Philo [7] describe philosophy as the gift of the gods or of heaven, and the Middle Platonist Atticus [8] speaks of Plato as "truly sent down from the gods". These ideas are based on Plato's own description (*Tim.* 47 b) of philosophy as a divine gift. These passages illustrate Justin's view that philosophy was "sent down"; other passages may be compared with his picture of its development. After Socrates the authority or authoritarian teaching of Plato led to the creation of two schools and more. The traditionalism and imitativeness of Plato are described by Apuleius. [9] "With effort and elegance Plato adorned the wisdom which Socrates handed down to him." Plato also "desired to imitate the constancy and continence of Pythagoras". Evidently Justin has taken Platonic sketches of the history of philosophy and abbreviated them to such an extent that they are almost meaningless. Presumably his description of Plato and Pythagoras as "like a wall and a support of philosophy" (*Dial.* 5) comes from the same source.

Of course Justin is not a pure Platonist, even a pure Platonist in terms of the eclectic philosophy of the second century. He is a Christian who finds that Plato and the Platonists (as well as the Stoics) have said many things well; and "whatever is said well by anyone" belongs to Christians too (*Apol.* ii. 13). This watchword of eclectic philosophy, already enunciated by Seneca, [10] is cited by Clement of Alexandria [11]

---

[1] Cic. *N. D.* i. 97.  [2] *Apol.* i. 55.  [3] *Riv. di storia della Filosofia* 1, 229–30; cf. Galen's criticism, p. 13 *supra*.  [4] *Apol.* ii. 12.  [5] *Dial.* 2.  [6] *Tusc.* i. 64 (probably Posidonius). [7] *Spec.* iii. 185; not original with Philo, as Wolfson (*Philo* I 160) argues.  [8] Eusebius, *Praep.* xi. 2. 4.  [9] *De Platone* i. 2, 3.  [10] *Ep.* 12. 11, 16. 7.  [11] *Str.* i. 37. 6.

7

as explicitly eclectic. This, then, is the philosophical-scientific milieu of Justin: the eclectic Platonism of the second century. In the New Academy the philosophers of nature were ridiculed;[1] Justin himself speaks of his ignorance of the encyclia (*Dial.* 2);[2] and what scientific knowledge he has is second-hand or worse. It is irrelevant to his main interests, which are theology and ethics.

Justin's pupil Tatian also rejects the encyclia as valueless (*Or.* 27). "What is the use of Attic style and the sorites of philosophers and the force of syllogisms and measurements of the earth and the positions of the stars and the courses of the sun? To investigate these matters is to dogmatize." He criticizes the doxographical opinions of those who call the sun a mass and the moon an earth, comparing them with the story of Herodorus about a lion who came down from an earth above ours. Similarly (*Or.* 20) he rejects the study of geography because no one has seen the edges of the world.[3] In a long attack he ascribes the cause of disease to demons and denies that medicines are of any value (*Or.* 16–18). It is obvious that Tatian knows more about science and philosophy than Justin does, but that he has no understanding of it whatever.

At the same time, Tatian wrote two "scientific" works, both of which are lost. The more important is his *Diatessaron*, a combination of the four canonical gospels into one. We are not here concerned with its content but with its title, which is apparently derived from Tatian's acquaintance with music. Just as in Irenaeus the four gospels correspond to the four regions of the earth and the four winds,[4] so for Tatian they correspond to the fourth harmony of music.[5] The difference between the two comparisons is that Irenaeus is concerned with four individual gospels, while Tatian insists on their harmonious unity, possibly relying on Philo's commentary on Genesis.[6]

Tatian's other scientific work is his lost treatise *On Animals*, to which he refers in his *Oration*. Some fragments (from the *Oration*) have been printed by Schwartz in his edition, and Wellmann has discussed them in his book *Der Physiologos* (Leipzig, 1930). The fragments are probably not complete and Wellmann's analysis is incorrect because he did not consider the philosophical background of Tatian in scepticism. We have to start with the passages which Tatian says he

[1] See p. 82 *supra*.   [2] Cf. the Hermetic *Asclepius* 13, with n. 115 of Nock–Festugière (p. 369).   [3] Cf. *VC* 3 (1949), 225–26.   [4] *Adv. haer.* iii. 11. 8.   [5] Cf. Plut. *Mus.* 22–23; Sext. Emp. *Adv. math.* i. 77.   [6] *Opif.* 48.

has discussed in the treatise on animals and deal with their probable context.

Tatian's purpose is to examine the ways in which man is like or unlike the animals. His own definition of man is "the image and likeness of God" (*Or.* 15). This image is not the soul but the spirit, which is given only to those who obey God (*Or.* 12–13). He then proceeds on purely sceptical grounds to criticize the Stoic definition of man as "a rational animal capable of intelligence and knowledge".[1] He argues that on Stoic grounds irrational animals are actually capable of intelligence and knowledge. In another passage he points out that men who use medicines are like animals who can cure themselves (*Or.* 18). The dog eats grass, the deer eats a viper, and the pig eats river-crabs. Thus man, apart from revelation, is no different from the animals.

Precisely the same line of argument is found in Sextus Empiricus.[2] The dog is so competent in matters of sense-perception and reasoning that it cannot be distinguished from man in this regard. It can even make various sounds, and when it is distressed by unwholesome humors it eats grass and recovers. The deer and pig of Tatian are found in such writers as Plutarch, Nepualius, and Aelian.[3] They are commonplace examples.

We see, then, that Tatian insists on the resemblance of man to the animals, just as Celsus does in writing against the Christians.[4] Wellmann thought that Tatian was a source of Origen; but this view is untenable, since Origen holds that the image of God is not the spirit but the reason of man and that animals find cures not by their reason but by instinct.[5] Tatian agrees with Celsus rather than with Origen. He does not rely on philosophy or science for anything but a negative kind of theology. As a sceptic rather than an eclectic he is a forerunner of Tertullian. His ideas on animals are not unlike those of Arnobius.[6]

Tatian's contemporary Athenagoras returns to the Platonic tradition of Justin, but it is for him a tradition combined with Peripatetic and Stoic ideas. Pohlenz[7] has shown that his stress on the close relation between body and soul is derived from the Peripatetics, and Lazzati[8]

[1] E. Schwartz, *Index Tatiani* 64 a.  [2] *Adv. math.* viii. 270–75, *Pyrrh.*i. 62–77.  [3] *Q.N.* 26; *V.H.* i. 7–9, *N.A.* v. 46, viii. 9; Nep 3.  [4] Origen, *C. Cels.* iv. 86.  [5] *Ibid.* iv. 85, 87.  [6] *Adv. gentes* ii. 16–18.  [7] *ZWT* 47 (1904), 241–50.  [8] *L'Aristotele perduto e gli scrittori cristiani* (Milan, 1938), 69–72.

has argued that he actually knows (perhaps indirectly) something of the early Aristotle. Athenagoras' argument for the possibility of resurrection (*Res.* 2) is apparently based on Posidonius' defence of divination. [1] His analysis of pagan miracles (*Leg.* 27) is derived largely from Stoic psychology. [2] We shall therefore expect to find his knowledge of science entirely second-hand, taken from commonplaces of philosophical debate. This expectation is fulfilled when we observe his discussion of the "law of nature" which prevents animals from attacking others of the same species and requires them to have intercourse only for the sake of offspring (*Leg.* 3). As Geffcken [3] has observed, these are commonplaces of Stoic discussions.

When Athenagoras endeavors to make a contribution of his own, the result is not very happy. He wants to prove that the flesh of Christians will rise even if it has been consumed by other human beings. He therefore gives an elaborate description of the process of digestion, probably derived from Stoic sources, [4] in which he shows how the body rejects unnatural foods. Then he proceeds to argue that since it is contrary to nature for animals to eat others of their own species, human digestive systems must reject human flesh. [5] The only difficulty with this conclusion is that it was not regarded as true even in antiquity. Athenagoras' enthusiastic acceptance of general principles should have been corrected by empirical observation.

Another apologist of the same period is Theophilus of Antioch. His philosophical background is a strange combination of Platonism and Stoicism with the scepticism of Carneades. [6] His lack of knowledge of philosophy is exceeded only by his confidence in attacking it. His scientific ideas are derived from an equally strange combination of cosmological, ethnographical, and chronological sources.

His picture of the universe is important because he is the first Christian writer to describe it. He believes that the sun, while undoubtedly bright and hot, is a very small planet. [7] The planets have no regular course but are so called because they wander about the sky. [8] The moon really waxes and wanes each month. [9] The earth is not spherical or cube-shaped. [10] He probably regards it as flat and

[1] Cicero, *N. D.* ii. 77.  [2] G. Bardy, *Athénagore* (Paris, 1934), 144.  [3] *Zwei griechische Apologeten* (Leipzig, 1907), 167–68.  [4] See chapter 15.  [5] *Res.* 5–6.  [6] Cf. *HTR* 43 (1950), 182–84.  [7] *Aut.* i. 5; Epicur. fr. 342–45 Usener; cf. Aristides, *Apol.* 6 : 2.  [8] *Aut.* ii. 15; cf. Epicur. *Ep.* ii. 92.  [9] *Aut.* i. 13, ii. 15; Epicur. *Ep.* ii. 94; cf. Aristides, *Apol.* 6 : 3.  [10] *Aut.* ii. 32; Epicur. fr. 302, pp. 214, 353 Usener.

hollowed out toward the center.[1] Finally, lightning precedes thunder in order to warn mankind of the sound.[2]

All these ideas can be found among the Epicureans rather than among Platonists and Stoics, and it is surprising to find Theophilus, a militant opponent of Epicurus, apparently deriving his cosmology from him. All these opinions reflect the crude phenomenalism of Epicurus.

Theophilus' ethnographical source is employed in his description of the gradual migration of mankind from its Arabian origin.[3] Mankind migrated in four directions: to the east; to the north, through the "great continent" (Europe) as far as Britain; to the south to Ethiopia, Egypt and Libya; and to the west along the shore of the Mediterranean to the "so-called" Gauls, Spains, and Germanies. This description of the populating of the world seems to be derived from a geography like that of Varro.[4] Unfortunately Theophilus has not troubled to combine this fourfold scheme with his own view, based on the three sons of Noah in the Old Testament, that the migrations took place in three directions. He states the view of his source and the view of the Old Testament as if they were the same.

Theophilus actually names his chronographical source, Chryseros the Nomenclator (*Aut.* iii. 27). This obscure figure[5] produced a list of kings, consuls, tribunes, and aediles from the foundation of Rome to the death of his patron, the emperor Marcus Aurelius (d. 180). From the list of Chryseros Theophilus takes enough information to calculate the length of time from Romulus to Marcus Aurelius. He connects this total with the biblical chronology by placing the death of Cyrus, king of Persia, in the sixty-second Olympiad, the 220th year from the foundation of Rome. Here his work is approximately correct, although elsewhere (*Aut.* iii. 29) he expresses the fear that he may have made errors of as much as two hundred years.

When we consider Theophilus' chronological work we cannot greatly regret our loss of his treatise *On History*, which he mentions in his extant work. He says that in it he discussed the genealogies of the sons of Noah (*Aut.* ii. 30). Presumably, if it ever existed, it was a

---

[1] *Aut.* ii. 13 („hollow places"); C. Bailey, *Titi Lucreti Cari De Rerum Natura* (Oxford, 1947), 1403. [2] *Aut.* i. 6; cf. Epicur. *Ep.* ii. 102 (without any idea of providence). [3] *Aut.* ii. 32. [4] Evidence for this point will be found in my forthcoming commentary on Theophilus. [5] Cf. Schenkl in *RE* Suppl. III 248–49.

midrashic treatment of the subject like the one we find in the *Clementine Homilies* and *Recognitions*. [1]

Theophilus, then, is no exception to the general picture of the second-century apologists which we have formed. They know little or nothing of science; they often misuse what little they do know; and they are not interested in science except as a subdivision of philosophy. This attitude toward science is common in their period and we should not criticize them for their lack of interest. It could also be said that the Christian church was not yet ready for a genuinely learned theology. The process of the integration of faith and reason still lay in the future, and, compared with the Alexandrians or Tertullian, the apologists must be classified as among the *simpliciores*, although they themselves would not have thought so.

With the apologists we must consider the anti-heretical work of Irenaeus of Lyons, the "father of western theology", whose thought has been influenced by them. His five books against heresies are not so remote from philosophy or science as is often supposed, [2] although his acquaintance with either is just as superficial as that of the apologists. He makes some use of doxographical materials for the history of philosophy, [3] criticizes Aristotelians for their pedantry and subtlety (*Adv. haer.* ii. 14. 5), and praises Plato for his piety (iii. 25. 5). At the same time he attacks Plato (ii. 33. 2) and philosophers in general (ii. 27. 1) as "dogmatists", adopting the viewpoint of the sceptics.

His criticism of Plato's doctrine of reminiscence reminds us of the arguments of the Peripatetic Strato, [4] who denied that it could be used to support the doctrine of the immortality of the soul. Irenaeus (ii. 33. 2—4) points out that souls do not remember what they previously were, while they do remember dreams. Plato may say that they have received a cup of oblivion (*Rep.* 621 b); how does he know? He is simply dogmatizing. Some Platonists say that the body is the cup of oblivion; [5] how then does the soul remember dreams and visions? It is evident that Irenaeus is relying upon some source sharply critical of Platonic teaching on the soul. [6] Elsewhere (ii. 19. 5) he compares the soul in the body to water in a jar; this comparison is probably Stoic. [7]

[1] Cf. H. J. Schoeps, *Aus frühchristlicher Zeit* (Tübingen, 1950), 11–19. [2] Cf. *HTR* 42 (1949), 41–51. [3] Diels, *Dox.* 171–72. [4] Fr. 122–27 Wehrli. [5] Cf. *Phaedo* 75 e; Albinus p. 178 : 10 Hermann. [6] As is Tertullian; cf. Waszink on *An.* 24 : 11. [7] Cf. Cic. *Tusc.* i. 52 (Posidonius).

Irenaeus knows something, though not very much, about geography. [1] In general, however, he shares the view of Tatian that scientific questions are irrelevant because they are not answered by revelation. He lists (ii. 28. 2) various items taken from a doxographical collection in order to show that such questions cannot be answered (see chapter 6). To be sure, the subjects were regarded as fairly obscure, but Irenaeus is willing to give up the investigation without beginning it. He is strongly influenced by scepticism. Only God can count the grains of sand, the waves of the sea, or the stars of the sky; only he can measure the earth (ii. 26. 3).

Irenaeus' only contact with science seems to be found in his criticism, which we have already discussed, of the miracles of the Valentinian Marcus. He clearly has no sympathy with the magician, and rejects the magic along with the use to which it was being put.

Thus we have seen that in orthodox writers of the second century there is practically no interest in science. Theology dominates their minds to the exclusion of almost everything else. The Marcosians were apparently interested in chemistry, but only for a severely practical purpose. Only at Rome among a small group of dynamistic monarchians was there any interest in secular learning. To this group we shall next turn.

[1] *VC* 3 (1949), 226.

## SCIENCE IN CHRISTIANITY

Our understanding of the dynamistic Monarchians at Rome has been considerably clarified by the recent study of Richard Walzer, *Galen on Jews and Christians*. In it he collects the passages which reflect Galen's interest in and criticism of Jewish and Christian theology and ethics, and relates the position of Galen to the attempts of Roman Monarchians to create a learned theology. The critical and scientific studies of these Christians are described by a contemporary opponent whose attack is reproduced by Eusebius. [1] They were notorious for their interest in textual criticism, their application of logic to the scriptures, and their study of geometry.

> Some of them make a laborious study of Euclid; they admire Aristotle and Theophrastus; and some of them almost worship Galen.

As Walzer points out, their interests and their enthusiasm for Galen are closely related. Galen was sometimes occupied with the study of the text of Hippocrates and Plato. He naturally recommended Euclid as a primer of geometry, and we know that he was greatly concerned with the logical writings of Aristotle and Theophrastus. [2]

Thus the first attempt within Christianity to combine faith with reason on genuinely rational grounds is due to the non-Christian physician and philosopher Galen. No wonder that the majority of simple believers distrusted the new methods! Nevertheless, these methods continued to be applied. At Rome itself we soon find the ecclesiastical writer Gaius applying literary criticism to the gospels, [3] and at Alexandria we find the combination of Christianity not with Aristotelianism but with Platonism. The impulse to create a learned theology is not due to the Roman Monarchians. It reflects a widespread feeling of the need of something beyond simple faith. But the Roman Monarchians deserve credit for being the pioneers.

[1] Eus. *H. E.* v. 28. 13–14.   [2] Walzer, *op. cit.*, 77–86.   [3] Cf. my article in *JR* 25 (1945), 183–96, esp. 188–89.

Some of the voluminous writings of Hippolytus, bishop of Rome at the beginning of the third century, reflect the new Christian interest in scientific questions. The first and fourth books of his *Refutation of All Heresies* are a hodge-podge of Greek sources. In the first book we find a collection of biographical and doxographical items on the history of philosophy. [1] The fourth book consists of a reproduction of a passage from Sextus Empiricus, [2] a part of a commentary on the *Timaeus* of Plato, [3] a treatise on arithmetic, [4] a treatise on astrology arguing that the constellations in the signs of the zodiac produce the physiognomy and character of men, [5] a short treatise against magic largely based on Anaxilaus, [6] something called Egyptian but really Neo-Pythagorean on the theory of numbers, [7] and part of a commentary on the *Phenomena* of Aratus. [8] The earlier *Chronicon* of Hippolytus begins with an ethnographical study, largely based on Jewish sources, of the way in which mankind developed from the migrations of the three sons of Noah. It includes lists of the most famous mountains and rivers and ends with the sources of the rivers of Paradise. [9] There follows next the *Stadiasmos* of the Mediterranean sea, a list of the distances from one port to another along the coast. This work, as A. Diller has pointed out, [10] is from the Augustan period; it is a part of the treatise ascribed to Menippus of Pergamon. Finally Hippolytus comes to the chronicle proper and traces the history of mankind from Adam to his own day. Another scientific-philosophical treatise of Hippolytus is preserved only in three ninth-century excerpts. This is the work *Against the Greeks and against Plato, or On the Universe.*

We must admit that the problem of Hippolytus is more difficult than might at first appear to be the case. The three works which we have mentioned are not ascribed to him in antiquity. The *Refutation* was transmitted under the name of Origen; the *Chronicon* is anonymous; and the treatise *On the Universe* is attributed by Johannes Philoponus, Photius, and the author of the *Sacra Parallela* to a certain Josephus. We shall see, when we consider his attitude toward miracles (p. 192), that Hippolytus' point of view in such a work as the *Commentary on Daniel* is quite different from that reflected in these scientific treatises.

---

[1] Diels, *Dox.* 144–56. [2] *Ref.* iv. 1–7 (Sext. Emp. *Adv. math.* v. 37–39). [3] *Ref.* iv. 8–13. [4] *Ref.* iv. 14. [5] *Ref.* iv. 15–27. [6] *Ref.* iv. 28–42; cf. Wellmann, *op. cit.*, (p. 95, n. 2) 57–62. [7] *Ref.* iv. 43–44. [8] *Ref.* iv. 46–50. [9] *Chron.* 235–39. [10] *Class. Philol.* 1949, 69.

For this reason (among others) P. Nautin has recently argued that the scientific treatises are wrongly ascribed to Hippolytus and that they were actually written by a certain Josephus, leader of a schism in the Roman church. [1] Nautin also holds that the statue of a Roman Christian which contains a list of his works is a statue not of Hippolytus but of this enigmatic Josephus.

For our present purposes we do not need to reach any positive conclusion as to the merits of Nautin's thesis, although on balance it seems less probable than the traditional view. In any event, these works reflect the degree of scientific culture which some Roman Christians had achieved at the beginning of the third century.They continue the tradition of the dynamistic Monarchians. The erudition of these works is somewhat disjointed, however; it serves more for display than for a synthesis of science and theology. At Alexandria, on the other hand, we find not only a more impressive display of second-hand erudition, in Clement, but also an attempt to unify philosophical learning with theology.

The beginnings of the school of Alexandria are lost in obscurity, although it must have had some relation to the earlier followers of Philo there. The figure of Pantaenus, said to be its founder, is somewhat shadowy, although Eusebius [2] tells us that he was formerly a Stoic and later evangelized the orient as far as India. Envoys actually came from India to various Roman emperors, [3] and we know that in this period there were Indians at Alexandria. [4] But it is difficult to state with certainty whether Pantaenus visited India or only South Arabia, which was also known by this name. [5] Possible confirmation of Pantaenus' visit to India might be found in the fact that his pupil Clement is the first Greek writer to mention the Buddha, but this mention probably comes from the work of Megasthenes. [6]

Clement frequently argues in favor of the study of the encyclia, and his writings reflect a considerable knowledge of details which he gleaned from such study. [7] What he knows of natural science seems to come from a slight acquaintance with the *Aphorisms* of Hippocrates, a little knowledge, presumably second or third hand,

---

[1] *Hippolyte et Josipe* (Paris, 1947); *Hippolyte Contre les hérésies* (Paris, 1949), esp. 215–30. For a detailed refutation cf. B. Capelle in *RTAM* 17 (1950), 145–74. [2] *H. E.* v. 10. 3. [3] J. O. Thomson, *History of Ancient Geography* (Cambridge, 1948), 299. [4] Dio Chrys. *Or.* xxxii. 40. [5] M. Höfner, *RAC* I 579. [6] O. Stein in *RE* XV 319–20. [7] *Str.* vi. 92–93, etc.; P. Camelot in *RSR* 21 (1931), 38–66.

of Aristotle's biological works, some curious information about
various animals, also derived from some manual or manuals, and
some gynecological ideas which have probably already passed into
a discussion of the wonders of teleology. On the last topic he deals
at length with the wonders of conception, of the origin of the embryo,
and of lactation. [1] Not without interest is a strange little passage on
breathing. [2] The following kinds of breathing are differentiated:
the breathing of demons, marine animals, insects, lunged animals,
and plants and hibernating animals. This topic also interested
Tertullian. [3]

We shall see when we come to deal with miracle that Clement is
sufficiently interested in science so that he corrects some strange
animal lore from sources ultimately derived from Aristotle. Of his
information about animals in general we can say that it is no worse,
and no better, than that of his contemporaries. It comes from the
same sources as that of Plutarch, Aelian, and Athenaeus. [4]

The scientific ideas of Origen are somewhat more fully integrated.
Following Clement of Rome, he holds that the earth is spherical. [5]
He believes in the orderly course of the planets, as we have seen in
examining his idea of nature (chapter 1). He states that motion is
caused either externally, as in the case of wood and stones, or internally, as in the case of animals, plants, fire, and springs. The rational
animal has a source of motion above both; this is its reason. Origen
therefore proceeds to argue that the stars are not moved by external
forces; their motion is caused internally, and it is due to free will. [6]
His whole picture of nature is thus Stoic, from the sphericity of the
world to the free will of the stars. [7]

Nevertheless, as Pohlenz has observed, Origen has no real interest
in the workings of nature. His *Commentary on Genesis* included no
explanation of the order of nature, and his only interest in it is as a
reflection of the idea of providence, with which he was greatly concerned. [8]

We see this interest in providence in his treatise *Contra Celsum*, in
which the old arguments for and against the rationality of animals

[1] *Paed.* ii. 83–97; i. 48–49; i. 39–41.　[2] *Str.* vii. 32–34.　[3] *An.* 10 : 5.　[4] On
his relation to Athenaeus cf. L. Nyikos, *Athenaeus quo consilio quibusque usus subsidiis
dipnosophistarum libros composuerit* (Basel, 1941), 99–112.　[5] *Pr.* ii. 3. 6 (1 Clem.
20 : 8).　[6] *Pr.* iii. 1. 2; *Orat.* vi. 1.　[7] SVF II 499, 989, 684–86; Cic. *N. D.* ii. 44.
[8] M. Pohlenz, *Die Stoa* II 205.

are brought forth. [1] Here again Origen follows the Stoics in holding
that the knowledge of animals is due simply to instinct. Celsus had
presented the old Academic arguments and the old Academic
examples, together with a few new emphases on the piety of animals.
Origen gives the traditional replies. Civilization among the ants
and bees merely imitates the rational and is no proof of rationality,
or of civilization. Bees and their hives exist to provide honey for men.
Ants collect food not by reason but because of "all-maternal nature".
Animals' remedies are due not to reason but to their natural constitution. Origen even criticizes Celsus' sources. "I know many
marvelous things about the nature of the animal [elephant] and its
habits, but I do not know of any reference to its oaths." [2] As Wellmann
points out, this note shows that Celsus' source is related to Juba of
Mauretania, in whose treatise this reference is found, while Origen's
is not. [3] We may add with Koetschau that Origen may actually
know something about bees from personal observation—although
this too may come from his Stoic source. [4] Origen's interest in the
subject, like Philo's, is due entirely to his desire to preserve providential care for mankind alone.

Like his contemporaries Origen believes in the spontaneous generation of snakes from dead men, bees from oxen, wasps from horses,
beetles from asses, and worms from many things. [5] He tentatively
accepts the generation of the first men from the earth. [6] And he
believes in parthenogenesis in the case of vultures, probably taking
the example from previous philosophical debates. [7] He also believes
that some animals have moral characters. The partridge, for example,
is wicked, while the turtle-dove is virtuously monogamous. [8] On the
question of non-existent animals his mind seems to have changed, for
in the early treatise *De principiis* he treats the goat-stag and griffin as
non-existent, [9] while in the late work *Contra Celsum*, while doubting
the existence of the phoenix, he accepts that of the griffin. [10] This
change could be due simply to his use of two different Stoic treatises.
The non-existence of the griffin was not a dogma.

[1] *C. Cels* iv. 73–99; cf. H. Chadwick in *JTS* 48 (1947), 34–49.   [2] *C. Cels*. iv. 98.
[3] M. Wellmann, *Der Physiologos* (Leipzig, 1930), 7–8; Juba, fr. 53 Jacoby.
[4] Koetschau, *Origenes Werke: Contra Celsum* xxvii.   [5] *C. Cels*. iv. 57; *Hom. in Luc.*
xiv, 101 Rauer.   [6] *C. Cels*. i. 37.   [7] *Ibid.*; cf. Ael. *N. A.* ii. 46.   [8] *Hom. in Jer.*
xvii. 1; *In cant. cant.* ii, 155 : 16 Baehrens; cf. *Hom. n Lev.* ii. 2; Tert *Monog.* 8;
Ael. *N. A.* iii. 44.   [9] *Princ.* iv. 3. 2.   [10] *C. Cels*. iv. 98; iv. 24; cf. Ael. *N. A.* iv. 27.

Origen's ideas on scientific subjects present the usual mixture of science and superstition which was common in the Graeco-Roman world. On the one hand, he is acquainted with the theory which explained the precession of the equinoxes—the gradual movement of the "fixed" stars—as due to a movement of these stars different from their daily circle around the earth. He has also heard that there is a sphere above that of the stars which is really fixed. [1] On the other hand, Origen firmly believes in magic. [2] He knows that the Egyptian magicians who contended with Moses could change water into blood, although he does not think that they could change blood into water. [3]

An even richer mixture is to be found in the fragmentary remains of the third-century polymath Julius Africanus. [4] He was interested in grammatical questions, both Homeric and biblical. In a fragment of his *Cesti* preserved in an Oxyrhynchus papyrus (P. Oxy. iii. 412), he discusses a magical incantation which he says is found in various Homeric manuscripts he himself has seen, and provides several hypotheses to explain its absence in other manuscripts. [5] A letter to a certain Aristides tries to explain the discrepancies between the genealogies of Jesus related in the gospels of Matthew and Luke. He has to invent some historical personages in order to reconcile the gospels, but he feels that "no clearer explanation could be found". [6] A letter to Origen on the story of Susanna is rather more satisfactory. Africanus is arguing that the story is "late and fictitious", and he proves his point by a series of arguments derived from rhetorical study (see chapter 4, page 59). To show the lateness of the story he points out that its style is like that of a mime, that it contains plays on Greek words, that it is not accepted by Jews, and that it differs in style and content from the book of Daniel. In Susanna a prophet cries out under the inspiration of the spirit, while in Daniel prophecies are made by means of visions and dreams and the appearance of an angel. To show the fictitious character of the story, he argues that since the Jews were captives among the Chaldaeans, no Jew could

---

[1] References and analysis in P. Duhem, *Le système du monde* II (Paris, 1914), 191–93. [2] G. Bardy in *RSR* 18 (1928), 126–42. [3] *Num. hom.* xiii. 4 (ii. 112 Baehrens). [4] Cf. W. Kroll–J. Sickenberger in *RE* XI 116–25. [5] Cf. E. Hefermehl in *BPW* 26 (1906), 413–15. [6] Cf. my article in *JR* 25 (1945), 192–93; the text of Africanus' letters: W. Reichardt, *Die Briefe des Sextus Julius Africanus an Aristides und Origenes* (Leipzig, 1909).

pronounce the death sentence, especially against the wife of Joachim, a king whom the king of Babylon had enthroned. And Joachim must have been a king; otherwise he would not have had such a fine house and garden. Here Africanus is quitting fact for fancy, but the general line of his argument is sound.

Africanus was not only a literary critic but also a great traveler. He claims to have seen manuscripts of the *Odyssey* at Aelia Capitolina (Jerusalem), at Nysa in Caria, and at Rome "in the beautiful library at the Pantheon which I myself designed for the emperor". J. G. Winter remarks that "the statement about the manuscripts is open to unlimited doubt", [1] but there is no reason for us to share his scepticism. Africanus visited the court of Abgar IX of Edessa (where he encountered Bardaisan), the places in Parthia and Phrygia where Noah's ark was said to have landed, and the Dead Sea. [2] Because of the reputation of Heraclas he went to Alexandria. [3] We must suppose that he was able to look at manuscripts if he wished to do so.

At the same time the fragments of his *Cesti* reflect an insatiable enthusiasm for magic, military stratagems, alchemy, and stories about horses (which he knows actually see demons). [4] In his *Chronicon* he denies that the darkness at the crucifixion could have been caused by an eclipse, for no eclipse is possible at the time of the full moon. The darkness was "God-made". [5] He includes a mention of an Egyptian lamb which spoke with a human voice; even Aelian had denied the credibility of this story. [6]

The oddness of the combination of various motifs in the work of Julius Africanus has led G. Björck [7] to argue that in his *Cesti* he was simply producing a parody of magical and paradoxigraphical literature. Björck contrasts Africanus' careful analysis of the story of Susanna with his acceptance as a part of the *Odyssey* of an incantation which even includes the names of Egyptian gods. He points out that some of the magical tricks described in the *Cesti* are simply ludicrous; they show the foolishness to which the study of magic can lead. Moreover, serious writers on such subjects employed a severe and unadorned style, while Africanus speaks of magic in the tones of Asiatic rhetoric.

[1] *Life and Letters in the Papyri* (Ann Arbor, 1933), 43. [2] *Cesti* vii, fr. 20 Viellefond; *Chron.* fr. 7, 13 Routh. [3] *Chron.* fr. 54. [4] J. R. Viellefond, *Jules Africain, fragments des Cestes* (Paris, 1932); demons in fr. 8, p. 24. [5] Fr. 50. [6] M. J. Routh, *Rel. sacr.* (ed. 2, 1846), II 260; Ael. *N. A.* xii. 3. [7] *Apsyrtus, Julius Africanus et l'hippiatrique grecque* (*Uppsala Univ. Årsskr.* 1944, no. 4), 13–25.

The thesis of Björck, who compares Africanus with the satirist Lucian, provides a way to explain the peculiar mixture which we find in Africanus. It must be admitted, however, that a similar mixture of science and superstition is present in many writers of the second and third centuries. And while horses see demons in the *Cesti*, which might be a parody, we must remember that in the serious *Chronicon* we read about the lamb with a human voice. Moreover, the use of Asiatic rhetoric does not necessarily imply the absence of seriousness. There may be elements of parody in the *Cesti*, but as a whole it reflects one of the many sides of Africanus' personality. [1]

Similar contact with what may be called general culture is to be found in the person of Bardaisan, whom Julius Africanus encountered at the court of Abgar. Africanus tells us that Bardaisan's skill in archery was such that he could outline a young man with arrows without touching him. [2] Out of his many writings we mention only two. First is his treatise *Indica*, known to Porphyry and Jerome, and based on information derived from an embassy of Indians who visited Syria in the reign of Elagabalus (218—22). [3] Second is the *Book of the Laws of Countries*, composed not by Bardaisan himself but by his disciple Philippus. It is a work intended to prove the futility of astrology from the existence of the various "laws of countries". The method of Bardaisan is not new, and most of his arguments are ultimately derived from Carneades. [4] More interesting is his emphasis on free will, which only man has because he was made in God's image. Bardaisan differentiates nature, fortune, and free will. Nature governs the actions of animals. Thus lions are carnivorous, and sheep herbivorous; bees make honey, ants lay up stores for the winter, and scorpions sting. The physical nature of man is governed by nature. He is born, is brought up, grows, begets children, grows old—all the while eating, drinking, sleeping and waking,—and dies. But his mind is free. He can choose whether to be carnivorous or herbivorous or to abstain from animal food. He can choose whether to take vengeance like lions and leopards and injure others like scorpions, or to be led like sheep. Since these changes and choices are possible,

---

[1] For the hypothesis that he built the third-century Christian basilica at Emmaus cf. L. H. Vincent–F. M. Abel, *Emmaüs: sa basilique et son histoire* (Paris, 1932), 257–62, 331–41. [2] *Cesti* vii, fr. 20; on Bardaisan cf. L. Cerfaux in *RAC* I 1180–86. [3] Cf. Porph. *Abst.* iv. 17; Stob. *Anth.* i. 3. 56. [4] Gundel in *RE* VII 2644; D. Amand, *Fatalisme et liberté dans l'antiquité grecque* (Louvain, 1945).

man is not governed by nature entirely. In matters of human conduct "nature has no law". [1] On the other hand, not everything is in man's power. Actually "men are governed by nature equally, by fortune differently, and by our freedom each as he wishes". [2]

If we examine the writings of the Latin apologists, we shall find very little interest in science among them. Minucius Felix, probably the earliest Latin apologist, is concerned with the philosophical idea of natural law (see chapter 2), but the only scientific items he offers are taken from school debates where they served to support arguments for the existence of providence. He speaks of divine providence as exercised not only for the universe but also for its parts. From Cicero [3] he derives the examples of the beneficence of the Nile, the Euphrates, and the Indus; and he adds the example of Britain, which lacks sunlight but is warmed by the surrounding sea. [4] This, as Thomson observes, is probably the earliest reference to the Gulf Stream. [5] Minucius also speaks of the work of divine providence in human conception and birth. [6] This too is philosophical commonplace.

In the case of Tertullian, we have already seen (chapter 2) his sceptical rejection of "laws of nature". He also attacks curiositas and holds that one must not investigate such matters as the shape of the world. Philosophers who study these things have a "lust for conjectures". [7] Like many of his contemporaries he denies the possibility of the existence of the antipodes. [8] His fairly extensive collection of stories about animals is largely derived from the Natural History of Pliny, although he occasionally uses other sources. [9] He takes as a model for his description of Pontus in his own day (Marc. i. 1) the description of the Massagetae given by Herodotus (iv. 121, 126) seven centuries earlier. [10] Even his description of a hydraulic organ comes from "popular philosophy in which Stoic conceptions played a prominent part". [11] In other words, Tertullian's science is all literary and philosophical. He has no interest whatever in it for its own sake. His lack of interest is reflected in the carelessness with which he used doxographical collections. [12]

[1] W. Cureton, Spicilegium syriacum (London, 1855), 10; cf. Eus. Praep. vi. 10. 10. [2] Cureton, op. cit. ,12. [3] N. D. ii. 130. [4] Oct. 18 : 3. [5] History of Ancient Geography (Cambridge, 1948), 358 cf. 151. [6] Oct. 18 : 2. [7] Pr. 7, Nat. ii. 4. [8] Nat. i. 8. [9] J. H. Waszink, Tertullian De Anima (Amsterdam, 1947), 46*. [10] E. Ivánka, Hellenisches u. christliches im frühbyzantinischen Geistesleben (Vienna, 1948), 31–34. [11] Waszink, op. cit., 216. [12] VC 5 (1951), 113–15.

There is a little more interest in scientific questions in the treatise *Adversus gentes* of Arnobius, written about the year 300, but much of his information comes to him through doxographical sources. After a list of such items (ii. 58–59) he concludes in the manner of Irenaeus with an appeal to revelation.

> What is to you, God says, to examine, to investigate ... whether the sun is larger than the earth or measures only a foot across; whether the moon shines by the light of another or by its own beams? There is no gain in knowing these things ... Leave these things to God (ii. 61).

From Herodotus and Tertullian [1] he repeats the story of an ideal experiment which by isolating an infant from outside contacts would determine what its true nature is (ii. 20–23). But, once again, the chief interest of this example lies in its usefulness for debate, not in the possibility of actually performing such an experiment.

His contemporary Lactantius argues that since philosophy consists of two elements, knowledge (*scientia*) and opinion, and since knowledge comes only through sense-perception, everything we may say on the subject of astronomy and meteorology is only a matter of opinion. It is like the description of a remote city which we know only by name. [2] From this standpoint he can criticize atomism. [3] "Who ever saw atoms? Who felt them? Who heard them? Or did Leucippus alone have eyes? Did he alone have a mind?" And he can argue, following Irenaeus, not only that the study of causes leads to uncertainty but that there is no blessedness (*beatitudo*) in knowing the source of the Nile. [4] From doxographical sources he gives a list of natural phenomena we cannot understand. [5]

Certainly Lactantius' own understanding of this topic was not very thorough. He attacks Xenophanes, "who most stupidly said that the moon was eighteen parts greater than the earth". This is a confusion of two passages in Cicero's *Lucullus*; Xenophanes said nothing of the sort. [6]

His information about animals seems to come largely from Cicero and Vergil, although for his understanding of human physiology he relies on the more dependable Varro. [7] But all his ideas are rhetorically and philosophically expressed; he has no interest in science except as a tool of apologetics.

This lack of interest leads him to a strange contradiction. He

[1] Herodotus ii. 2; Tert. *Nat.* i. 8.  [2] *Div. inst.* iii. 3. 1–5.  [3] See p. 147.  [4] *Div. inst.* iii. 8. 29.  [5] *Div. inst.* iii. 3. 4; *VC* 3 (1949), 228.  [6] *Div. inst.* iii. 23. 12; Cic. *Luc.* 82, 123; Diels, *Dox.* 121 n. 1.  [7] E. g. *Opif.* 12.

8

claims that if the world were spherical it would have to be uniform in appearance, [1] and asks, "Is there anyone so stupid as to believe that there are men whose footprints are higher than their heads?" [2] On the other hand, he uses a proof of the existence of God which is based on the sphericity of the universe and ultimately on the sphericity of the world. This is the famous example of the "sphere" or orrery of Archimedes, which Lactantius takes from Cicero. [3]

This machine was turned by a crank and made models of the sun and the other planets go about their courses with a fair degree of accurate imitation. As Cicero says, [4] Archimedes "had thought out a way to represent accurately by a single device for turning the sphere those various and divergent movements with their different rates of speed". Posidonius later used Archimedes' manufacture of this sphere as an analogy to the work of God. [5]

Two things are peculiar in Lactantius' use of the analogy. In the first place, it not only suggests a picture of the heavens which he elsewhere rejects but also argues for a knowledge of the heavens which he declares impossible. In the second place, he triumphantly concludes that if a Stoic had seen the machine in operation he would not have believed that the world moves automatically but instead that it was governed by the mind of its maker. This is an odd conclusion to draw from an example invented by a Stoic teacher; and in any event the Stoics did not hold that the world is moved automatically—that was the Epicurean view. [6]

It is not too sweeping a generalization to state that among Latin Christian writers interest in natural science and in nature itself was much slighter than it was among their Greek compatriots. Proof of this statement is to be found not only in the writings we have just discussed, but also in the treatise on nature by Dionysius of Alexandria, briefly summarized in our first chapter. Latin writers and, we must assume, their readers were more concerned with rhetoric than with nature. It is not pure coincidence that Minucius Felix, Arnobius, and Lactantius were rhetoricians while Tertullian was a lawyer also (and all the more) trained in rhetoric. Certainly Greek Christian writers are devoted to rhetoric too, but they seem to retain some interest in the subject-matter which underlies their speeches.

---

[1] *Div. inst.* iii 24. 8.  [2] *Ibid.*, iii. 24. 1.  [3] *Ibid.*, ii. 5. 18; Cic. *N. D.* ii. 88.  [4] *Rep.* i. 21–22.  [5] Cic. *N. D.* ii. 88, *Tusc.* i. 63; cf. Sext. Emp. *Adv. math.* ix. 115, Galen *U. P.* xiv. 5, p. 295: 7.  [6] Cf. Cic. *N. D.* i. 53–54.

The difference is also present in their attitudes toward philosophy. Roman Christian writers often seem to have retained the Roman suspicion, now outmoded, of Greek learning as subversive and lacking seriousness. Greek writers, on the other hand, use philosophy and in what science they know in constructing a synthetic theology which does not exclude speculation and does not depend to so great an extent on authority.

In the latter half of the third century we find much scientific information and something of a scientific spirit in the homilies on the six days of creation by Basil, bishop of Caesarea in Cappadocia. Their sources have been analyzed most recently by S. Giet in the introduction to his edition. [1] They consist of Plato (especially the *Timaeus*), Aristotle (usually through an intermediary), to a lesser extent the Stoics (perhaps Posidonius), and some items from paradoxographical sources, including the pseudo-Democritean literature (Bolos). On the relative importance of these sources, we may say that Basil owes most to Peripatetic writings, though he certainly does not understand the Peripatetic point of view. [2]

We have already seen (chapter 2) that Basil has a high regard for the laws of nature. What is he to do when he meets opponents whose laws are different from his? For one thing, he can follow his predecessors in their sharp attack on the utility of science. He can say that his opponents speak of "logical necessities" (11 c) or "geometrical necessities" (24 a) which are either self-contradictory (11 c) or overruled by divine power (24 b). He can say that their ideas are impossible or fictitious (26 e). He can insist on logical consistency (29 e).

Unfortunately his attack leads him to be inconsistent himself. At one point he argues that we must have proof from sense-perception (24 d), but at another he attacks sense-perception with an hypothesis (25 a–b) and rejects an argument based on experience (36 a–b).

On the positive side it is significant that Basil takes such obvious pleasure in describing and discussing the workings of nature. As God's creation, it is good; most of it has a moral meaning, but Basil's interest in it goes beyond moral allegorizing. He is fascinated by the theories of Greek science even when he must reject them all in order to follow the book of Genesis.

In the last third of the third century we find a Christian bishop

[1] *Basile de Césarée: Homélies sur l'hexaéméron* (Paris, 1950), 47–69.  [2] Cf. 29a–30a.

who may have been master of the Aristotelian school at Alexandria.
This is Anatolius of Laodicea, described by Eusebius in glowing
terms. [1]

> He was an Alexandrian who for his achievements in rhetoric, the encyclia
> and philosophy, had attained the first place among our most illustrious
> contemporaries, for in arithmetic and geometry, in astronomy and other
> sciences, whether logical or physical, and in the rhetorical arts as well, he
> had reached the pinnacle. It is recorded that because of these achievements
> the citizens considered him worthy of teaching in the Aristotelian school at
> Alexandria. [so Rufinus].

Eusebius then quotes from his *Canons on the Pascha*, in which he upheld
a nineteen-year cycle of reckoning against the earlier efforts of
Hippolytus and Dionysius of Alexandria. [2] He also mentions Anatolius'
*Introductions to Arithmetic*, which consisted of ten complete treatises.
Perhaps the beginning of this work is represented by his little tract
*On the Decad* published by Heiberg and translated with further
observations by Tannery. [3] Other fragments exist in the *Theologumena
arithmetica* attributed to Iamblichus.

Tannery observes that the tract on the decad contains practically
nothing really new when compared with Theon of Smyrna, and that
all Anatolius has done is to exclude speculations on the relation of
the numbers to the Greek gods. This is the way in which he Christi-
anizes his source, which probably goes behind Theon to the Hellenistic
age. [4]

The importance of Anatolius lies not in his teaching, or even in his
attempt to use astronomical data for ecclesiastical purposes, but in
the fact that in the third century a Christian could be head of a
Peripatetic school. The gap between Christianity and science was
narrowing as Christian learning advanced and antique science
declined.

Late in the fourth century we find the compilation of the allegorical
animal lore of late antiquity in a collection known as the *Physiologus*. [5]
To give a precise date to the *Physiologus* is extraordinarily difficult.
Wellmann, however, has shown that it was not known to any of the
Greek fathers before the end of the fourth century, although animal

---

[1] *H. E.* vii. 32. 6; cf. 14–20.  [2] The treatise of Hippolytus is mentioned on the
base of his statue; cf. Gentz in *RE XVIII* 1, 1650–51.  [3] P. Tannery, *Mémoires scienti-
fiques* III (Paris, 1915), 12–30.  [4] *Ibid.*, 29–30.  [5] Greek text ed. F. Sbordone,
Milan, 1936; discussion by B. E. Perry in *RE* XX 1074–1129.

stories later found in it are often told by earlier writers, including
Clement, Origen, and Basil. The first traces of its use are in Ambrose
and in Eustathius, the translator of Basil's homilies on the Hexaemeron
into Latin. [1] A little later Augustine implicitly recommends its study
for expositors of scripture. [2]

The *Physiologus* is based on a combination of Christian allegorical
exegesis with some source ultimately derived from the paradoxo-
graphical-magical treatises of Bolos on sympathies and antipathies
(see chapter 1). [3] It tells fantastic stories, mostly about animals but
sometimes about plants and stones, in order to illustrate biblical
verses. In the first chapter the lion is identified with Christ. Its concealment of its tracks is then identified with the concealment of his
divinity. It sleeps with open eyes. So the Lord's body, but not his
divinity, slept on the cross. The lion cub is born dead, but on the
third day its father breathes on its face and raises it. In the fourth
chapter there is the story of the pelican, which feeds its offspring with
its own blood. When the young strike the faces of their parents, the
parents beat and kill them. Later the parents are sorry; they mourn
for the young for three days, and raise them on the third day. In the
eleventh chapter we read that when the snake grows old, it fasts
for forty days and forty nights until its skin loosens; then it finds a
rock and scrapes its skin off, becoming new. It does not poison a spring
while it is drinking from it. It is afraid of a naked man. And when
attacked it guards only its head. [4] These points are supposed to
illustrate the saying of Jesus, "Be wise as serpents" (Matthew 10 : 16).
The seventeenth chapter describes the whale. When it is hungry it
opens its mouth, and the sweet aroma which emerges attracts little
fish but not large and mature ones. This whale is the devil or the
heretics. The whale is also as large as an island. Sailors land on it and
build fires; unfortunately it soon dives and they are lost.

These examples will suffice to show the general character of the
*Physiologus*. The stories are given in translation by Perry, who also
provides a brief commentary. [5] The details about the various animals

---

[1] M. Wellmann, *Der Physiologos* (Leipzig, 1930), 3–11; on the date of Eustathius
(c. 400), B. Altaner in *ZNW* 39 (1940), 161–70. Perry 1103 prefers a second-
century date for the *Physiologus*, but without evidence. [2] *Doctr. christ.* ii. 24. [3] Perry
1105–11. [4] The second and fourth items are found in a catena fragment ascribed
to Origen (*Comm. in Matt.* fr. 202 Klostermann, p. 98), but both have parallels in
non-Christian literature (Perry 1083). [5] Perry 1078–96.

can usually be paralleled in other books about animals, but occasionally the author's enthusiasm for allegory causes him to invent stories to suit the requirements of the Christian history.

The influence of the *Physiologus* was very great. It passed through many redactions and was translated into Ethiopic, Syriac, Armenian, Coptic, [1] Arabic, and Latin, as well as into Slavonic and other languages. [2] Its influence on Christian art was also pronounced. [3]

That such a book could flourish to such an extent is a clear indication of the extent to which zoology had declined. The influence of Bolos, already strong in the first century (see chapter 1), had completely conquered that of Aristotle. The symbolical meaning of animals was more important than the facts about them. The "eyes of the soul" had blinded the eyes of sense-perception.

By the end of the fourth century Christian interest in natural science, like natural science itself, was practically dead. In Syria we find Nemesius of Emesa writing his treatise *On the Nature of Man*, in which he makes use of Aristotle and Galen in addition to Neoplatonic sources. [4] In the west, however, the triumph of Neoplatonism was almost complete. Some of the leading ideas of Ambrose, as Courcelle has shown, are derived from Plotinus, [5] even though Ambrose vigorously attacks philosophy. [6] What he knows of the workings of nature is taken from Vergil and other poets and from popular philosophy, although he also knows something about physiology. [7] As for Jerome, we must agree with Courcelle that "although he has read Pliny the Elder, he knows the non-Christian Greek naturalists only by name; the notions of the natural sciences indispensable for his commentaries he borrows from Greek or Latin ecclesiastical authors". [8] He has also read the principal works of Galen. [9]

The case of Augustine is somewhat more complicated. We have already seen (chapter 2) that he speaks of natural law with great respect. We shall later observe (chapter 10) that he criticizes the Manichaeans for their inability to explain solstices and equinoxes

[1] New fragments edited by A. van Lantschoot in *Coptic Studies in Honor of Walter Ewing Crum* (Boston, 1950), 339–63.  [2] Perry 1116–28.  [3] Perry 1128–29.
[4] W. Jaeger, *Nemesios von Emesa* (Leipzig, 1914); E. Skard in *RE* Suppl. VII 562–66.  [5] P. Courcelle, *Recherches sur les Confessions de saint Augustin* (Paris, 1950), 106–38.  [6] F. H. Dudden, *The Life and Times of St Ambrose* (Oxford, 1935), I 13–15.
[7] *Ibid.*, 16–20.  [8] P. Courcelle, *Les lettres grecques en occident* (Paris, 1943), 77–78.
[9] *Ibid.*, 74–75.

and eclipses. But what does he actually know of natural science? He does not give lists of philosophical opinions about the universe. As Marrou observes, [1] his learning would not have gained anything had he done so. But Augustine's knowledge of the world about him is above all else literary. His few statements on geographical matters seem to come from books, even commentaries on poets. For natural history he usually relies on folklore, although he believes that sometimes his experience has confirmed the strange stories he tells about stones and animals. In the case of medicine he has some exact knowledge, but he has paid especial attention to bizarre and abnormal cases. For physics and astronomy he relies not only on philosophers but also on the learned men who described natural phenomena; he is especially interested in the latter group. [2]

There is nothing new about this attitude, for we have found almost exactly the same viewpoint in Philo. What characterizes Augustine's thought, however, is his interest in the strange and unusual in nature which, he believes, makes belief in miracle a logical necessity (see chapter 13). This "curiosity" is typical of the literary life of the Roman empire and was only accentuated in the fourth and fifth centuries. [3]

His emphasis on novelty could be used, again, against the many persons even within the church who accepted the iron laws of astrology. Augustine admits that farmers and travelers must study the stars, but they must not study them too thoroughly. [4] At the same time, because of the strength of the classical tradition he can say that the order of nature revealed by astronomy is "a great proof of religion and a torment of the curious". [5]

Augustine's starting point, once he had become a Christian, was not scientific knowledge but the Bible. His efforts to relate miracles to natural law in the commentary *De Genesi ad litteram* arise because of difficulties in the biblical story, not because of an interest in science as such. Augustine like Plotinus was ultimately concerned only with God and with man, not with the stage on which the drama of salvation was being enacted.

There are no grounds on which one can blame those who live in another period of history for not sharing one's own interests. It might

[1] H. I. Marrou, *Saint Augustin et la culture antique* (Paris, 1949), 681.  [2] *Ibid.*, 135–47.  [3] *Ibid.*, 148–55.  [4] *Ep.* 55 : 15; L. de Vreesse, *Augustinus en de Astrologie* (Maastricht, 1933), 115.  [5] *Ord.* ii. 42.

be argued that in late antiquity life would have been longer, or more comfortable, or more cultivated had more attention been paid to natural science as a means for controlling nature by understanding it. The answer the ancients themselves would have given is very simple. Human life does not need to be longer, or more comfortable; if it were longer or more comfortable it could not be cultivated. The rise of asceticism and the introversion on which it was necessarily based tended to exclude a scientific interest in the world of nature.

Some ancient writers could imagine a kind of ascetic pursuit of science for its own sake. But a pure science which produces no practical results whatever is not likely to last, and on the other hand the kind of knowledge which men came to seek was not knowledge about the world but knowledge about themselves.

At the same time the old social structure was gradually breaking up and interest in the soul was given fresh impetus as men saw that they could do little to uphold the empire.

It certainly cannot be said that Christians or Christianity killed natural science, except in so far as Christianity answered the psychological needs of the new era as science did not. We have found Christians who vigorously opposed the old learning and those who vigorously defended and transmitted it. The reason ancient science died was presumably its excessive concern with logic rather than with facts, and especially its failure to combine logic with observation. It was given to premature generalization and to inadequate study of phenomena. In the absence of microscopes and telescopes its conclusions remained unverifiable, and it was easy for its opponents to say that they were mere conjectures. Some Christians attacked science without much knowledge, but had Christianity accepted ancient science wholeheartedly modern science might not yet have been born.

It must also be observed that at least in some respects Christians were far less credulous than their contemporaries, at least in the period before Augustine. While we have found (chapter 5) many writers of the second, third, and fourth centuries accepting the most absurd stories of mythology and miracle, the Christian attitude as expressed by theologians is much more reserved. It is significant that in his life of Alexander, Lucian represents him as opposed by Christians and atheists alone. [1] On what we may call a sub-theological level,

[1] *Alex.* 25, 38 (the atheïsts were Epicureans).

Christians shared the intellectual decadence of their contemporaries; their leaders, however, attacked polytheism and its mythologies with great vigor. [1]

Undoubtedly there were Christians who made use of magic, astrology, and all the other pseudo-scientific methods of the age. The leaders of the church, however, vigorously denounced these methods. [2] If sometimes they included what we regard as genuine science in the pseudo-science they rejected, we must remember the extent to which such science was actually conjectural and the low state which it had already reached.

---

[1] For Christian attacks on mythology cf. G. Stählin *TWzNT* IV 799–800. [2] Cf. W. Gundel in *RAC* I 825–31. Note Basil's contempt for magicians who claim to be able to draw down the moon (*Hex.* vi. 11).

# PART II
# CHRISTIANITY

# FRONTISPIECE—PART II

This fourth-century marble figure from Tarsus, at present in the Metropolitan Museum of Art in New York, depicts two episodes in the life of the prophet Jonah. To the right the ship's company is carefully placing him in the jaws of a sea monster; to the left he is being thrown up on the shore after his miraculous journey. It is significant for our purpose that the prophet is being placed in the monster's mouth feet first so that without undue effort he can later come out head first. This represents the partial rationalization of the miracle. It would strain one's credulity to imagine Jonah turning around inside a monster as narrow as this one was. Therefore, although earlier portrayals of Jonah's journey are willing to have him go in and come out head first, our sculptor reflects the ideas of those who on the one hand treat miracles as facts and on the other try to limit the degree of their miraculousness.

As we should expect, the magical papyri stress the omnipotence of God. [1] The power described in them is to be controlled by the magician, who like the gods can do "whatever he wishes". A magical papyrus of the second or third century of our era lists some of the conventional achievements of a magician. [2]

> [The sun] will stand still, and if I command the moon, it will come down, and if I wish to hold back the day the night will stay for me, and again, if we want daylight, the light will not go away; and if I wish to cross the sea, I do not need a ship, and if I wish to go through the air, I shall be lifted up.

A very similar list is given in the *Metamorphoses* of Apuleius. [3] We may note that these achievements are substantially the same happenings which poets normally regarded as impossibilities. They are not new: the same promises were made by the magicians criticized in the Hippocratic treatise *On the Sacred Disease*. (c. 4).

All this is on a lower level than philosophical thought, and philosophers (in spite of Plato, *Leg.* x. 901 d–e) were not hesitant about finding examples of things which God could not do. For example, Aristotle cites the poet Agathon in support of his view that not even God can change the past. [4] Epicurus and the Peripatetic Strato agree that divine power was not used in the formation of the universe. [5] And the Epicurean poet Lucretius argues that "nothing can come out of what does not exist, even by divine power (*divinitus*)". [6] Palaephatus is probably speaking ironically when he says that Artemis can do whatever she wishes, for he immediately adds that it is not true that a man (Actaeon) turns into a deer or vice versa. The poets invented this story for piety's sake. [7]

In the first century before Christ the idea of power became a leading conception, especially because of the increasing concentration of power at Rome, and it plays a considerable part in the system of Posidonius. [8] In his thought we find great emphasis laid upon the omnipotence of God. "There is nothing which God cannot do, and that without any effort." [9] He held that Zeus was above nature and fate—in other words, above natural law and in control of it. [10] But Posidonius also said that the "substance" of God was the cosmos,

---

[1] ZP iv. 641, vii. 582, xii. 250. [2] ZP xxxiv. [3] *Met.* i. 8; cf. R. Helm, *Incantamenta magica*, nos. 99–103. [4] *Eth. nic.* vi. 2. 6. [5] D. L. x. 76; Cic. *N. D.* i. 35, *Luc.* 121. [6] *Rer. nat.* i. 150. [7] *Incred.* 6. [8] M. P. Nilsson, *Greek Piety*, 103. [9] Cic. *N. D.* iii. 92 (cf. ii. 77). [10] Diels, *Dox.* 324; Cic. *Div.* i. 125; see p. 22.

and explicitly denied the posibility of creation *ex nihilo*. [1] His emphasis
on omnipotence, therefore, is a limited emphasis. He cannot reject
science in favour of theology. And he tries to prove the omnipotence
of God by analogies with the human mind and will, and by a reference
to the flexibility of nature.

Other philosophers were unwilling to follow the lead of Posidonius.
An Academic opponent of the Stoics suggests ironically that if God
is omnipotent he should have made the Stoics wise so that they would
not be so superstitious. [2] The eclectic Academic philosopher Antiochus,
who owed much to the Stoic school, parted company with them at
this point and vigorously rejected their idea of omnipotence. [3] In
the first century of our era the Roman Stoic Seneca accepts divine
omnipotence—probably reflecting the thought of Posidonius—but
is aware that it is a highly debatable question. [4]

Seneca's contemporary Pliny gives a list of things which God cannot
do, in order to prove that God does not exist outside nature. He
cannot die, give mortals immortality or recall the dead, change the
past, or—to use "facetious arguments"—make twice ten unequal to
twenty. [5] This list, presumably not original (for Pliny says that he is
omitting *multa similiter*), contains the elements of later discussions of
the topic.

These later discussions, like that of Pliny, are based primarily on
two points, the observed order of nature and the truth of arithmetic
and geometry. Relying on the observed order of nature, philosophical
writers state that God cannot change the past; he cannot make snow
black or fire cold; he cannot form a man out of stone or a horse or
bull out of ashes. Similarly they hold that God cannot make twice two
equal to five; he cannot make the diagonal of a parallelogram equal
in length to its side; he cannot make what is horizontal vertical or
vice versa. [6]

At the end of the second century two writers, Galen and Alexander
of Aphrodisias, discuss this topic in more detail. Galen is criticizing
the Jewish idea of the omnipotence of God. [7]

> To Moses it seems enough to say that God simply willed the arrangement
> of matter and it was presently arranged in due order, for he believes that
> everything is possible for God, even if he should wish to make a horse or a

---

[1] D. L. vii. 148; Diels, *Dox.* 462 : 14.    [2] Cic. *Div.* ii. 86.    [3] Cic. *Luc.* 50.
[4] *N. Q.* i. pr. 16.    [5] *N. H.* ii. 27.    [6] [Plut.] *Cons. ad Apoll.* 26; Diels, *Dox.* 299;
Gal. *Us. part.* xi. 14; Alex. Aphrod. *Fat.* p. 200.    [7] *Us. part.* xi. 14.

bull out of ashes. We, however, do not hold this; we say that certain things are by nature impossible, and that God does not even attempt to undertake such things; he chooses the best out of the possibilities of becoming.

What Galen is criticizing is not the idea of creation out of nothing, but the idea of something happening contrary to the ordinary course of nature. [1] Aristotle had already argued that the form of a man is his nature, because a man produces a man [2] (*Phys.* ii. 1, 193 b 8, 11) while a bed does not produce a bed. Later philosophers were accustomed to use the examples of the man and the horse when they dealt with the way in which "becoming" takes place by generation. [3] In the Peripatetic treatise *De spiritu* we find the horse and the bull. [4]

Similarly Alexander of Aphrodisias tells us that "according to nature" and "according to fate" a man is produced from a man and a horse from a horse. [5] This result is not "from necessity", however; some external cause could produce a result "contrary to nature". [6] On the other hand, twice two makes four "of necessity", though not "by fate", [7] and similarly the diagonal of a parallelogram "by necessity" cannot equal its side in length. [8] And since—as Plato himself testifies (*Theaet.* 176 a)—the gods cannot overcome necessity, they cannot accomplish what is necessarily impossible. [9] If the world is necessarily perishable, the gods cannot make it imperishable. [10] Things which are by nature impossible preserve this nature even with the gods, who cannot, therefore, make the diagonal of a parallelogram equal in length to its side or make twice two equal to five or cause anything which happened not to have happened. [11] Moreover, if the limitless is (necessarily) immeasurable, the gods cannot measure it. [12]

We may observe that for Galen, a physician, the significant examples are the man, horse, and bull, while for Alexander, a speculative philosopher, these examples are not "of necessity"; he prefers to use the examples which he regards as "necessary".

Among Platonists another kind of argument was employed. We find it set forth by the Middle Platonist opponent of Christianity, Celsus, who denies that "everything is possible for God". God cannot perform shameful acts and he does not will to do anything contrary

[1] Against R. Walzer, *Galen on Jews and Christians*, 27. [2] Cf. *Gen. anim.* iv. 4. [3] Max. Tyr. *Diss.* xvi. 4; M. Aurel. viii. 46. [4] *Sp.* 9. [5] *Fat.* p. 169. [6] P. 170. [7] *Qu.* ii. 5, p. 52. [8] *Qu.* i. 18, p. 31. [9] P. 32. [10] P. 31. [11] *Fat.* p. 200. [12] P. 201.

to nature. He is the rational principle of all existing things; therefore he will do nothing irrational or contrary to himself. [1]

The Christian opponent of Celsus, Origen, agrees with both the Peripatetic and the Platonic criticisms of unqualified omnipotence. In his theological treatise *De principiis* he states that God's power cannot be limitless. The limitless is by nature incomprehensible, and if God had unlimited power he would necessarily be unaware of it. [2] He also agrees with Celsus that God does not work contrary to nature, although—following Aristotle—he holds that God produces some effects "beyond (the ordinary course of) nature". [3] At another point Origen argues that God's power is limited by his justice. As far as his power alone is concerned, all things are possible for him. God is not merely powerful, however; he is also just. Therefore only just actions are possible for him. [4]

In Neoplatonism we find these questions discussed in much the same manner. The views of Porphyry are not altogether consistent. At one point he tries to avoid the theoretical question of omnipotence by pointing to the actual course of nature. No doubt God can permit navigation on land or labor and industry on the sea; he can make virtue vice and vice virtue; he can place wings on man and set the stars beneath the earth. God can do all these things—impossibilities often used by poets, perhaps here an ironical concession to Christian theologians—but he does not. [5] At another point, however, Porphyry states his own view with complete clarity. [6]

> All things are not possible for God. He cannot bring it about that Homer should not have been a poet or that Troy should not have been taken. He cannot make twice two, which equal four, to be reckoned as a hundred, even though this may seem good to him.

These are the traditional Peripatetic arguments. With them Porphyry combines the axiom of Platonists.

> God cannot ever become evil, even though he wishes to do so. He cannot sin, since he is by nature good.

Here Porphyry entirely agrees with Origen [7] in holding that these limitations reflect not the weakness but the nature of God. For these theologians the primary attribute of God was not power but good-

[1] Orig. *C. Cels.* v. 14.  [2] *Princ.* ii. 9. 1; cf. Plotinus, *Enn.* iv. 4. 9.  [3] *C. Cels.* v. 23.  [4] *Comm. ser. in Matt.* 95; cf. 1 Clem. 27 : 2.  [5] Mac. Magn.iv. 2.  [6] *Ibid.* iv. 24.  [7] *C. Cels.* v. 23.

ness. They held fast the tradition of Plato rather than that of Posidonius (see p. 128).

The later Neoplatonist Iamblichus returns to the ideas of Posidonius, [1] and brushes aside all such objections to the axiom of divine omnipotence. The true followers of Pythagoras, he says, believe all miracle stories, for they know that God can do anything. They are not like the "sophists" who think that God can do some things and not others. [2] In the thought of Iamblichus simple faith in religious tradition and—incidentally—in magic has triumphed over philosophical understanding. His Christian contemporaries often lay less stress on omnipotence than he does. Tertullian, of course, provides an exception (see p. 196).

Among Christian writers we need mention only two examples. Macarius Magnes agrees with Porphyry that God cannot change the past. Were he to do so, he would be denying his character as creator, for he would be changing the created into the uncreated. [3] Similarly Augustine teaches that if God were able to die he would obviously be diminishing his power. If he were able to be deceived or to make mistakes (such as regarding twice two as unequal to four), his knowledge would be diminished rather than increased. [4] The view of the Christian fathers is well summarized by the seventeenth-century Anglican bishop Beveridge. [5] Of God he says that

> it is impossible that he should please to do what implies a contradiction, for then he would will what is false, which being truth itself, it is a contradiction he should do. He cannot do that which no power can do.

For the fathers generally, both Greek and Latin, the omnipotence of God is not arbitrary and must be qualified by his other attributes. From another point of view it can be said that "any development of Greek theology, if it is to remain consistent with the presuppositions of Greek natural science, must stop short of the attribution to God of an omnipotent power over nature". [6] This stopping short sometimes takes strange forms.

The literalness with which non-literal statements in the New Testament came to be taken can be seen in some Christian exegesis of Mark 10 : 25 (Matt. 19 : 23, Luke 18 : 25). "It is easier for a

[1] K. Reinhardt, *Kosmos u. Sympathie* 255. [2] *Pyth.* 139; cf. Clem. *Ecl. proph.* xvi. 3. [3] Mac. Magn. iv. 30. [4] *Civ. dei* v. 10. [5] *Ecclesia Anglicana Ecclesia Catholica* 36–37. [6] M. B. Foster in *Mind* N.S. 43 (1934), 456.

camel to pass through the eye of a needle than for a rich man to enter the kingdom of God." The context clearly shows that the comparison is an *adynaton*. "With men it is impossible, but not with God; for all things are possible with God." [1] Some exegetes as early as the fifth century were unwilling to treat it as an *adynaton*. They wanted the impossible to be a little more possible; and in a *Tractatus de divitiis* we find the suggestion that the Latin word *camellus* means not only the camel but also a ship's cable. [2] In the tenth and eleventh centuries, but not earlier, the same explanation is given for the Greek word.

This kind of interpretation reflects the rationalizing exegesis of many early Christians who treat hyperbole as literal statement and make New Testament symbolism ridiculous by interpreting it as if it were fact.

Such theological refinements are not, of course, to be found in early Hebrew and Christian writers. In the Old Testament, as in Homer, the omnipotence of God is taken for granted. "The Lord did everything he wished in the heaven and in the earth" (Ps. 134 : 6). There are limits to his power, but they are not discussed. As in Homer, God like man cannot overcome death, except in a few special cases such as the assumptions of Moses and Elijah. Only gradually does the idea of God's power over death develop, as we shall see when we discuss the doctrine of resurrection (chapter 14).

The basic axiom is that God can do anything. When Sarah questions the possibility of conception at the age of ninety, God asks her, "Is anything too difficult (or wonderful) for the Lord?" (Genesis 18 : 14). In the Septuagint this question is rendered, "Shall anything be impossible with the Lord?" The whole emphasis on divine power in the Bible leads directly to the idea of omnipotence. [3]

Philo describes Jewish children as learning the axiom (*dogma*) of divine omnipotence from birth, [4] and it is reflected in the sayings of Jesus in the New Testament. "All things are possible with God" (Mark 10 : 28, 14 : 36). "Things impossible with man are possible with God" (Luke 18 : 27). This axiom is reflected in and supported by faith in God's power as manifested in the creation of the universe,

[1] Other *adynata* beginning with 'it is easier": Mark 2 : 9 (Matt. 9 : 5, Luke 5 : 23); Luke 16 : 17 ('it is easier for heaven and earth to pass away...."); cf. Sir. 22 : 15. [2] Cf. J. Denk in *ZNW* 5 (1904), 256–57. [3] Cf. P. Heinisch, *Theologie des Alten Testaments* (Bonn, 1940), 47–49, 128–29. [4] *Abr.* 112.

in nature miracles, and in the resurrection of the body. It leads immediately to highly complicated philosophical problems because of the qualifications of omnipotence which we have already mentioned.

In the next seven chapters we shall examine the ways in which these problems were faced in ancient Christian theology.

# 10

# CREATION

At the beginning of the Christian rule of faith there stands a brief statement of the miracle which most clearly differentiates the Christian idea of God and nature from Greek philosophy. This is the miracle of creation. It is intended to show that God is the sole lord of nature and history. He it is who created the world and man out of nothing, and who rules over both. There is no world of preexistent matter, independent of God, from which man's soul, a divine spark, will eventually be rescued. God made it all, and he saw that it was very good (Genesis 1 : 31). Just as the Bible begins, "In the beginning God created heaven and earth", and ends with a vision of a new heaven and a new earth after the resurrection, so the ancient symbols of faith begin with God the Almighty Creator and end with the life of the age to come. It is God in action, lifting and bringing down the curtain of history—but also creating the stage and the actors—who is "Alpha and Omega, the first and the last, the beginning and the end" (Revelation 22 : 13).

The doctrine of creation in Christianity was not worked out in philosophical or even theological reflection. It is the expression of religious insight which finds in God the source of all existence. Erich Frank accurately interprets the nature of this insight when he writes: [1]

> The Christian philosophers were fully aware of the fact that their idea of creation, just as their idea of God, was based on their religious faith, on revelation, not on intellectual reasoning. No matter how earnestly they tried to find a philosophical justification for their religious creed, the creation of the world remained a mystery beyond human understanding, the miracle of all miracles.

This miracle points toward the goodness of the creation, the meaningfulness of history in the created world, and the completeness of God's victory which must eventually come. It is a symbol of God's freedom and omnipotence.

---

[1] E. Frank, *Philosophical Understanding and Religious Truth* (New York, 1945), 59.

Nevertheless this miracle is not clearly or certainly set forth in the Hebrew Bible. The opening verses of Genesis, indeed, have often been understood, especially by the church fathers, as demonstrating the creation *ex nihilo*. But many others, in antiquity and in modern times, have taken them to prove the coeternity of matter with God. Driven by the compulsions of controversy, and by its own inner understanding of the relation of God to the world, the ancient church proclaimed belief in creation out of nothing. We shall first examine the way in which this idea arose in the Old Testament and in Judaism; next we shall consider the philosophical development which it encountered; and finally we shall turn to trace the idea of *ex nihilo* creation from Philo to Augustine.

Within the Old Testament the concept of creation was only gradually developed. [1] Perhaps the most ancient affirmation of God's creative power is to be found in the book of Job, where two chapters are devoted to the creation of the world through wisdom out of pre-existent chaos. Here God is clearly the orderer of chaos, as in Greek thought of the same period (sixth-fifth century B. C.), not the creator out of nothing. [2]

In the contemporary or slightly later Second Isaiah we find God as lord not only over Israel but also over all nations. He is creator of the whole universe of heaven and earth. He alone stretched forth the heavens. He alone creates. [3] His omnipotence is absolute.

> I am Yahweh, and there is none else; beside me there is no God.... I form the light and create darkness; I make peace, and create evil; I am Yahweh who does all these things (Isaiah 45 : 5–7).

He created the heavens, formed the earth and made it, established it and created it (Isaiah 45 : 18). Could the author tell us more plainly that matter was not preexistent?

A century later, the author of the Priestly Code tells the story of creation in a way which stresses "God's absolute sway over all that exists and his transcendent exaltation over the works of creation". [4]

> (1) In the beginning God created heaven and earth.
> (2) And the earth was waste and void, and darkness was upon the face of the deep, and the spirit of God moved upon the face of the waters.
> (3) And God said, Let there be light; and there was light.

[1] W. Eichrodt, *Theologie des Alten Testaments* II (Leipzig, 1935), 45–57.   [2] Job 28 and 38; R. H. Pfeiffer, *Introduction to the Old Testament* (New York, 1941), 704–6.   [3] W. Foerster in *T. W. z. N. T.* III 1007.   [4] Pfeiffer, *op. cit.*, 194.

These first three verses of Genesis became the foundation of all later Jewish and Christian explanations of the origin of the universe.

As Gunkel observes, [1] the second verse is not unique. The idea of preexistent chaos ordered or arranged by God is found not only elsewhere in the Bible, but also in the mythology of many other peoples. It is the first verse, with its statement that God created (*bara*, the word used by Second Isaiah) heaven and earth, which makes the Genesis story distinct from the others.

But even in this proclamation of the majesty of God it is not expressly stated out of what he made the universe. The ambiguity of the juxtaposition of the first two verses has troubled commentators, not only in modern times but also in antiquity. Does the second verse describe the situation existing at the time described in the first verse? Should we read, "in the beginning of God's creating heaven and earth"? Or is a sequence of events implied? Clearly the philosophical problem of creation *ex nihilo* did not enter the Priestly writer's mind. It seems likely, however, that had he been concerned with the question he would have insisted on the omnipotence of God and its corollary, the dependence of matter on him.

The same lack of interest in philosophy is found in the Psalms. Gunkel [2] points out that in them "the thought of the act of creation performed by the omnipotence of God is a principal theme". But it is never clearly stated precisely in what way his act took place. Theoretical, philosophical ideas are alien to the genius of the Hebrew Old Testament.

Not only in the Bible, but also in post-biblical Judaism, faith in God's act of creation was of primary importance. It is prominent in the apocryphal and pseudepigraphical writings. The ambiguity of the Old Testament, however, permitted interpretations which found pre-existent matter in Genesis. A philosophical opponent said to Rabbi Gamaliel, "Your God was a great artist, but he found excellent colors at his disposal". The rabbi asked what they were. "Chaos and darkness and water and wind and abysses." Gamaliel found it necessary to prove from scripture that each one was created by God. [3]

In the apocrypha we find two important statements of the doctrine. The naively religious 2 Maccabees represents the martyr mother of

[1] H. Gunkel, *Genesis* (ed. 3, Göttingen, 1917), 101.    [2] *Einleitung in die Psalmen* (Göttingen, 1933), 77.    [3] *Genesis Rabbah* i. 9; G. F. Moore, *Judaism in the Age of the Tannaim* I (Cambridge, 1927), 380–82.

the seven Maccabaean martyrs as confessing her faith in creation *ex nihilo*. God made the heaven and the earth and everything in them "not out of things existent" (2 Macc. 7 : 28). It is significant that 2 Maccabees also stresses the miraculous and the resurrection of the flesh.

On the other hand, the consciously Hellenizing Wisdom of Solomon is somewhat ambiguous in its attitude. Wisdom 11 : 17 describes God's omnipotent hand (Wisdom) as making the world out of "formless matter". What is formless matter? Two interpretations are possible. The author may simply be giving an "elegant rephrasing of Genesis 1 : 2 (= Heb. tohu wa bohu)" (R. Marcus). On the other hand, "formless matter" is the traditional Platonic description of the eternal matter out of which the Demiurge shaped the universe. Possibly the author is attempting an apologetic compromise, as he apparently does elsewhere. For example, in Wisdom 8 : 19–20 antithetical Hebrew and Greek ideas of the nature of the soul are simply placed side by side. [1]

In the Christianity of the New Testament period, emphasis was laid on creation only in relation to the new, eschatological creation effected in Christ. The emphasis is almost entirely on Christology. But in several instances it is suggested that the Christian view will eventually be that of a creation out of nothing. This was not only a natural conclusion for those to draw who had not encountered Greek philosophy, but also a conclusion required on the grounds of a dynamic eschatological faith in God. Christ, who is the Wisdom of God, is the one through whom all creation came into being.

> For us there is one God the Father, from whom are all things, .... and one Lord Jesus Christ, through whom are all things (1 Cor. 8 : 6). [2]

Christ is the new and creative act of the God who said, Out of darkness light shall shine (2 Cor. 4 : 6). The same thought is expressed in Colossians 1 : 16:

> By him were all things created .... and for him; he is before all things, and by him all things consist. [3]

As Cullmann rightly observes, [4] this is the same teaching as that in

---

[1] On Greek philosophy in Wisdom cf. J. Fichtner in *ZNW* 36 (1937), 113–32, esp. 117, 127–29. [2] Philosophical parallels in J. Weiss, *Der erste Korintherbrief* (Göttingen, 1910), 223–27. [3] Rabbinic parallels in C. F. Burney in *JTS* 27 (1925–26), 160–70. [4] O. Cullmann, *The Earliest Christian Confessions* (London, 1949), 51–52.

John 1 : 3 ("all things were made through him, and apart from him nothing at all was made") and Hebrews 1 : 2–3 ("by whom he made the worlds").

If we were to inquire of these various New Testament writers what it was out of which God made the universe, we should find in the first place that they never explicitly state that he made it "out of nothing". When Origen [1] wishes to provide scriptural authority for this doctrine the only passages he can adduce are 2 Maccabees 7 : 28 and Hermas, *Mandates* 1 : 1. There is no statement in the New Testament that God made the universe "out of nothing". In the second place, when we examine the passage in 1 Corinthians to which we have referred, we find that if we regard it as an exact statement using philosophical terminology, it says that God is himself the "matter" out of which the universe emanates. [2] Practically all philosophical writers regarded "out of" as a preposition denoting the material cause of a thing. On the other hand, as Theiler notes, [3] the pseudo-Aristotelian *De mundo*, using religious language, speaks of the ancient doctrine that "from God is everything", an expression which probably does not imply emanation. Elsewhere Paul speaks of God, saying that "from him and through him and for him are all things" (Rom. 11 : 36) or, more briefly, "all things are from God" (1 Cor. 11 : 12). These passages do not imply a philosophical analysis of causes but religious faith in God who is the cause of all. In the ordinary Greek language of the period the word "out of" is used both for the origin and for the cause of events. [4] Therefore Paul's language in 1 Corinthians 8 : 6 cannot be pressed to prove his teaching of an emanation doctrine. On the contrary, it looks forward to the eventual expression of the doctrine of creation "out of nothing".

We may add that in the Fourth Gospel and in Hebrews the creation is implicitly, though not explicitly, *ex nihilo*. Rudolf Bultmann sets forth the Johannine teaching when he points out that "creation is not the ordering of a chaotic matter". [5] And the Epistle to the Hebrews states that creation is something we can apprehend only through faith. What is seen was made out of things which do not appear (Heb.

---

[1] *Princ.* ii. 1. 5, *Ioh.* i. 17; see p. 146 below.　[2] So J. Weiss, *op. cit.*, 224; cf. C. M. Walsh, *The Doctrine of Creation* (London, 1910), 125.　[3] W. Theiler, *Die Vorbereitung des Neuplatonismus* (Berlin, 1930), 24 n. 1.　[4] J. H. Moulton–G. Milligan, *The Vocabulary of the Greek Testament* (London, 1929), 189–90.　[5] *Das Johannesevangelium* (Göttingen, 1937–41), 20.

11 : 3). It might be thought that this verse implies the ordering of disorder, the formation of a visible from an invisible world, as in the Septuagint translation of Genesis 1 : 2. But since the creation is known only by faith rather than by philosophical investigation, we may assume that the author refers to an absolute creation of matter, whether it passed through invisibility to visibility or not.

When we pass beyond the New Testament but continue to examine only those writers who are largely uninfluenced by philosophy, we find our best example in the Roman writer Hermas, who composed his work during the first half of the second century. He lays down as the first of his "commandments" the requirement of belief in the omnipotent creator.

> First of all, believe that there is one God, who created and formed everything, and created everything from non-existence into existence.

If these commandments, as I have elsewhere [1] suggested, are Hermas' substitute for the Decalogue, he is making more precise the commandment, "Thou shalt have none other gods but me", in the light of creation. This statement by Hermas was extremely influential in Greek patristic theology. It is quoted admiringly by Irenaeus, Origen, Methodius, and Athanasius, among others.

From a religious point of view, the Christian doctrine of creation was intended to express the transcendence of God and the absolute dependence of the universe upon its Creator. Only this omnipotent Creator is worthy of worship. The tragedy of the gentiles' worship is that it is directed toward the creation rather than toward the Creator (Rom. 1 : 25).

Augustine sums up the religious meaning of the doctrine of creation in his *Confessions*. [2]

> All these things praise You, the Creator of them all. But how do You create them? How, O God, did You create heaven and earth? Obviously it was not *in* heaven or on earth that You made heaven and earth; nor in the air nor in the waters, since these belong to heaven and earth; nor did You make the universe in the universe, because there was no place for it to be made in until was made. Nor had You any material in Your hand when you were making heaven and earth: for where should You have got what You had not yet made to use as material? What exists, save because You exist? You spoke and heaven and earth were created; in Your word You created them.

[1] *HTR* 40 (1947), 11.  [2] *Conf.* xi. 7 (tr. F. J. Sheed).

Thus Augustine sets forth the essential meaning of the biblical doctrine of creation as coordinate with omnipotence

Hellenistic Jewish and Christian theologians could not, however, simply assert that God created the universe *ex nihilo*. They were confronted with the unanimous teaching of Greek philosophers that the world was made out of eternally existent matter (chapter 3). It was necessary, therefore, for them to develop philosophical arguments in support of their own view and in opposition to Greek philosophy. To those arguments we now turn.

Like the author of the book of Wisdom, Philo of Alexandria speaks of God's creation of the universe "out of formless matter". [1] As in the case of Wisdom, it is very difficult to determine precisely what he means. His language seems to reflect the Middle Platonic doctrine which we have already discussed (chapter 3). The statement in Wisdom, as we have said, may be intentionally ambiguous; and Philo too may be veiling his true belief. But in Philo's case he is drawing a veil over his genuine, but philosophically disreputable, belief that matter was created by God.

That Philo actually believed in God's creation of matter seems certain because of Wolfson's careful analysis of his reinterpretation of the *Timaeus*. [2] In the *Timaeus* there is a "receptacle" in which the world came into being. In Middle Platonism this receptacle was identified with matter, and Albinus [3] tells us that Plato calls matter "space". Now Philo explicitly says [4] that "God created space and place simultaneously with bodies". Thus his view on the crucial question of the meaning of the *Timaeus* can be discovered. His God is a genuine creator who does not impose forms on a pre-existent matter but creates the matter himself.

Later Christian theologians only gradually came to realize the importance of the createdness of matter. Justin represents himself as rejecting the idea of an uncreated universe even before he became a Christian; [5] but this rejection has to do not with the origin of matter but with the shaping of the universe in time. He quotes the first three verses of Genesis to prove that Plato borrowed his teaching from Moses. Plato taught, as Genesis teaches, that "God made the world, having rotated matter that was formless". [6] Justin does not

[1] *Heres* 140, *Spec.* i. 328.  [2] H. A. Wolfson, *Philo* (Cambridge, 1948), I 300–10.
[3] *Eisag.* 8, 162 : 26 Hermann; cf. Aristotle, *Phys.* 209 b 11.  [4] *Conf.* 136.  [5] *Dial.* 5; cf. Witt, *op. cit.*, 120.  [6] *Apol.* i. 59. The Neopythagorean Numenius (fr. 10 Leemans) also held that Plato followed Moses.

really understand the difference between Platonism and Christianity.

When we find in Justin occasional additions to New Testament verses, stressing the creative power of God, we must conclude that they probably are not his own but come from the traditional teaching of the church in his time. For example, to Mark 10 : 18, "No one is good but God", Justin adds "who made all things". [1] In Mark 12 : 30 he reads that the God who is to be served with all one's powers is the God "who made thee". [2] (This addition, found in a similar context in Didache 1 : 2, is derived from Sirach 7 : 30, as the Archbishop of Quebec has observed.)

Justin's former pupil Tatian reacts vigorously against his master in his militant attack *Against the Greeks*, in which he argues that everything of value in Greek philosophy has been borrowed from the Orient and also claims that the inconsistencies and follies of philosophers nullify their teaching. He then presents his own faith in God, a faith opposed both to Platonism and to Stoicism. [3]

> Our God has no place in time, since he alone is without beginning and is himself the beginning of all. God is a spirit; he does not extend through matter but is the founder of material spirits and the forms in matter. He is invisible and intangible, since he is the father of sensible and visible things. We know him through his creation and we understand the invisible working of his power through what he has made. I am not willing to worship the creation which he made for us.

Similarly Tatian rejects any dualism in the universe. [4]

> Matter is not without a beginning as God is, nor is it equal in power to God by being without beginning. It is a created thing, though it was not created by any other than the fashioner of all.

For this reason, Tatian says, we must reject the Stoic theory of cycles in history and believe in the resurrection. His God is an absolutely free and omnipotent creator, not a mere demiurge.

The most thorough analysis of the problem of creation in early Christianity is given by Theophilus, bishop of Antioch, in his second book *To Autolycus*. Here he elaborately analyzes the Platonic view and argues that it is a denial of the omnipotence of God in creation. If God is uncreated and therefore immutable, matter if uncreated would also be immutable, and therefore equal to God. And if God

[1] *Apol.* i. 16. 7.   [2] *Apol.* i. 16. 6.   [3] *Or.* 4 (pp. 4 : 29–5 : 8 Schwartz).   [4] *Ibid.* 5 (p. 6 : 12–15).

made the world from uncreated matter he would be no greater than a human being who makes something out of materials he receives from someone else (ii. 4).

Next Theophilus turns (ii. 5–7) to question the authority of the Greek poets as theologians. This passage is presumably aimed at the Stoics. He begins with a quotation from Homer (*Iliad* xiv. 201, xxi. 196).

> Ocean, origin of the gods, and mother Tethys.... whence come all rivers and the whole sea.

Theophilus rightly observes that "in these statements he does not set forth God". Ocean is water, not God the creator of water. Similarly the Academic philosopher Clitomachus had argued that if Zeus is a god, then his brother Poseidon is a god; if Poseidon is a god, then rivers are gods; where is a line to be drawn (Sextus Empiricus, *Adv. math.* ix. 182–83)?

Of Hesiod, Theophilus remarks that "he said that the world was created, but neglected to say by whom". Approximately the same question is raised in Sextus Empiricus, *Adv. math.* x. 18. We find chaos at the beginning of Hesiod's poem. Where did it come from? Theophilus also observes, quite in the manner of Clitomachus, that since Zeus and Cronus came into existence much later than the universe, they could not have created it. And the Muses, the daughters of Zeus, could hardly have had authentic information.

Finally Theophilus mentions the Orphic theogony in the *Birds* of Aristophanes. He considers it ridiculous but does not say why. Similarly in Sextus, *Adv. math.* ix. 15, Orpheus is quoted, but without criticism. Therefore Theophilus has no criticism to make!

Of course the Stoic reply to his criticisms would be simple. Hesiod received what knowledge he had from divine inspiration. But Theophilus reserves divine inspiration for the prophets among the Hebrews and the Sibyl among the Greeks. By the Sibyl he means the Alexandrian Jewish writings ascribed to her and widely read by Christians in his day.

Theophilus' interest in the problem of creation was given impetus by an obscure artist and philosopher named Hermogenes, against whom both he and Tertullian wrote treatises. The work of Theophilus is entirely lost, but it was used by Tertullian, and we may suspect that the philosophical elements in Tertullian's work are derived from him. (The *reductio ad absurdum* with which Tertullian ends is his own.)

Hermogenes apparently represents the confluence of Middle Platonism with either Judaism or Christianity. Were it not for a fragment dealing with the ascension of Jesus, we should be inclined to place his arguments entirely outside the framework of early Christianity. In any event, his interest for us lies in his interpretation of Genesis in the light of the *Timaeus*. Hermogenes offers us three possibilities concerning the origin of the universe. God made all things (1) from his own being, (2) from nothing, or (3) from pre-existent matter. The first two must be rejected. (1) God is immutable, and therefore could not have made the world from himself. (2) God is immutable, and therefore could not ever have begun the work of creation. Moreover, God is perfect and the creation is imperfect; this imperfection must be due to some other cause, viz. matter. Therefore the third possibility must be accepted.

The world came into existence out of matter, which is eternal, for God is always Lord, and must have been Lord over something. The "matter" was completely undefined, as in the *Timaeus*; its behavior was like the boiling of water in a kettle. God acted on it simply by approaching it, just as beauty is influential by its mere approach, and as a magnet works on an object. But the creation is an "eternal task"; matter always remains partly evil and disordered. In this description we find a cosmology very similar to that of the *Hermetica*. In these tractates matter is often regarded as evil. After Plato the preexistent matter is described as in disorder (i. 4). The "image of God" works on those who are drawn to it just as a magnet influences iron (iv. 11). And the work of God is eternal; God always creates all things (v. 9). The *Hermetica* state, however, as Hermogenes does not, that God himself *is* all things. Here is evidence of Hermogenes' partial conversion to Christianity. Theophilus and Tertullian felt that he had not abandoned enough of his previous convictions.

Tertullian replies to Hermogenes by stating that in Genesis the term "Lord" is not applied to God before the fifteenth verse of the second chapter. The biblical text from which Tertullian drew this conclusion was that of Theophilus. [1] Perhaps Theophilus had pointed out the same fact. The "matter" out of which God made the world was his Wisdom, as the prophets have said. This probably comes

[1] Cf. *VC* 3 (1949), 228–29.

from Theophilus, who like Tertullian identifies Wisdom with the Spirit or Logos or Son of God. [1] We need not linger over Tertullian's largely second-hand arguments against Hermogenes. The significant item in his argument is his constant insistence on the freedom of God. [2]

> It is more suitable for God to have created by his free will than by necessity, that is, from nothing rather than from matter. It is more worthy to believe that God is free, even though the author of evils, than to believe him a slave.

Here is the foundation of all (or most) of Tertullian's irrationalism, and perhaps of his conversion to Montanism. Divine and human freedom are the most meaningful dogmas of his theology.

Elements of Middle Platonism are also to be found in the creation doctrine of Clement of Alexandria. As Claude Mondésert rightly points out, [3] the world is called "created" (Str. iii. 105); it came into being and on this point Plato (Timaeus 28 b) agrees with Genesis (Str. v. 92). But what Mondésert does not observe is that these statements merely reflect the orthodox Middle Platonic interpretation of the Timaeus, in which the universe actually had a beginning, though not in time. They say nothing whatever about the origin of matter. In fact Clement nowhere sets forth his doctrine on the subject. He quotes philosophical opinions on the first principles of the universe, however, and after citing the doxographical statement,

> The Stoics and Plato and Pythagoras presume matter as existent in the beginnings,

goes on to praise Plato for having spoken in the Timaeus (48 c) of the difficulty of the subject. He then cites Genesis 1 : 2 as providing some ground for philosophical opinion. [4]

Elsewhere Clement is arguing against heretics who say that God has some physical relationship to mankind. He denies their claim "whether he made the world out of nothing or fashioned it out of matter". "Nothing" is non-existent and therefore entirely unlike God, and matter is completely different from him. [5] We might imagine that Clement is arguing on his opponents' grounds, and that this accounts for his indifference to the question; but his unclear statements

---

[1] Tert. Herm. 18; Theoph. Aut. ii. 10.   [2] Tert. Herm. 14, cf. 16.   [3] Clément d'Alexandrie (Paris, 1944), 198–99.   [4] Str. v. 89. 5–90. 1.   [5] Str. ii. 74. 1.

and clear silences on the subject suggest that he actually accepted the Middle Platonic doctrine rather than that of Philo. [1]

Clement's successor at the school of Alexandria was Origen, the greatest theologian of ancient Christianity. Like most of his contemporaries Origen was influenced by the Platonism of his day. Some of his doctrines are strikingly similar to those of Hermogenes. God is not absolute, but perfect; and perfection is itself a condition; therefore he created only as much matter as he could fashion into a cosmos. [2] But the world is not coeternal with God, and matter was certainly made by him. He attacks the Platonists and Stoics for their idea of matter coeternal with God, asking how they can possibly complain about the Epicurean teaching of a fortuitous universe. [3]

On this point the excellent book of Daniélou on Origen is somewhat misleading. He states [4] that

> it seems that Origen admitted not a creation of matter in time, but an eternal existence of matter regarded as primal material.

In this case we should be entirely within the sphere of the Middle Platonism of Albinus. But we are not within the sphere of Middle Platonism, for in his *Commentary on John* [5] Origen explicitly contrasts the Christian view of creation with that which derives the world from preexistent matter, and cites two scriptural texts to prove his point (2 Macc. 7 : 28, Hermas, *Mand.* 1 : 1). And in a fragment of his *Commentary on Genesis* preserved by Eusebius, [6] he states that God, unlike a human workman, is not in need of materials; he himself made the materials, viz. matter.

At the same time Origen attempts to avoid the idea that the omnipotent God was ever in solitary omnipotence by postulating his eternal creative activity. For God to be omnipotent, there had to be something over which he could exercise his power. [7] Later theologians understood this doctrine to imply the eternity of matter; but Origen was trying to avoid precisely that conclusion. For him God is eternally dynamic and creative.

Origen did not however, accept the full implications of divine

[1] In his lost *Hypotyposes* Clement regarded matter as not created in time (frag. 23, vol. iii, p. 202 Stählin). [2] *Princ.* ii. 9. 1. This is Philonic; cf. Eus. *Praep.* vii. 21. [3] *Princ.* ii. 1. 4; cf. Eus. *Praep.* vii. 22. 6–7. [4] J. Daniélou, *Origène* (Paris, 1948), 216–17. [5] *Ioh.* i. 17. [6] *Praep.* vii. 22; cf. Chalcidius, cc. 276–78 (derived from Origen; B. W. Switalski, *Des Chalcidius Kommentar zu Plato's Timaeus* [Münster, 1902], 45–48). [7] *Princ.* i. 2. 10, iii. 5. 3.

omnipotence, and accepted with Hermogenes the philosophical theory that since God is immutable he cannot begin to do anything. [1] This theory had been upheld by the Epicureans against Platonists and Stoics. [2] From a religious point of view, a more satisfactory statement is made by Irenaeus, who says that God made the matter out of which he made the world, and that we should not ask what God was doing before creation for scripture does not give us the answer. [3]

Methodius, writing at the end of the third century, has no difficulty in demolishing the position of Origen, for he holds that *ex nihilo* creation does not involve a change in the immutable God. He then proceeds to identify Origen's view with Greek philosophy or Manichaeism and attacks the latter as if it were Origen's doctrine. [4]

In the fourth century Basil of Caesarea simply disregards the Origenist view while rejecting the eternal matter of Greek philosophy. [5] On the other hand, his brother Gregory of Nyssa solves the problem of the origin of matter by following the Platonic and Neoplatonic idea of a primal matter consisting of intelligible spiritual elements, a matter without qualities such as we find in Chalcidius (see p. 39). [6]

Among Latin theological writers such complexities tended to be brushed aside. Lactantius emphatically asserts that the world was created *ex nihilo*. [7] He rejects the atomist doctrine. "Who ever saw atoms? Who felt them? Who heard them? Or did only Leucippus have a mind?" [8] At the same time he appeals to Epicurus and Democritus for support in teaching that the universe had a beginning and will have an end. [9]

The most important Latin theologian was, of course, Augustine. When he passed from Manichaeism into Christian faith he went by the way of Academic scepticism and Neoplatonism. Thus his career serves to illustrate the course of much ancient Christian thought. The Academy helped prepare the way for a thorough theological analysis of such problems as creation, whereas the science or rather pseudo-science of the Manichees was the heir of Greek and oriental

---

[1] *Princ.* i. 2. 10; Tert. *Hermog.* 2.  [2] Cic. *N. D.* i. 21–22.  [3] *Adv. haer.* ii. 10. 2, 28. 7.  [4] *Creat.* 2, 494 Bonwetsch.  [5] *Hex.* ii. 2.  [6] *Hex.*, PG 44, 69C; cf. K. Gronau, *Poseidonios und die jüdisch-christliche Genesisexegese* (Leipzig, 1914), 113-14.  [7] *Div. inst.* ii. 8. 8.  [8] *Ira* 10 : 3 (against Epicurean empiricism; cf. Plut. *Adv. Col.* 28, Arnob. *Adv. gent.* ii. 10).  [9] *Div. inst.* vii. 1. 10.

dualism. Christians had to reject this dualism in order to defend the freedom of God. [1]

Augustine's Manichaean period is as important for what he accepted during it as for what he later believed. His teachers held that from all eternity there had been two "roots" or first principles, the light and the dark. [2]

> The difference between these two principles is like that between a king and a pig. Light dwells in a royal abode in places suitable to its nature, while the Dark like a pig wallows in mud and is nourished by filth and delights in it.

In such a dualistic theology there is no place for a doctrine of *ex nihilo* creation, and Titus of Bostra quotes Mani as saying, "There were God and Matter, Light and Darkness, Good and Evil, absolute opposites in every respect, so that in no way did they communicate with one another". [3] As Epiphanius observes, this doctrine is close to the general view of late Greek philosophy. And as the *Acta Archelai* point out, it involves the idea of two gods coeternal and equal, one good, the other evil. [4]

Early in his career Augustine found such concepts very satisfactory. With Mani he shared a strong feeling for dualism. The Manichaean scheme seemed to explain the world to him in psychologically meaningful terms. Throughout his life Augustine was obsessed by the problem of evil. Yet when he came to compare Manichaean "science" with what he had learned in his encyclical education, he found the Manichees unscientific. Mani was unable to explain solstices and equinoxes and eclipses. [5] Again, the Manichaean bishop Faustus was not scientifically trained; he was "not learned in any of the liberal sciences except literature, and not especially learned even in that". [6] Augustine soon turned from Manichaeism to scepticism. The rationalism which had led him into Manichaeism [7] led him out again.

He could not, however, become a Christian. While he says that he

---

[1] E. Gilson, *Introduction à l'étude de saint Augustin* (Paris, 1931), 242–67; C. J. O'Toole, *The Philosophy of Creation in the Writings of St. Augustine* (Washington, 1944; inadequate on Manichaeism and Neoplatonism). [2] F. C. Burkitt, *The Religion of the Manichees* (Cambridge, 1925), 17, quoting Severus of Antioch. Cf. H.–C. Puech, *Le manichéisme* (Paris, 1949), 74–75. [3] Epiph. *haer.* 66. 14. 1; cf. Polotsky in *RE* Suppl. VI 245. [4] *Act. Arch.* 7, 9 : 12 Beeson. [5] *Conf.* v. 6. [6] *Ibid.*, v. 11 [7] P. Courcelle, *Recherches sur les Confessions de saint Augustin* (Paris, 1950), 65.

tried to find help in the Catholic faith, he claims that he could not find it "because the Catholic faith was not what I thought it was". Because of his previous training he was compelled to think of evil not merely as a substance, but as a corporeal substance. This was the view of the Manichees. Augustine continued to believe in the existence of two opposing powers, each infinite (although somehow the evil power was weaker than the good). He could not believe in one good God, for a good God could not have created any nature evil. [1]

Finally, as he turned to a synthesis between Neoplatonism and Christianity, [2] he became convinced that both God and his creation were good. If corruptible things "were supremely good they could not be corrupted, but they could not be corrupted if they were not good at all". Therefore whatever exists is at least partly good; and evil is not a substance but the absence of good. [3] This doctrine, which comes from Plotinus, [4] reached Augustine through the sermons of Ambrose.

Augustine had rejected, as had almost all the Christian theologians we have discussed, the doctrine of the eternity of matter, coequal with God. Two possibilities remained for him. He could follow Plotinus in teaching that matter emanated from God; he could follow the Christian tradition in holding that God created matter *ex nihilo*. At this point his doctrine is clearly Christian rather than Neoplatonic.

Because of his understanding of the danger of Manichaeism Augustine strongly emphasized the importance of the creation story in Genesis. He wrote no fewer than six commentaries on it. These are the treatise *De Genesi contra Manichaeos* (388–90); the incomplete *De Genesi ad litteram, Liber imperfectus* (393); the eleventh, twelfth, and thirteenth books of the *Confessiones* (about 400); the long commentary *De Genesi ad litteram* (401–15); and finally the eleventh and twelfth books of the treatise *De civitate dei* (413–26). The sixth work is the lost fragment on Genesis as far as the creation of man. [5]

The question with which we are concerned in investigating these commentaries is that of the origin of matter. Augustine's answer is always that God made matter out of nothing. The appeal which Manichaeism had for him is gone. He admires the teaching of Plato in the *Timaeus*; in the treatise *De civitate dei* he can say that the Platonic

[1] *Conf.* v. 20.  [2] Courcelle, *op. cit.*, 138.  [3] *Conf.* vii. 18–19.  [4] *Enn.* i. 8. 11; cf. Basil, *Hex.* ii. 4–5, and Ambrose, *De Isaac* (cf. Courcelle, *op. cit.*, 106–7).  [5] *Retract.* i. 18.

idea of creation is like the Hebrew; [1] but he is reading Plato in the light of Christian doctrine.

In his first commentary he answers criticisms of the Manichees. They read the first verse of Genesis, "In the beginning God made heaven and earth", and they ask three questions originally asked by the Epicureans. [2] In what "beginning"? What was God doing before creation? Why did he suddenly decide to create? Augustine replies to the first question by giving the traditional exegetical answer: the "beginning" was not temporal; it refers to Christ, who as the Wisdom of God is the "beginning of his ways" (Prov. 8 : 22). Why did God create?

> Because he willed to do so. For the will of God is the cause of heaven and earth, and for that reason the will of God is greater than heaven and earth. Now he who says, "Why did he will to make heaven and earth?" asks for something greater than the will of God; but there is nothing greater. [3]

Augustine also explains why the earth is called invisible and chaotic in the Greek and Latin versions of Genesis 1 : 2. It had not yet been formed, shaped, and set in order; for Wisdom 11 : 7 speaks of "formless matter". [4]

> And for this reason God is most rightly believed to have made everything out of nothing, because even if everything was made by formation out of that matter, still the matter itself was made out of absolutely nothing. For we should not be like those who do not believe that the omnipotent God could have made anything out of nothing, when they consider that carpenters and other artisans cannot make anything unless they have materials.... But the omnipotent God was helped by no material which he himself had not made, in order to make what he willed to make. For if, in making those things which he willed to make, anything which he himself had not made helped him, he was not omnipotent—which it is sacrilegious to believe. [5]

Here Augustine seems to have in mind the Middle Platonic view as set forth by Cicero; he refutes it (as Christian theologians after Theophilus had refuted it) by an appeal to omnipotence.

In the *Confessions* Augustine raises an interesting exegetical problem. His opponents have criticized his interpretation of Genesis. "The Spirit of God, who wrote these words by his servant Moses, did not mean by them what you say, but something else, which we say." [6]

---

[1] *Civ. dei* viii. 11.  [2] *Gen. contra Manich.* i. 3–4; Cic. *N.D.* i 22.  [3] *Ibid.*, i. 9.
[4] He observes that some manuscripts read „invisible matter".  [5] *Gen. contra Manich.* i. 10; cf. Cic. *N. D.* fr. 2; see chapter 3.  [6] *Conf.* xii. 17.

He replies that it was ultimately God who revealed the true interpretation to him. Other interpretations are perhaps possible, but verbal debate over them is unprofitable. He sets forth his basic principle in a passage which explains how it was possible for Christian theologians to use exegesis as a theological method. [1]

> All of us who read are trying to see and grasp the meaning of the man we are reading: and given that we believe him a speaker of the truth, we should obviously not think that he was saying something that we know or think to be false. While, therefore, each one of us is trying to understand in the sacred writings what the writer meant by them, what harm if one accepts a meaning which You, Light of all true minds, show him to be in itself a true meaning, even if the author we are reading did not actually mean that by it: since his meaning also, though different from mine, is true.

The acceptance of this principle means that historical exegesis is irrelevant.

The use of this principle also means that the starting point is not to be the book one is interpreting but the theological principles which one tries to read into the book. The *Imperfectus liber* begins with a brief survey of the Catholic faith and continues with a discussion of the four exegetical methods to be employed in finding the faith in the Bible. [2] Similarly in the longer commentary *De Genesi ad litteram* Augustine tells us that both the Catholic faith and most certain reason teach that God created matter. [3]

His thought on this subject is summed up in the treatise *De civitate dei*. In discussing the question of miracle he points out that

> whatever marvelous thing takes place in this world is much less marvelous than this whole universe of heaven and earth and everything in them, which God certainly made. Like him who made it, the mode of making is hidden and incomprehensible to man. [4]

Later in the treatise the customary problems are discussed, along with the usual analysis of the authority of scripture. The world and everything in it, Augustine concludes, were created by the will of God. [5]

Augustine's doctrine, like that of Christians generally, was not so much a product of reason as a corollary of his fundamental faith in the omnipotent will of God. It reflects the religious insight that the

[1] *Ibid.*, xii. 27 (tr. F. J. Sheed). [2] *Liber imperf.* i. 2–4; cf. E. v. Dobschütz in *Harnack–Ehrung* (Leipzig, 1921), 1–13. [3] *Gen. ad litt.* i. 28–29. [4] *Civ. dei* x. 12; cf. Philo, cited p. 186 *infra*. [5] *Civ. dei.* xi. 3–6.

Creator, not the creation, must be worshipped. In the work *De civitate. dei* we find a clear expression of this doctrine, which distinguishes Christianity from Greek philosophy (see chapter 3). [1]

> We shall worship God, not heaven and earth, the two parts of which this world consists: not the soul or souls diffused throughout all living creatures, but the God who made heaven and earth and all things which are in them, who made every soul, whatever may be its mode of life, whether living a life of any kind without sense or reason, or not only living but sentient, or intelligent as well as living and sentient.

This is the God who creates and is omnipotent, the God of early Christianity.

[1] *Ibid.*, vii. 29.

# NATURE MIRACLES IN THE BIBLE

While the cardinal miracle of the Hebrew religion is God's act in creation, we should not suppose that God abandoned his world after making it. On the contrary, in Hebrew thought God was constantly at work, guiding the course of nature and of history by frequent interventions in the "natural" order of events. Sometimes, indeed, his miraculous works are described in language which recalls the original act of creation. When the earth opens to receive the rebel Korah, God is "creating a creation" (Numbers 16 : 30). More often, we find three words used for the wonderful acts of God. They are *'oth* ("sign"), *mopheth* ("portent"), and *niphla'oth* ("wonders"). A "sign" need not be truly extraordinary. It is something in which the observer sees by faith the hand of God. A "portent", while extraordinary, is not what Greek theologians would call supernatural rather than natural. The regular course of the sun is a sign, while something like an eclipse is a portent (cf. Joel 2 : 31). "Wonders" are merely extraordinary happenings which arouse awe or admiration. [1] Another fairly common word is *geburah*, which means "act of power". [2]

Two commonplaces of Old Testament theology sum up the ideas of God and the world which underlie these terms. In the first place, as we have said, the God of the Old Testament is known above all as the creator and ruler of the universe. By his will everything is governed. When he wishes to reveal himself, he does so. It makes little difference whether he reveals himself in nature or acts in history. "All things are possible for God." In the second place—a corollary of the first—there are no "laws of nature" which can possibly check his freedom. As Robinson expresses it, "nature and history are simply different aspects of the continued activity of God, and miracles are

[1] H. W. Robinson, *Inspiration and Revelation in the Old Testament* (Oxford, 1946), 34–47. [2] W. Eichrodt, *Theologie des Alten Testaments* II (Leipzig, 1935), 83–86.

the representative occasions on which that activity especially impresses human consciousness". [1]

This is not to say that there is no underlying order. After the flood God swore that there would never again be such a deluge (Genesis 9 : 15).

> While the earth endures, seedtime and harvest, cold and heat, summer and winter, day and night shall not cease (Genesis 8 : 22).

The sun and moon stood still for Joshua, but "there was no day like that either before it or after it" (Joshua 10 : 14). It would have been easy for the shadow on Hezekiah's sundial to go forward ten steps, but difficult for it to go back (2 Kings 20 : 10). Moreover, miracle stories are centered around Moses, Elijah and Elisha, and in fact are relatively infrequent in the Old Testament. [2] If the events described were not unusual, no one would notice them. As Pritchard observes, "the average Israelite knew that iron was heavier—always heavier —than water".

At the same time, there are no limits to God's power. "Is anything too hard for the Lord?" (Genesis 18 : 14). "He spoke and it was done" (Psalm 33 : 9). The idea that all things are possible for God is clearly expressed in the Old Testament (Job 42 : 2) and reiterated by Philo and in the New Testament, as we have seen. Indeed, the New Testament teaching on God's omnipotence is simply repeated from the Old Testament. Things impossible with men are possible with God (Luke 18 : 27).

The New Testament reflects the Old Testament ideas of miracle. [3] It also makes use of most of the Old Testament words to describe miracles. A word often employed for miracle is "power" or "mighty work" ($\delta\acute{v}\nu\alpha\mu\iota\varsigma$). Derived from the Greek Old Testament, it emphasizes the creative power of God and his control over his creation. [4] Oddly enough, in view of Mark's high view of the person of Jesus, he uses this word in the story of the rejection at Nazareth. "He could do no mighty work there." But this solitary example of impotence is an exception to the general picture of the power of Jesus and his disciples.

Also related to God's work of creation is the word "work" ($\check{\epsilon}\rho\gamma o\nu$), which in the Old Testament refers to creation and in the New

---

[1] Robinson, *op. cit.*, 39.   [2] J. B. Pritchard, „Motifs of Old Testament Miracles", *Crozer Quarterly* 27 (1950), 97–109.   [3] Cf. A. Richardson, *The Miracle Stories of the Gospels* (London, 1942).   [4] W. Grundmann in *TWzNT* II 302.

Testament is practically confined to the gospel of John. [1] Here it refers especially to the miracles as works or deeds of salvation.

Another word which is especially common in the gospel of John is the Old Testament "sign" ($\sigma\eta\mu\varepsilon\tilde{\iota}o\nu$). The word is frequently employed in the collection of seven great signs found in John 2—12 and perhaps concluded in John 20 : 30–31. Of the first it is said,

> This beginning of signs did Jesus in Cana of Galilee, and he manifested his glory (John 2 : 11).

These "signs" are essentially the same as "works". [2] The Johannine collection may be compared with the records of epiphanies current in the Hellenistic world, [3] as well as to the ten "signs" worked by Moses and remembered by Jews and Christians alike. We may note that we are no longer in the old world of Hebrew thought, where a "sign" is not necessarily contrary to ordinary experience. John's seven signs begin with the changing of water into wine and end with the raising of Lazarus, dead for four days.

Frequently associated with "sign" is "wonder" or "portent" ($\tau\acute{\varepsilon}\varrho\alpha\varsigma$). Moses' ten miracles were "signs and portents" (Exod. 11 : 9–10). In the New Testament with one exception which is an Old Testament quotation (Acts 2 : 19), "portent" is never found apart from "sign". The word for portent could easily lead to confusion, for in the Hellenistic world it was often employed to classify strange or unusual animals, "monsters" (cf. pp. 6–7), and anything unusual or startling. [4] Another meaning it possessed was in reference to untrue or exaggerated stories. It was used in this sense by Polybius, Strabo, Plutarch, and Lucian. [5]

Other words less frequently employed are "wonders" ($\theta\alpha\nu\mu\acute{\alpha}\sigma\iota\alpha$, Matt. 21 : 15, cf. Exod. 3 : 20) and "paradoxical events" ($\pi\alpha\varrho\acute{\alpha}\delta o\xi\alpha$, Luke 5 : 26). The latter word is rare in the Greek Old Testament but common in Hellenistic Greek, where it sometimes bears the connotation of falsity [6] but more often simply expresses the amazement of the person who witnesses the event or hears of it. [7] Thus in Luke it is a substitute for Mark 2 : 12, "We never saw it happen thus". Another common Hellenistic term, $\mathring{\alpha}\varrho\varepsilon\tau\acute{\eta}$, is found only once in the New Testament in reference to miracle (1 Pet. 2 : 9). [8]

[1] G. Bertram, *ibid.* II 633–36, 639. [2] Cf. John 6 : 30. [3] Cf. F. Pfister in *RE* Suppl. IV 300. [4] P. Stein, TEPA$\Sigma$ (Marburg, 1909), 7–11, 17–19. [5] *Ibid.*, 30–31. [6] E. g., Plato, *Politicus* 281 a. [7] Cf. O. Weinreich, *Antike Heilungswunder* (Giessen, 1909), 198–99. [8] Cf. R. Herzog, *Die Wunderheilungen von Epidauros* (Leipzig, 1931), 49–50.

It is significant that the word *aretalogos*, which means "one who tells miracle stories", comes to have a bad meaning among more highly educated persons. Thus Juvenal [1] speaks of a "lying *aretalogus*" who tells stories for which there are no witnesses, and Porphyrio [2] describes a poet as so garrulous that he might be called an *aretalogus*. On the other hand, the Greek Old Testament speaks of the *aretai* of God and Sirach goes so far as to ask God to fill Sion with his *aretalogia* (36 : 17). This is the popular usage. [3]

From this cursory examination of the principal words used in the Bible for miracles we cannot assume, as so many writers have assumed, that there is something uniquely distinctive about the biblical view. The word "sign" is found in Hellenistic writers with much the same meaning as in the New Testament; so is "portent"; so is "wonders". The difference does not lie in the words but in the basic world view underlying the biblical writers' expressions. It lies in the context of their thought, and miracle in itself is not the distinctive characteristic of their point of view. The inner meaning of miracle is more significant than miracle itself.

The cardinal miracle of the Old Testament is the act of God in the creation of the universe, which we have already discussed. In the more primitive story of the creation two startling miracles are recounted, that of the formation of Eve from a rib of Adam, and of the talking serpent in the garden of Eden (Gen. 2 : 21–22 and 3 : 1). The first of these is an etymological legend intended to explain the name "woman" (*issah*) as derived from "man" (*ish*). The second explains not only how it was that Adam and Eve were led astray, but also why it is that reptiles creep and seem to eat dirt, and why men and serpents live in enmity (Gen. 3 : 14–15). In later Jewish writings the serpent is sometimes identified with the devil (e.g. Rev. 12 : 9, 3 Bar. 9 : 7), but this does not seem to be the intention of the original story.

From the sixth through the ninth chapter of Genesis we find two narratives of a great flood which covered the whole earth. They are not very artfully joined together; in one the flood lasts for forty days and nights (Gen. 7 : 17); in the later story, the waters continue for a hundred and fifty days (Gen. 7 : 24). In the earlier story seven males

---

1 *Sat.* xv. 16, 26; cf. Crusius in *RE* II 670–72; R. Reitzenstein, *Hellenistische Wundererzählungen* (Leipzig, 1906), 6–8. ² *Schol. ad Hor. Serm.* i. 1 120. ³ Crusius, *loc. cit.*, 671–72; W. Aly in *RE Suppl.* VI 13–15.

and seven females of clean beasts and birds and only pairs of the
unclean animals are admitted (Gen. 7 : 2–3); in the later, a pair
of every species of animal is taken into the ark (Gen. 6 : 20). Everything outside the ark is drowned (Gen. 7 : 21–23).

In both forms of the story this flood is depicted as unique. In the
earlier, the Lord smells the sweet savor of Noah's sacrifice and
declares that he will not curse the ground again nor will he ever again
smite everything living. "While the earth remains, seedtime and
harvest, cold and heat, summer and winter, day and night shall not
cease" (Gen. 8 : 21–22). After the flood God himself ensures the
regularity of natural phenomena. The later story is less detailed and
simply states that God's covenant with Noah bound him never to
bring another flood to destroy the earth (Gen. 9 : 11). Of this covenant
the rainbow is the token (Gen. 9 : 12).

Another miracle among the legends of Genesis is Sarah's con-
ceiving at the age of ninety when her husband Abraham is one
hundred (Gen. 17 : 17). When Sarah hears God's promise she laughs
inwardly, but the Lord says to Abraham, "Why did Sarah laugh
and say, 'Shall I really bear a child in my old age?' Is anything too
difficult (or wonderful) for the Lord?" This saying is rendered in the
Septuagint, "Shall anything be impossible with the Lord?" (Gen. 18:14).

In the light of this question God's statement to Lot, who desired
to escape from the plain of Sodom to a little town named Zoar, "I
cannot do anything until you arrive there" (Gen. 19 : 22), must
mean only that God has chosen to wait for Lot. God is not bound
by anything but his own promises. Had there been ten righteous
men in Sodom he would have spared it (Gen. 18 : 32). Lot's wife,
who disobeys God's command and looks back at the rain of fire and
brimstone, is turned into a pillar of salt (Gen. 19 : 26). Evidently
this incident is a legend intended to explain the desert land near the
Dead Sea and the existence of some peculiar rock formation there.

The legends of Genesis do not include a great number of nature
miracles. A few myths in the creation story, a flood, a miraculous
conception, and the story of Sodom—these are not very prominent
in a narrative to which all nature is miraculous. In the book of
Exodus the situation is different. Here Moses is presented as a great
thaumaturge who enters into competition with the magicians of
Egypt and defeats them in their own craft. [1]

[1] Cf. T. Hopfner, *Griechisch-ägyptischer Offenbarungszauber* II (Leipzig, 1924),
§§ 10–11.

God's call to Moses took place from a burning bush, miraculously not consumed, on Mount Horeb (Exod. 3 : 2). The bush attracts Moses' attention, and he says, "I will turn aside and see this great sight, why the bush is not burned" (Exod. 3 : 3). After the call Moses expresses his doubt that the people will believe that the Lord has appeared to him, and the Lord provides him with two signs "that they may believe that Yahweh the God of their fathers, the God of Abraham, the God of Isaac, and the God of Jacob has appeared to you" (Exod. 3 : 5 cf. John 20 : 30–31). The first is the miraculous transformation of Moses' rod into a snake or a crocodile [1] and the second is leprosy which can appear or disappear when Moses puts his hand into his bosom or removes it. Should these two signs fail to bring conviction, Moses is to pour river water on the dry land; it will then become blood (Exod. 4 : 2–9). However, since Aaron is a more accomplished speaker than his brother Moses, the rod is to be given to him (Exod. 4 : 17). These signs are to be worked before the king of Egypt so that he will let the people go. The Lord also informs Moses that he will harden the king's heart so that he will not let the people go until his first-born son is slain (Exod. 4 : 21–23). Aaron soon performs the signs before the people and they believe (Exod. 4 : 30–31).

Later we find the reiteration of God's promise: "I will harden Pharaoh's heart, and multiply my signs and my wonders in the land of Egypt" (Exod. 7 : 3). There follows a contest between Moses and Aaron and the magicians of Egypt. They too are able to turn rods into serpents, although Aaron's rod swallows up their rods (Exod. 7 : 12). Moses and Aaron smite the river water and turn it into blood; so do the magicians with their enchantments (Exod. 7 : 22). Proof of the miracle is found in the death of the river fish and in the wells which the Egyptians had to dig by the river (Exod. 7 : 21, 24).

The next miracle is the swarming of frogs over the whole land, a wonder which the magicians also accomplished (Exod. 8 : 7). At the king's request Moses asks the Lord to take away the frogs, and the Lord does so; but Pharaoh is hard of heart once more (Exod. 8 : 12–15). This time the magicians are unable to duplicate the miracle, and they tell the king, "This is the finger of God" (Exod. 8 : 18–19). Once more, swarms of flies come and go; the magicians

[1] Cf. H. Gressmann, *Mose und seine Zeit* (Göttingen, 1913), 88; on the Exodus miracles generally, 66–154.

are not mentioned. The king still refuses to release the people (Exod. 8 : 32).

Now the situation is more serious. The Lord kills all the cattle of Egypt on a fixed day predicted by Moses, but touches none of the cattle of the Israelites. When the king remains obdurate, Moses takes soot and scatters it in the air. It is blown through all the land and produces boils on animals and men. The magicians are unable to stand before Moses (Exod. 9 : 11).

Finally the Lord decides to send all his plagues against the stubborn Egyptians. Rain, hail and thunder follow; then locusts come and eat what the hail has left; then Moses raises his hand toward heaven and produces thick darkness for three days. "But all the children of Israel had light in their dwellings" (Exod. 10 : 23). The king still refuses to let them go, even though these ten signs and wonders have taken place.

Therefore the Lord gives his final and greatest sign, which, according to the story, is commemorated in the feast of Passover. At midnight the Lord smites all the first-born in the land of Egypt "from the first-born of Pharaoh that sat on his throne to the first-born of the prisoner in the dungeon, and all the first-born of cattle" (Exod. 12 : 29). Pharaoh thereupon lets the people go.

When he changes his mind once more, the Israelites, guided by a pillar of cloud and a pillar of fire, have encamped "between Migdol and the sea, before Baal Zephon" (Exod. 14 : 12). Two sources describe their crossing. In the earlier form of the story, a strong east wind blows the water back all night long, and the Israelites cross, followed by the Egyptians who drown when Moses stretches out his hand over the sea and the waters return. The "song of Moses" expresses the miracle vividly:

> "With the blast of thy nostrils the waters were piled up,
> The floods stood upright as a heap;
> The deeps were congealed in the heart of the sea" (Exod. 15 : 8).

Again in the more ancient "song of Miriam" the stress is laid not on the dryness of the Israelites but, as in the rest of the "song of Moses", on the wetness of their foes.

> "Sing to Yahweh, for he has triumphed gloriously;
> Horse and rider has he thrown into the sea" (Exod. 15 : 21).

The later form is more magical. Pursued by the Egyptian army, Moses raises his rod over the sea and divides it so that the Israelites can pass through on dry ground (Exod. 14 : 16, 22). The Exodus miracles do not come to an end in the crossing. Wonder succeeds wonder as the people journey onward to the promised land. They are fed in the wilderness by the daily dew of *manna*, literally, "what is it?", which obligingly arrives in double measure on the day before Sabbath. In Exod. 16 : 31 it is said to be "like coriander seed, white; and its taste was like wafers made with honey". When the Israelites are thirsty Moses strikes a rock with his rod, and water comes out of it (Exod. 17 : 6). The rod is also useful in battle. When Moses holds it up, the Israelites prevail over the Amalekites; when Moses drops his arm the Amalekites succeed (Exod. 17 : 11). In the hand of Aaron the rod puts forth flowers and almonds (Num. 17 : 8). [1]

When Korah and his companions rebel against Moses' government, Moses reiterates his claim to a divine mission. "If these men die the common death of all men ... then the Lord has not sent me. But if the Lord makes a new thing (lit. creates a creation) and the ground opens its mouth and swallows them up ... then you shall understand that these men have despised the Lord" (Num. 16 : 29–30). An earthquake immediately follows and these men are buried alive.

In the story of the diviner Balaam we find an episode in which an angel of the Lord blocks the way of the ass on which Balaam rides. When Balaam beats the ass in an effort to have it go on, the Lord opens its mouth and it has a brief conversation with its master (Num. 22 : 28–30).

As Israel enters into the promised land more miracles take place. Joshua's crossing of the Jordan is explicitly compared to Moses' crossing of the Red Sea (Josh. 4 : 23). After seven days of trumpet blowing around Jericho, only the shout of the people is needed to make its walls fall in ruins (Josh. 6 : 20). Most remarkable of all, when Joshua is fighting the Amorites he addresses the sun and moon:

"Sun, be silent on Gibeon, And thou, Moon, in the valley of Aijalon.
And the sun was silent and the moon stayed
Until the nation had avenged themselves of their enemies."

This story is said to be written in the Book of Jashar (Josh. 10 : 13). What it seems to mean is that darkness and a hail storm were desired by Joshua (cf. Josh. 10 : 9, 11) for his victory. The prosaic author of the book of Joshua takes the passage differently, however. "The

[1] Cf. P. Saintyves, *Essais de folklore biblique* (Paris, 1922), 61–137.

sun stayed in the midst of heaven and did not hasten to go down
for a whole day. And there was no day like that before it or after it,
when the Lord listened to the voice of a man" (Josh. 10 : 13–14).
In later stories there is sometimes an appeal to God to renew his
wonderful works as at the Exodus (Judges 6 : 13; a miracle follows,
6 : 21). The story of Manoah's wife and her miraculous conception
(Judges 13 : 2–7) reminds us of the story of Sarah and was apparently in the mind of the evangelist Luke (1 : 26ff).

Nature miracles like those of Moses are renewed in the cycle of
stories about Elijah and Elisha, the "men of God". Elijah prevents
rainfall for "some years" (three and a half, according to later tradition,
James 5 : 17, Luke 4 : 26), is miraculously fed by ravens, constantly
replenishes a jar of meal and a cruse of oil, restores a dead child to
life, brings down fire from heaven, and predicts the return of the rain
(1 Kings 17–18). An angel feeds him with a meal which sustains
him for forty days and nights (1 Kings 19 : 5–8). At the end of his
life he brings down fire from heaven which consumes two companies
of fifty soldiers each (2 Kings 1 : 9–12), and finally goes up into
heaven in a whirlwind or chariot of fire (2 Kings 2 : 1, 11) after he
has crossed the Jordan on dry ground (2 Kings 2 : 8).

His successor Elisha, receiving a "double portion" of his spirit,
performs similar feats. He too divides the waters of the Jordan
(2 Kings 2 : 14) provides water without rainfall (3 : 17–20), and a
miraculous supply of oil (4 : 6), causes a barren woman to conceive
(4 : 32, 37), and miraculously multiplies food (4 : 42–44). He also
cures leprosy (5 : 14) and causes it (5 : 27); he makes an iron axe-
head float (6 : 6). The last of his miracles takes place after his death.
A dead man, cast into the sepulchre of Elisha, touches his bones and
immediately stands up (13 : 21). [1]

The great prophets have little to do with miracles of this sort. The
only significant example is found in Isaiah 38 : 7–8 and 2 Kings
20 : 8, 11. Its miraculousness is expressed more clearly in the account
in 2 Kings. Isaiah offers to give king Hezekiah a sign from Yahweh:
the shadows on a sundial will either go forward ten steps or go backward ten steps. The king replies that it is easy for the shadows to go
forward, but hard for them to go back. Isaiah thereupon cries to
Yahweh and the shadow goes back ten steps.

[1] Cf. H. Duhm, *Der Verkehr Gottes mit den Menschen im Alten Testament* (Tübingen,
1926), 68–70.

11

A prayer in the book of Nehemiah (9 : 5–38) recalls the signs and wonders of the Exodus (9 : 10–12, 15, 19–21) but does not seem to expect anything similar in a later period. Similarly the psalms are full of praises for the wonder-working God of Israel (e.g. 66 : 5–6, 78 passim, 105—107, etc.). But there is no expectation of wonders to be worked through the psalmists themselves. In the book of Job the wonders of God are exemplified primarily in the miracle of creation, though there is an allusion to his control over the sun, perhaps a reference to Joshua (Job 9 : 7).

The book of Jonah tells the story of a great fish which God prepared to rescue Jonah from the sea; he was in its belly three days and nights. When the Lord spake to the fish it vomited Jonah forth upon the dry land (Jonah 2 : 1, 10). Inserted in the brief story is a psalm which Jonah is supposed to have said inside the fish. It does not suit its context, and may well be older than the story which frames it. Early Christians found this story strikingly similar to the death and resurrection of Christ, as we shall see (see p. 168 *infra*); perhaps its mention of Sheol as comparable to the fish encouraged the idea of the *descensus ad inferos*.

Three wonders are found in the first part of the apocalyptic book of Daniel, written during the reign of Antiochus Epiphanes of Syria (c. 165 B. C.). The author places them in the Persian period, perhaps because they will thus seem more credible. In the first, three Jewish youths are cast into a "burning fiery furnace" which does not burn them or singe their hair or blacken their clothing; after emerging unscathed they do not even smell of fire (Dan. 3 : 27). The second wonder takes place at Belshazzar's feast, when human fingers are seen writing on the plaster of the wall (Dan. 5 : 5). In the third, Daniel himself is cast into a den of lions, but after spending a night there is released unharmed. His accusers (with their children and wives) are then thrown in, and the lions break their bones in pieces before they reach the bottom of the den (Dan. 6 : 24). In a somewhat later addition to the book of Daniel, the story of Bel, Jewish shrewdness is contrasted with pagan credulity. The king of Babylon believes the statement of the priests of Bel to the effect that great quantities of food are needed daily for the idol. Daniel observes that since the idol is made of clay covered with bronze it cannot eat. Actually the priests enter the temple at night through a trap door and consume the food with their families. Daniel exposes the fraud by pointing out their footprints to the king.

The Maccabaean period itself, with its atmosphere of intense religious feeling, was conducive to the rise of miracle stories. In the relatively sober history provided by 1 Maccabees, however, there are no stories of miracles. As Pfeiffer remarks, [1] "God intervenes to give victory not through miracles but through natural means". In 2 Maccabees, on the other hand, there are frequent miraculous epiphanies; God is the omnipotent wonder-worker (2 Macc. 15 : 21). This emphasis on miracles can be explained in several ways. In the first place, 2 Maccabees is a theological tract rather than a work of historical research. It lays emphasis on three doctrines often later associated in Christianity: creation *ex nihilo* (7 : 28), wonder-working, and the resurrection of the flesh (7 : 11, 14 : 46). In the second place, the epitomist to whom the book owes its present form explicitly states that he has mingled historical fact with attractive style in an effort to please his readers (15 : 39). Precisely this mixture is often criticized, as we shall see, by historians who distrust stories of the miraculous.

With the rise of apocalyptic, miracles came to be expected in the imminent reign of God, when he would renew his favor toward Israel as in the days of the Exodus. "As in the days of your coming forth out of the land of Egypt, I will show them marvelous things" (Micah 7 : 15). The miracle-worker Elijah would return. "Behold, I will send you Elijah the prophet before the great and terrible day of the Lord come" (Malachi 4 : 5). "I will show wonders in the heavens and on the earth: blood and fire and pillars of smoke. The sun shall be turned into darkness and the moon into blood before the great and terrible day of the Lord come" (Joel 2 : 30–31). It is obvious that these future wonders are modeled to a considerable extent on the miracles of Israel's past. And it is generally true that the ages of miracles are the past and the future. The Wisdom of Solomon provides a general theory to explain miracles (19 : 18; see *infra*, p. 184), but the miracles are all in the future (5 : 17–23) or in the past (11 : 16–19). Some miracles are possible in the present, as the stories of the rabbis' healongs and of those of Jesus and his adversaries remind us. But the truly great and stupendous miracles do not now occur.

The wisdom of Jesus son of Sirach places proof of God's omnipotence squarely on the wonders of the past. Whatever God com-

[1] *History of New Testament Times* (New York, 1949) 494.

mands shall take place (Sir. 39 : 16). No one can say, "What is this? Why is that?", for "at his command the waters stood as a heap . . . . at his command is done whatever pleases him" (Sir. 39 : 17f.). The miracles of Moses are mentioned, but stronger emphasis is laid on the stupendous events in the time of Joshua, Elijah and Elisha.

> Did not the sun go back by his means? And was not one day as long as two? (46 : 4).
>
> By the word of the Lord he shut up the heaven, and also three times brought down fire. O Elijah, how you were honored in your wonderful deeds! and who may glory like you! Yo raised up a dead man from death, and his soul from the place of the dead, by the word of the Most High (48 : 3–5).
>
> Elijah it was who was covered with a whirlwind, and Elisha was filled with his spirit.... He did wonders in his life, and at his death his works were marvelous (48 : 12–14).
>
> In his (Hezekiah's) time the sun went backward (48 : 23).

"Therefore bless the God of all", the author concludes, "who alone does wonderful things everywhere" (50 : 22). The examples he gives, however, are not contemporary; they are "acts of old" (51 : 8).

If we turn now to ask how such stories would be regarded in the Graeco-Roman world, we shall have to point out that attitudes toward such stories would vary from century to century and from group to group. A simpler question to ask is whether Greek mythology contained similar tales. The answer to this question is obvious. The formation of Eve from Adam's rib is no more remarkable than the story of Deucalion and Pyrrha, who after the deluge of which they were the sole survivors cast stones behind them from which the human race emerged. But as Ovid [1] ironically remarks, "Who would believe this story were not antiquity its witness?" Both Philo and Origen hasten to treat the biblical story as allegory. Again, the biblical flood is like the flood from which Deucalion and Pyrrha escaped. Therefore Philo and two Christian apologists identify Noah with Deucalion. [2]

Weather portents like those in the Old Testament are exceedingly common in classical mythology and history. Eclipses of sun or moon often accompanied important historical events. The reversal of the sun's course is more unusual, although Herodotus was informed

[1] *Metam.* i. 400.  [2] Philo, *Praem.* 23; Just. *Apol.* ii. 6. 2; Theoph. *Autol.* ii. 30, iii. 18–19.

by Egyptian priests that it had happened twice. [1] Magicians claimed to be able to effect the same change. [2] The other wonders ascribed to Moses, Joshua, Elijah and Elisha are typical of wonderworkers at any time, and would be accepted or rejected on the same grounds.

For example, the "divine men" of the Graeco-Roman world reveal their divinity through the miracles which accompany their births, characterize their lives and make them triumph over death. [3] These miracles were very similar to those ascribed to some of the heroes of the Old Testament, and when Greekspeaking Jews came to rewrite the Old Testament stories for a Greek audience they described the Old Testament "divine men" in terms of the Graeco-Roman equivalents. [4] Thus the way was prepared for the Christian interpretation of Jesus and Paul in similar terms.

We should also observe that in the rhetoric of Neoplatonism it became so customary to describe the miracles of philosophical heroes that when no miracles are available a biographer will apologize for not having provided any stories about them. [5] Many people in antiquity felt that miracles had to accompany the lives of great men. The idea of cosmic sympathy was only one part of this feeling; Diogenes Laertius (iv. 64) tells us that a lunar eclipse at the death of Carneades reflected the "sympathy" of the moon; but it was an important feature for philosophical debates. On a lower level no arguments would be required.

When we turn to the nature miracles of the New Testament we must first of all consider their historical setting. In the Old Testament we found miracles in the distant past and in the future, though rarely in the actual present. The miracles of the Old Testament are concentrated around Moses and the "men of God" Elijah and Elisha. In the later prophets future miracles were predicted. In 2 Maccabees miracles were described as having happened in Maccabaean times. When we come to the New Testament period, however, we find an eager expectation of miracles not so much among the rabbis as among apocalyptic-eschatological writers who believe that the fulfilment of prophecy is imminent.

[1] *Hist.* ii. 142; cf. Apollodorus, *Epit.* ii. 12 with Frazer's notes. [2] A. S. Pease, *Aeneid IV* (Cambridge, 1935), 403. [3] H. Windisch, *Paulus und Christus* (Leipzig, 1934), 24–89; L. Bieler, ΘΕΙΟΣ ΑΝΗΡ I (Vienna, 1935). We give examples, p. 173 *infra*. [4] Windisch, *op. cit.*, 89–114. [5] Eunapius (*Vit. phil.* p. 471 Boissonade) explains that a certain Antoninus had no tendency to theurgy *perhaps* because of imperial opposition to sorcery; cf. Mark 5 : 6?

Apocalyptic writing flourished in Judaism in the period between the Maccabaean revolt and the destruction of Jerusalem in A. D. 70. Under Roman rule the Jewish people constantly prayed that God would free them from their slavery. [1] Only God was their king, and God was about to take up his power and reign over them. For apocalyptic writers the new age itself would be the greatest of miracles, although it would be accompanied by other wonders. [2] These miracles would be a reassertion of the free creative power of God, to whom "all things are possible". [3]

In the troubles which preceded the Jewish war of 66–70 expectation of such miracles played a prominent part. Around the year 45 a Jewish prophet named Theudas assembled many followers by the river Jordan. He informed them that at his command the waters would part and they could then march through, presumably to Jerusalem. The Roman procurator, however, did not wait for the miracle to take place but sent a cavalry troop which killed many of Theudas' followers and beheaded him. [4] Here we may possibly see a mixture of science and religion. The elder Pliny, who had actually visited Judaea, tells us that there is a brook there which dries up every Sabbath. [5] If the procurator possessed such information, he could not have afforded to take chances.

About ten years later an Egyptian persuaded four thousand enthusiasts to come to the mount of Olives outside Jerusalem because at his command the walls of the city would fall. Again the Romans did not wait upon the event but attacked. The Egyptian lost six hundred of his men and disappeared into the desert. [6] Again, a later prophet claimed that in the desert God would provide "signs of liberty" or "evident wonders and signs". [7]

In all three cases we seem to find an eschatological understanding of the Old Testament. The crossing of the Jordan had been made easy for Joshua, Elijah, and Elisha; why should not such an event occur again? Joshua had broken down the walls of Jericho in a miraculous way, and signs and wonders had been given Moses and the children of Israel in the desert. [3] Throughout the first century,

[1] On one of the principal causes of this atittude cf. F. C. Grant, *The Economic Background of the Gospels* (Oxford, 1926). [2] 2. Esdr. 7:27, 13:49; 2 Bar. 29:6, 51:7. [3] See chapter 9. [4] Jos. *Ant.* xx. 97–98. [5] Plin. *N. H.* xxxi. 24. [6] Jos. *Bell.* ii. 262; Acts 21:38 (cf. *Bell.* ii. 259). [7] Jos. *Bell.* ii. 259–60. [8] The desert remained a place of eschatological expectation; cf. Matt. 24 : 26; Hippol. *Comm. in Dan.* iii. 18; G. Kittel in *TWzNT* II 655–57.

apocalyptists both Christian and non-Christian expected such miracles to take place when the reign of God was inaugurated.

Such a belief seems to be reflected in the sayings of Jesus. The story of the cursing of the fig-tree contains the statement (Mark 11 : 23) that "whoever says to this mountain, Be lifted up and cast into the sea, and does not doubt in his heart but believes that what he says is taking place, it will take place for him". The mountain in question may perhaps be the mount of Olives, which according to Zechariah 14 : 4 is to be split and moved to the east and to the west "in that day". The Hebrew word for "to the west", perhaps misunderstood in a Greek translation, is "to the sea". [1]

The same saying is handed down in a different context in Matthew and Luke. [2] "If you have faith like a grain of mustard [3] you will say to this mountain . . . ." Luke alters the "mountain" to a "sycamine tree", and thus interprets the saying as an *adynaton*; poets sometimes spoke of the impossibility of trees being in the sea. [4] Matthew makes the statement still more general by adding, "and nothing will be impossible for you". [5] The same idea is expressed in the saying, "Ask and it will be given you", [6] which means "Ask in faith, doubting nothing". [7] This is the kind of faith which can "move mountains". [8] It is first of all an attitude of complete trust in God and in his eschatological promises. By the time of Paul it has become objectified as a unique kind of spiritual gift, a wonder-working faith. [9]

Just at this point we are able to contrast the attitude of Christian believers with that of a contemporary philosopher. In his *Scientific Problems* the Roman Stoic Seneca discusses the question of the causes of earthquakes. [10]

> Countless "miracles" move and change the face of the earth in various places, bring down mountains, raise plains, swell valleys, raise up new islands in the deep. It is worth while to investigate the causes from which these things happen. You may ask, "What will the value of the endeavor be?" The greatest value of all, to know nature.

This is a very different point of view from that of the early Christians. The event, an earthquake, is presumably the same in each case.

---

[1] Cf. *JBL* 67 (1948), 297–303; for rabbinic parallels cf. H. Strack–P. Billerbeck, *Kommentar zum Neuen Testament* I (Munich, 1922), 759. [2] Matt. 17 : 20, Luke 17 : 6. [3] The smallest of seeds, Matt. 13 : 32 (Mark 4 : 31). [4] See p. 58. [5] Cf. Mark 9 : 23. [6] Matt. 7 : 7, Luke 11 : 9. [7] James 1 : 6. [8] 1 Cor. 13 : 2. [9] 1 Cor. 12 : 9. [10] *N. Q.* vi. 4. 1–2.

Seneca sees in it an occasion for scientific investigation or philosophical speculation; Jesus looks forward to it as an event in which the hand of God will be revealed.

Christians believed that God was going to perform great signs and wonders. Indeed, Jesus "by the finger of God" was already casting out demons and thus demonstrating the presence of the reign of God. [1] The tradition of his healing miracles is unquestionably reliable. [2] Does the earliest tradition, however, include nature miracles? In his *Geschichte der synoptischen Tradition* [3] Bultmann has endeavored to show that the earliest tradition, that of the common source of Matthew and Luke, does not include such stories, and that they are derived from non-Jewish, Hellenistic sources. They reflect the power of God at work in Jesus, but they are "somewhat separate from his individual will and function rather automatically". Earlier critics had suggested that they were derived from the Old Testament, but Bultmann claims that only a few elements in the stories have such an origin.

Fascher attacked Bultmann's method in a critique which includes the observation that the origin of the miracle stories still remains dark. He adds that one's attitude toward the question of their authenticity depends largely on his presuppositions. The same point has been made by Vincent Taylor and by many other writers. [4]

It can probably be said, however, that there are two strands of thought in the synoptic gospels. In the story of the temptations of Jesus, he explicitly refuses to perform such nature miracles as the turning of stones into bread or the defiance of gravitation by jumping off the wing of the temple. [5] To the Pharisees who ask for a "sign from heaven", he replies that to this generation no sign will be given. [6] In the Matthaean account of the same event he adds the exception of the "sign of Jonah", [7] but this exception probably does not refer to nature miracles. In what may be a reflection of this saying, the apostle Paul describes the Jews as seeking signs and the Christians as replying with the proclamation of Christ crucified, a "scandal" to the Jews and foolishness to Greeks. [8] Similarly in the Acts of the

[1] Luke 11 : 20, Matt. 12 : 28; cf. Exod. 8 : 19. [2] Cf. L. J. McGinley, *Form-Criticism of the Synoptic Healing Narratives* (Woodstock, Md., 1944); also in *Theological Studies* 4 (1943), 53–99, 385–419. [3] Göttingen, 1921, 1931; first ed., 135–50. [4] *Die formgeschichtliche Methode* (Giessen, 1924), 130; *The Formation of the Gospel Tradition* (London, 1933), 119–41. [5] Matt. 4 : 3–6, Luke 4 : 3–4, 9–12. [6] Mark 8 : 12. [7] Matt. 16 : 4. [8] 1 Cor. 1 : 22–23.

Apostles the "mighty works and wonders and signs" of Jesus seem to be not nature miracles but his "going about doing good and healing all those who were under the power of the devil". [1]

On the other hand, it is obvious that the synoptic gospels include stories of nature miracles. These are (1) the stilling of the storm (Mark 4 : 37–41), (2) the walking on the sea (Mark 6 : 45–52), (3) the multiplication of bread (Mark 6 : 34–44, 8 : 1–9), (4) the cursing of the fig-tree (Mark 11 : 12–14, 20), and (5) the coin in the fish's mouth (Matt. 17 : 24–27). To these we may add the Johannine story of the changing of water into wine (John 2 : 1–11) and the other "signs" which the evangelist knows but does not relate (John 20 : 30). The darkness at the crucifixion (Mark 15 : 33) and the rending of the temple veil (Mark 15 : 38) are illustrations of cosmic "sympathy" rather than nature miracles.

We are not concerned with the question of the historicity of these miracles but with the ways in which this question was raised and answered in antiquity. We may say, however, that probably these stories were originally told in an atmosphere of apocalyptic eschatology They are fairly closely related to the Old Testament, which was regarded as a book of prophecy as well as a record of God's dealings with his people in the past. [2] The use of the Old Testament as prophecy inevitably controlled not only details of these stories but also the whole way in which they were told. For example, the framework of the stilling of the storm is based on the story of Jonah; [3] the walking on the sea seems to be related to the description of God in the book of Job; [4] and the multiplication of bread is close to a similar story about Elisha in 2 Kings 4 : 42–44. The cursing of the fig-tree is probably based on the expectation of a period of miraculous fruitfulness in the last days (see p. 167, n. 1). The darkness at the crucifixion, which Luke (23 : 45) apparently explains as due to an eclipse, [5] is perhaps based on the prophecy of Amos 8 : 9, "I will cause the sun to go down at noon, and I will darken the earth in the clear day". The rending of the temple veil signifies the end of the cultus at Jerusalem, and perhaps the departure of the presence of God, as in the case of the portents before the destruction of the temple. [6]

---

[1] Acts 2 : 22, 10 : 38.  [2] Cf. J. Daniélou, *Sacramentum Futuri* (Paris, 1950). [3] Cf. Jerome, *Comm. in Matt.* i. 9 (PL 26, 55A).  [4] Job 9 : 8, „God alone.... treads on the waves of the sea"; 9 : 11, „he goes by me and I do not see him" (cf. Mark 6 : 48–49).  [5] On the eclipses in this period cf. F. Boll in *RE* VI 2360. [6] E. Lohmeyer, *Das Evangelium des Markus* (Göttingen, 1937), 347.

The Johannine story of changing water into wine may be simply a popular tale, but in view of John's symbolical treatment of the multiplication of bread we must agree with Cullmann that it may be a symbolical picture of the miracles of baptism and the Eucharist. [1]

Another miracle story which is also eschatological is that of the virginal conception of Jesus. According to Matthew and Luke [2] his conception by Mary was due to the Holy Spirit. In the Old Testament, especially in the legends of the patriarchs, conception is often attributed to God; and in the Septuagint translation of Isaiah 7 : 14 we read the prophecy, "Behold a virgin shall conceive and bear a son". [3] On the other hand, the virginal conception is not found in the gospel of Mark, where it almost seems to be excluded by the story of the attempt of Jesus' family to seize him and his rejection of them. [4] In John 1 : 45 a disciple of Jesus speaks of him as son of Joseph, and in primitive Jewish Christianity there were many who regarded Jesus as the son of Joseph and Mary. [5] The idea of the virginal conception, however, rapidly became a dogma of Catholic Christianity.

All these stories reflect the belief that the last days have already dawned and that the last days are characterized by miracles. God has at last taken up his power and the miracle stories at first reflect this belief and then are used to confirm it. In the gospel of John we find these stories employed as evidences of the divine power of Jesus. [6]

> If I do not do the works of my Father, do not believe me; but if I do them, even if you do not believe me, believe the works, so that you may know and recognize that the Father is in me and I am in the Father.

Such eschatological miracles (although we do not find nature miracles mentioned) were to be found in the Christian community; Paul speaks of his own miracles [7] as well as those of others. [8]

When we say that these miracles have eschatological significance we must also point out the implications of eschatology. The new age of Jewish apocalyptic-eschatological writers was to be brought about by the omnipotent God, who created the first creation and

[1] *Urchristentum und Gottesdienst* (Zurich, 1949), 67ff.; contrast K. L. Schmidt in *Harnack-Ehrung* (Leipzig, 1921), 42. [2] Matt. 1 : 18, 20; Luke 1 : 35 (see p. 176). [3] Hellenistic Jewish parallels in W. L. Knox, *Some Hellenistic Elements in Primitive Christianity* (London, 1944), 22–25. [4] Mark 3 : 21, 31–35. [5] H. J. Schoeps, *Theologie und Geschichte des Judenchristentums* (Tübingen, 1949), 71–74. [6] John 10 : 37–38. [7] 2 Cor. 12 : 12, Rom. 15 : 19. [8] 1 Cor. 12 : 9–10, 29–30, Gal. 3 : 5.

will create a second. The underlying axiom which made prophecy credible was the omnipotence of God. No matter how stable the present world might seem, no matter how apparently unbreakable the chain of cause and effect, God would act and nothing could resist his power.

Thus the miracle stories at the same time reflect this belief and are used to confirm it. And since the community within which they are told is a community which believes that in Christ God has acted, and that Christ will soon return, no questioning of these stories is possible, at least in the earliest days of Christianity. It is only when two new factors are introduced that the question of credibility arises. In the first place, the passage of time forces Christians to rethink their conception of the immediate return of Christ. For some reason there is a delay, and people ask the question, "Where is the promise of his coming?" and argue that the process of nature is always the same (2 Peter 3 : 4). The author of 2 Peter has to argue that the miracle of the transfiguration was not a myth but an eye-witness report. [1] In the second place, the passage of Christianity from Palestine to the Graeco-Roman world and its increasing contact with Greek philosophy and history raises the question of credibility with increasing sharpness. Conflict arises not only between Christian and non-Christian, but also between the educated Christian and "the many". In this debate the underlying problem of divine omnipotence is sometimes brought to the surface and always plays a part in forming the thought of proponents and opponentsa like.

Our explanation of the miracle stories as eschatological events (some historical, others perhaps entirely symbolical) is very similar to the interpretation given them by Johannes Weiss and the "eschatological school" in Germany fifty years ago. At that time it was vigorously attacked by Paul Fiebig in his *Jüdische Wundergeschichten des neutestamentlichen Zeitalters* (Tübingen, 1911). He argued that miracle stories are characteristic of the first century. They were not told just about the promised Messiah but about rabbis who lived in Palestine then. These stories are fairly similar to those told about Jesus. Among the examples Fiebig gives are the multiplication of bread and the stilling of a storm. Though what he claims as the raising of a dead man sounds more like a misunderstood metaphor, [2]

[1] Cf. G. Stählin in *TWzNT* IV 791. [2] *Op. cit.*, 22–24, 33 (bread, storm); 36–38 (resurrection).

we must admit that he does provide a few examples of miracles ascribed to the rabbis.

Most of the examples he cites, however, come from the period after the destruction of the temple and after the decline of eschatology within Judaism. They therefore do not adequately represent the earlier period. [1] Rabbinic Judaism, purged of its apocalyptic wing, does not altogether correspond to the environment of the earliest church. And we have already found in Josephus (p. 166) a reliable witness for the linking of miracles with apocalyptic hopes. It is true that belief in the miraculous is found in ancient Judaism generally. But the kind of belief which passes into early Christianity is given its impetus by eschatology.

The primary reason why miracle stories are so prominent in early Christianity, then, is that it was an eschatological movement within Judaism. The omnipotence of God was already effective and would soon be more effective still. The content of the stories, however, is not uniquely Jewish or eschatological. The stories can be paralleled in Greek and Roman literature, and would thus be subject to criticism by those trained in rhetoric or philosophy.

Before we turn to the parallels to the nature miracles of the New Testament, we must answer the objections raised by W. Grundmann [2] to regarding them as parallels. He argues that (1) while most non-Christian miracles are associated with magic, those of the New Testament have nothing to do with magic or magical means. In response to this argument we may reply that (a) most of the parallels we shall discuss are not associated with magic, while (b) the early attacks on the miracles of Jesus usually treated them as magical. He also argues that (2) the New Testament miracles are brought about by a powerful word of Jesus or his disciples, a word which has nothing to do with a magical formula. This argument is, of course, only a variant of the first one. It is still more erroneous, for (a) most of the New Testament nature miracles are not "brought about by a powerful word" but simply happen; and (b) the Aramaic words occasionally preserved (Mark 5 : 41, 7 : 34) are not entirely unlike the *nomina barbarica* of magic. Grundmann finally argues that (3) the New Testament miracles present faith as a necessity; this is a

[1] So A. Schlatter, *Das Wunder in der Synagoge* (Gütersloh, 1912), 55–56. [2] *Der Begriff der Kraft in der neutestamentlichen Gedankenwelt* (Stuttgart, 1932), 65–68; repeated in *TWzNT* II 303.

personal relationship which excludes impersonal magic. Again we can reply that (a) sometimes faith is necessary in the miracle stories, sometimes it is not; and (b) sometimes outside Christianity faith is necessary too.

The fundamental difficulty with Grundmann's arguments is due to his identification of (non-Christian) miracle with magic. This identification cannot be justified, and a thoroughgoing distinction between Christian and non-Christian miracle stories cannot be made. The contexts are different; the phenomena are somewhat similar.

The similarity between Christian and non-Christian stories of virginal conception is noted by Origen, who points out that Speusippus, Plato's nephew, said Plato was the son of Apollo and a human mother. [1] A more complete collection of sources is given by Jerome in his work *Adversus Jovinianum*. The Indian Gymnosophists say that a virgin produced Buddha from her side, while three Greek writers (Speusippus, Clearchus, and Anaxilides) relate that Perictione the mother of Plato was overcome by a vision of Apollo; they think he would not have been the greatest of philosophers had he not been born of a virgin mother. [2]

The same Greek writers are cited by Diogenes Laertius (iii. 2), who says, however, that the vision appeared in a dream to Ariston, who was ordered by the god to keep Perictione pure until the birth of Plato. Presumably these are different episodes in the same story.

The source from which Jerome derives his information is the Neoplatonic philosopher Porphyry, as Bickel has shown. [3] Bickel doubts that his reference to the Buddha is related to the Indian Buddha, for no other ancient writer mentions his virginal conception. He claims that this is really a certain Buddha from Persia who was said to be the teacher of Mani in the third century. [4] On the other hand, Jerome's notice has nothing to do with Manichaeism, and he could have derived it from the *Indica* of Bardaisan, which Porphyry knew and used (see p. 111). We conclude that all of Jerome's statements come from Porphyry.

It is difficult to determine whether Porphyry actually accepted these stories of virginal conception or not. In his *Life of Pythagoras* (2)

[1] *C. Cels.* i. 37.  [2] *Adv. Jovin.* i. 42 (PL 23, 285).  [3] E. Bickel, *Diatribe in Senecae philosophi fragmenta* I (Leipzig, 1915), 133–41.  [4] *Ibid.*, 147–52; cf. H. C. Puech, *Le manichéisme* (Paris, 1949), 22–26.

he says that "some" say that Pythagoras was the son of Apollo and Pythais. They cite a poet of Samos to prove their point.

Pythagoras, beloved of Zeus, whom to Apollo bore
Pythais, most beautiful of Samian women.

Porphyry does not criticize this story; he simply relates it.

On the other hand, Porphyry's successor Iamblichus, whose credulity we have already discussed (p. 75), cites the same verses but criticizes them because they led to the popular belief that Pythagoras was not the son of his real father Mnesarchus. [1] Iamblichus knows that three Greek writers (Epimenides, Eudoxus, and Xenocrates) have said that Apollo had intercourse with Pythagoras' mother, whose name was not Pythais but Parthenis, and that he predicted Pythagoras' birth through the Pythian oracle. Their story "must be absolutely rejected".

Iamblichus himself provides a reconstruction of the true narrative. Mnesarchus' wife, whose name was Parthenis ("virginal"), was already pregnant when the Pythian oracle told him that she would bear a marvelous child. In honor of the Pythia he changed her name to Pythais, and when the boy was born named him Pythagoras ("predicted by the Pythia"). Pythagoras was certainly not the physical son of Apollo. His soul, not his body, was divine, and only it was "sent down to men". [2]

Iamblichus' reconstruction, of course, is not his point of departure. His basic principle is the impossibility of the union of the divine with the human, and this leads him to criticize the traditional stories of Pythagoras' birth. Because of this principle he contradicts another principle set forth in the same treatise: "Doubt no marvel concerning the gods". The contradiction shows us the danger of making generalizations about credibility in antiquity.

If we turn back to the legends of early Roman history and their treatment by historians, we shall find similar ambiguities. These legends sometimes tell of the divine origin of great men. Romulus and Remus were thought to be the sons of Rhea Silvia and Mars, while Scipio Africanus was called the son of Jupiter. These stories were subject to considerable criticism. Livy assures us that he does not intend either to confirm or to refute poetic legends. [3] Antiquity

[1] *Pyth.* 4–7.  [2] *Ibid.*, 8.  [3] Livy i. praef. 6–8; on confirmation and refutation in rhetoric see p. 59.

must be permitted to mingle the human with the divine and thus make the foundations of cities more venerable. Moreover, the military glory of Rome is so great that those who do not take it hardly should accept the story of Mars as the father of Romulus. The question of fact is not important. On the other hand, when Livy relates the story itself he admits that the fact is really in question. [1] We have already seen (p. 55) that the Greek historian Dionysius of Halicarnassus has difficulties with the story; we may add that he refers his readers to philosophers for help on the problem. [2] Plutarch ascribes the story to Greek sources, and while he relates it without criticism, we shall presently see that he regards similar tales as incredible. [3] Dio Cassius, writing early in the third century, does not criticize the story, although he does explain away the divine origin of Scipio Africanus. The general, he says, always went to the Capitol before doing businesss; the rumor therefore arose that Jupiter was his father. He encouraged the rumor for political reasons. [4]

A somewhat similar account of the relation between the human and the divine is given concerning the ancient Roman king Numa. According to Livy (i. 19. 5) Numa thought that the fear of the gods could not be instilled in the minds of the Roman people without some miraculous event. He therefore pretended to have meetings with the goddess Egeria. Livy's analysis finds the origin of the story in politics. Plutarch, on the other hand, examines it from the standpoint of science (*Numa* iv. 3–4). After observing that it is difficult to believe that a divine being would enjoy a human body and its beauty, [5] he goes on to give an Egyptian theory which explains such cases. The Egyptians argue that "it is not impossible for a spirit of God to approach a woman and implant some beginnings of procreation". Their theory, however, does not explain the case of Numa and Egeria, for they do not think that a man can thus approach a goddess. Plutarch, who in any event regards the story as mythical, [6] criticizes their view on the ground that both male and female contribute in procreation.

The Egyptian theory is described more fully in *Quaestiones conviviales* viii. 1. 3. Here it is said that the Egyptians allow the possibility of intercourse between a male god and a mortal woman, but not

---

[1] *Ibid.*, i. 4. 1.    [2] Dion. Hal. i. 77. 3.    [3] Plut. *Rom.* 3–4; on Greek sources cf. Rosenberg in *RE* I A 1085.    [4] Dio Cass. xvi. 57. 39.    [5] Similarly Celsus argues that even if the mother of Jesus was beautiful, the nature of God does not allow him to love a corruptible body; see p. 177.    [6] *Fort. rom.* 9.

between a mortal man and a female goddess. The reason for their rejection of the second case is that they suppose the substance of the gods to consist only of air and spirits and a certain heat and moisture.

Eduard Norden [1] has compared this Egyptian theory with the stories of the conception of Jesus in the infancy narrative of Luke. It is difficult, however, to suppose that these stories were written under the influence of Graeco-Egyptian theosophy. The theory would prove valuable to Christians only when they were defending stories already in existence, although we must admit that we know of no instances of its use.

Alexander the Great was regarded in his lifetime as the son of Zeus Ammon; he journeyed to the oasis of Siwah so that the oracle there might proclaim the story of his origin. Arrian, who tells this story, does not doubt that he was the son of Philip of Macedon and Olympias, and he describes divine portents as accompanying only his death. [2] In more legendary stories such portents were assigned to his birth. [3] Finally the story was told that he was the son of the Egyptian magician Nectanebo, who had managed to impregnate Olympias in a dream he had caused her to have (Pseudo-Callisthenes i. 5).

> The many are deceived (says Pseudo-Callisthenes i. 1) when they call him the son of king Philip. This is not true, for he was not his son, but the wisest Egyptians say that he was the son of Nectanebo.

This story, as Ausfeld long ago observed, [4] is an Egyptian patriotic reworking of an older story in which the god Ammon was Alexander's father. As is often the case, we cannot tell how literally the tellers or the hearers of the story understood it. It belongs to romance rather than history. Alexander is the hero of Alexandrian plebeians in the Ptolemaic period, [5] although as Kroll observes, [6] Pseudo-Callisthenes is not a popular tale but a learned romance, a work of some sophistication.

Similarly the birth of Augustus was foreshadowed by portents. Julius Marathus, followed by Suetonius (*Aug.* 94), reports a decree of the Senate that no child born in that year should be allowed to live. [7]

---

[1] *Die Geburt des Kindes* (Leipzig, 1924), 76–82.  [2] Arrian, *Anab.* iii. 3. 2, vii. 30. 2.  [3] Plut. *Alex.* ii. 2–iii. 3; from Timaeus? Cf. A. S. Pease on Cic. *Div.* i. 47 (pp 177–78).  [4] A. Ausfeld, *Der griechische Alexanderroman* (Leipzig, 1907), 227–28.  [5] *Ibid.*, 237–38, 242.  [6] W. Kroll, *Historia Alexandris Magni* I (Berlin, 1926), xiv–xv.  [7] We may compare the biblical stories in Exodus 1 : 16 and Matthew 2 : 16. Cf. L. Bieler, *ΘΕΙΟΣ ΑΝΗΡ* I (Vienna, 1935), 41.

He adds that prospective fathers prevented its publication. Suetonius also relates a story from the *Theologumena* of Asclepiades of Mendes. The mother of Augustus had been sleeping in the temple of Apollo when a snake approached her. When she awoke she cleansed herself, but a snake-shaped mark appeared and remained on her body. Augustus, born in the tenth month after this experience, was considered the son of Apollo. It is not clear whether Suetonius believes this story or not. A similar tale is told of Olympias, the mother of Alexander. [1]

Such stories were treated with a certain scepticism by those who knew of the frauds perpetrated by priests. [2] Herodotus had already doubted the authenticity of divine epiphanies of this sort. [3] Josephus tells us of a certain Paulina who believed that she was going to sleep with the god Anubis; her companion turned out to be the Roman knight Decius Mundus. [4] And from such cases Ovid draws the conclusion, "In the gods' name many have entered chaste marriage-beds". [5]

On more philosophical grounds Celsus the opponent of Christianity refuses to accept the story of the virginal conception of Jesus. Like Plutarch he argues that God would not fall in love with a human woman, no matter how beautiful she might be; and Mary was actually neither wealthy nor of royal birth. The story is incredible and has nothing to do with the kingdom of God. [6] From a more scientific point of view Marcion criticized the prophecy of Isaiah 7 : 14, stating that "nature does not permit a virgin to bear a child". [7] In Marcion's opinion nature was immutable. [8]

An explanation of this virginal conception is given by Celsus, apparently from Jewish sources. The father of Jesus was a Roman soldier named Panthera. [9] While Panthera is a real name, it is at least possible that it represents a play on $\pi\alpha\varrho\vartheta\acute{\epsilon}\nu\sigma\varsigma$, the Greek word for "virgin". Another explanation may be reflected in a strange story told by Aelian. [10] He relates that "in the time of king Herod" a beautiful Jewish girl was loved by a snake which used to sleep with her. We may recall that in Christian circles before the end of the

---

[1] Plut. *Alex.* ii. 4; cf. Pease on Cic. *Div.* ii. 135 (p. 565).  [2] O. Weinreich, *Der Trug des Nectanebos* (Leipzig, 1911), 17–42.  [3] Herod. i. 182.  [4] Jos. *Ant.* xviii. 65–80.  [5] *Metam.* iii. 281–82.  [6] Orig. *C. Cels.* i. 39.  [7] Tert. *Marc.* iii. 13; cf. Galen, cited p. 13.  [8] A. v. Harnack, *Marcion* (ed. 2, Leipzig, 1924), 260*.  [9] Orig. *C. Cels.* i. 32.  [10] Ael. *N. A.* vi. 17.

second century the parallel was drawn between the virgin Eve and the virgin Mary, [1] and that some Jewish interpreters of the Old Testament taught that the serpent actually seduced Eve. [2] Aelian's story may conceivably reflect a popular version of Jewish criticism. On the other hand, no conception is recorded, and it may be simply a story about a friendly animal.

Another kind of miracle in the New Testament has many parallels in Greek and Roman writers. This is the control over storms and waters which the gods shared with the divine men of antiquity. Stories of such control were very common. [3] On the other hand, belief in the possibility of walking on water was relatively rare. Such belief is to be found in India in pre-Christian times, [4] but Greek writers generally regard it as foolish. Water bears up only what is lighter than itself. [5] The poet Menander [6] speaks of the kind of stories told about Alexander in which anything can happen. "If I need a way through the sea it will immediately be provided for me." This statement may reflect popular belief in something like walking on water. On the other hand Dio Chrysostom describes impossibilities possible only to the gods, and gives as one example walking on the sea. He says that Xerxes achieved this by crossing the Hellespont on a bridge of boats. [7] Actually it is only in dreams that men walk on the sea. [8] Two stories told by Lucian parody the belief in walking on water. In one he describes men with cork feet who walk on water; [9] in the other he says that a Pythagorean could walk on water "with ordinary shoes". [10] An epitome of the Greek attitude is found in the *Hieroglyphica* of Horapollo, who says that the Egyptians depict the idea of the impossible by a hieroglyph of human feet walking on water. Since, as Sbordone observes, this is not actually the case, his interpretation reflects Greek rather than Egyptian ideas. [11]

Stories of the multiplication of bread are not common, but we have an example in the story told by Pomponius Mela [12] about a miraculous table in Ethiopia whose supplies never ran short.

There are several ancient stories of changing water into wine.

[1] H. Koch, *Adhuc Virgo* (Tübingen, 1929), 12–13; Justin, *Dial.* 100, 358 Otto. [2] L. Ginzberg, *The Legends of the Jews* V (Philadelphia, 1925), 133. [3] E. S. McCartney in *Class. Weekly* 27 (1933), 19. [4] W. N. Brown, *The Indian and Christian Miracles of Walking on the Water* (Chicago, 1928), 15. [5] Cf. Sen. *N. Q.* iii. 25. 5–7. [6] Fr. 924 K. [7] *Or.* iii. 30–31. [8] *Or.* xi. 129. [9] *Ver. hist.* ii. 4. [10] *Philops.* 13. [11] *Hier.* i. 58, 121 Sbordone. [12] *Chor.* iii. 87; cf. Philemon and Baucis (Ovid, *Metam.* viii. 618–715).

Diodorus Siculus (iii. 66. 2) describes a spring which proves to the people of Teos that Dionysus was born there, for at fixed intervals (presumably on his festival) it changes into wine. Pliny tells us that on the island of Andros water turned into wine in the temple of Dionysus every January 5th. He gives as his authority a man who was consul for the third time in the year 72. [1] Finally Pausanias (vi. 26) describes a wonder at Elis in considerable detail. [2] The priests brought three pots into a building and set them down empty in the presence of citizens of Elis and any strangers who might happen to be there. They then sealed the doors of the building with the assistance of volunteer witnesses. The following morning they inspected the seals and then, upon entering the building, found the pots filled with wine.

> I was not there [says Pausanias] but the most respected citizens of Elis, and strangers too, swore that this is true.

Pausanias also recounts the Andrian story of wine flowing from the sanctuary of Dionysus, but expresses considerable hesitation over both tales.

We know that mechanical devices to produce miraculous effects were fairly common in antiquity, [3] and they were probably used at Elis, as at Corinth. [4] The fourth-century Christian writer Epiphanius [5] tells us that in his day water was still turned into wine at Cibyra in Caria and at Gerasa in Palestine. Unfortunately recent excavations suggest that the miracle at Gerasa not only was the continuation of an earlier pagan wonder, but was contrived by an elaborate system of pipe lines. [6]

Ascension stories are told of Romulus, Empedocles, Augustus, and Drusilla, the sister of Caligula. Dionysius of Halicarnassus contrasts the "more mythical" accounts of the ascension of Romulus with the "more plausible" stories of his genuine murder (*Ant.* ii. 56. 2–3). Livy, [7] followed by Dio Cassius, [8] ascribes the ascension story to a certain Julius Proculus, who wished to avoid political disturbances among the people by telling them of Romulus' deification. Dio

[1] N. H. ii. 231.   [2] The same miracle is related in Ps.-Arist. *Mirab. auscult.* 123.
[3] A. de Rochas, *L'art des thaumaturges dans l'antiquité* (ed. 2, Paris, 1922).   [4] C. Bonner, "A Dionysiac Miracle at Corinth", *AJA* 33 (1929), 368–75.   [5] *Pan. haer.* li. 30. 2, p. 301 Holl.   [6] C. H. Kraeling, *Gerasa City of the Decapolis* (New Haven, 1938), 63, 212.   [7] Livy i. 16. 5–8.   [8] Dio Cassius i. 5. 12.

Cassius [1] also relates the political or rather economic origin of the stories about Augustus and Drusilla. Numerius Atticus was paid a million sesterces by Livia, Augustus' widow, to say he had witnessed Augustus' ascension; Livius Geminus received the same sum from Caligula for his testimony to the ascension of the emperor's sister Drusilla.

The true meaning of these reports has been concealed by Dio Cassius, a convinced opponent of the imperial cult. When "divine men" die and become gods, they must disappear and ascend into heaven, just as Heracles and Empedocles disappeared and ascended. Some proof of this disappearance and ascension is required, especially in the case of deified emperors or their relatives. We therefore find oaths sworn in order to confirm the assumptions of Augustus, Drusilla and Claudius. [2] Dio Cassius is simply rationalizing this religious theme.

We may mention also that another element of proof is provided by the visible flight of the soul in the form of a bird. In the case of Roman emperors the bird was an eagle; [3] Lucian satirizes this kind of story by having a vulture fly away from the dying Peregrinus. [4] An interpolator of the *Martyrdom of Polycarp* (16 : 1) describes a dove as departing from the dying bishop of Smyrna. [5] These birds represent the rationalization of a religious motif.

The story of Empedocles' ascension aroused much criticism. One description of his death tells us that he jumped into the crater of the volcano Etna, thus dying in fire like Heracles. [6] This narrative was widely ridiculed in antiquity on the ground that Empedocles' desire for fame overcame his reason. [7] Another description, provided by Heraclides of Pontus, shows Empedocles sleeping one night in a field and disappearing during the night. Reports from some slaves revealed that at midnight a loud voice called Empedocles and a heavenly light shone forth. The third-century historian Timaeus criticizes this story as an example of the credulity of Heraclides, who was so naive that he also tells of a man who fell from the moon. [8]

In spite of such criticisms, ascension stories were popular. Only

[1] *Ibid.*, lvi. 46. 2, lix. 11. 4. [2] D. M. Pippidi in *Studi e materiali di Storia delle Religioni* 21 (1947–48), 94. [3] *Ibid.*, 101; Dio Cass. lvi. 42. [4] Luc. *Peregr.* 39. [5] J. B. Lightfoot, *The Apostolic Fathers* II. iii. 390–91. [6] D. L. viii. 61; cf. Pippidi, *op. cit.*, 87. [7] Cf. J. H. Waszink on Tert. *An.* 32 : 1 (p. 384). [8] D. L. viii. 67–68, 72.

philosophers and historians criticized them, as Plutarch criticizes the story of Romulus' ascension because the body cannot rise with the soul. [1] We shall later consider such objections when we deal with apologetic arguments for resurrection (chapter 15). Here it is enough to say that all these miracle stories became increasingly popular, and that the number of writers who criticized them steadily diminished.

[1] *Rom.* 28.

12

# NATURE MIRACLES IN HELLENISTIC JUDAISM AND CHRISTIANITY

When we speak of credibility we must remember that it is a problem faced primarily by those who live under the influence of more than one world-view. It arises largely in relatively sophisticated circles whose members ask the question, "Did it really happen?" For the credulous person who accepts hearsay reports without weighing them, the problem does not arise. But our use of the word "credulous" as a term of reproach should remind us that a person's credulousness is to be evaluated in relation to his mental environment. What is credulity in one age may be clear perception in another. Even in the same period, as we observed in our investigation of Hellenistic attitudes, points of view will vary. But in general the attitudes of those who lived under the influence of the biblical world-view were not the same as the opinions of the philosophers and historians with whom we have dealt (chapter 4). The problem of the relation between such world-views is the problem of apologetic, and it was especially relevant to ancient Hellenistic Jews and Christians, determined to express their native world-view in terms of Greek philosophy.

Such apologetic necessarily treated miracles as objective happenings, discerned by the senses, since it was defending them against the attacks of those who treated them in the same way. Both sides took stories which were at least in part symbolical and used them as if they contained only a crudely literal meaning. "Did it really happen?" Thus the question was asked in the wrong way—for "really" and "happen" were left quite undefined—and therefore answered in the wrong way.

In his *History of the Warfare Between Science and Theology*, A. D. White devoted a chapter to the curious attempts of ancient Jews and Christians to "prove" the truth of the story of Sodom and Gomorrah by the dust about the Dead Sea and a peculiar rock formation which could be called a pillar of salt. [1] This is only one example out of many which were used to show that "archaeology confirms the Bible". According to Josephus (*Ant.* i. 92–95) the remains of Noah's ark were still extant in the first century A. D. The *Clementine Recognitions* (i. 29) tell us that huge ancient bones must obviously be identified with those of the giants in Genesis. Two of the more extreme examples of such "proof" are provided by Irenaeus, [2] who states—on what authority?—that the "pillar of salt" exudes blood monthly, and by the tourist Cosmas Indicopleustes, [3] who says that the tracks made by the Israelites' wheels near the Red Sea are still visible, in the sixth century!

Let us turn back to an earlier period before nonsense flourished to such an extent.

The Hellenistic Jewish tragedian Ezekiel [4] seems to be aware of the scepticism which his rewriting of the Exodus will encounter, but he proceeds to emphasize the miraculousness of the events, admitting their incredibility to mortals and their impracticable nature but at the same time insisting upon this element in the stories. [5] He even goes so far as to introduce the wonder bird of popular imagination, the phoenix! [6] This is hardly philosophical, but it illustrates how far literary men could go in stressing miracle.

Before turning to philosophy we may mention the historian Josephus. It is sometimes said that he "constantly" expresses a non-committal attitude toward the wonder stories of the Old Testament. [7] The proof of this is supposed to be his statement, "Let each reader think as he will", which is borrowed from Dionysius of Halicarnassus (p. 55 above). Josephus employs this formula for the ages of the patriarchs, the crossing of the Red Sea (which he compares to Alexander's crossing of the Pamphylian Sea), Moses' vision on Sinai, and the story of Balaam and his talking ass. [8] Belief in Moses' vision is explicitly stated, even though it is stated in a speech ascribed to

---

[1] "From the Dead Sea Legends to Comparative Mythology", Vol. ii (New York, 1896), 209–63. [2] *Adv. haer.* iv. 31, 254 Harvey. [3] PG 88, 196 D. Cf. the footprints of Heracles (Herodotus iv. 82, Luc. *Ver. hist.* i. 7) and of the Elkasaite angel (Hippolytus, *Ref.* ix. 13. 2); cf. also H. Delahaye, *Les légendes hagiographiques* (ed. 2, Brussels, 1906), 48–49; R. de Vaux in *Revue biblique* 47 (1938), 383–87. [4] Cf. J. Weineke, *Ezechielis Iudaei poetae . . . fragmenta* (Münster, 1931). [5] Eusebius, *Praep.* ix. 29. 7, 8. [6] *Ibid.*, 16; cf. J. Hubaux–M. Leroy, *Le mythe du phénix* (Liège, 1939), 45–50. [7] H. St. J. Thackeray, *Josephus the Man and the Historian* (New York, 1929), 57. [8] *Ant.* i. 108, ii. 348, iii. 81, iv. 158.

Moses. [1] On the other hand, in retelling the story of Isaiah and Hezekiah's sundial, he states that "irrational events which are greater than one could hope for are believed because of similar occurrences". [2] He also says that "by the will of God" Balaam's ass received a human voice. [3] This hardly reflects scepticism.

Two further examples may be found in his paraphrases of the book of Daniel. The fire which might have burned the three young men was weak because of their righteousness and because God was stronger than the fire. [4] The story of the lions' den is actually heightened. The enemies of Daniel thought that the lions had not touched him because they had already been fed; therefore the king put the enemies into the den to prove the contrary. [5]

Of course, in view of Josephus' frequent employment of the technique of the Hellenistic romance [6] we cannot be entirely certain that he actually accepted any of these stories as true. On the other hand, no evidence exists which definitively proves that he rejected them.

The first attempt we find to explain the Old Testament miracles on scientific or philosophical grounds is given in the Wisdom of Solomon. Here the Stoic idea of the transmutation of elements is employed. On this theory, the qualities of one element could be transferred to another. [7]

> The whole creation in its several kinds was fashioned again,
> Obeying thy several commandments, that thy servants might be kept
> without hurt (Wisdom 19 : 6).

> The elements being changed in order among themselves,
> As in a psaltery the notes vary the character of the tune,
> While always adhering to the sound, which one may accurately divine
> from the sight of things that have happened (19 : 18).

In view of the fact that the description of divine Wisdom in Wisdom 7 : 22–23 is almost certainly based on the Stoic Cleanthes' description of "the good" (SVF I 557), we may well imagine that this theory of miracle is based on Cleanthes too. And in fact there is a passage from Cleanthes (SVF I 497) which describes the intermingling of the elements and the origin of the world in a manner which might well underlie the theory of Wisdom. In it we find the same word,

[1] *Ant.* iii. 85.  [2] *Ant.* x. 28.  [3] *Ant.* iv. 109.  [4] *Ant.* x. 215.  [5] *Ant.* x. 260.
[6] M. Braun, *Griechischer Roman und hellenistische Geschichtschreibung* (Frankfort, 1934), 118.  [7] SVF II 405–11; cf. Epict. *Diss.* iii. 24 (cited by Goodrick on Wisdom).

*anothen*, "again" or "from above", which Wisdom uses in the first passage cited above. Moreover Cleanthes used the image of the plectrum and the lyre to describe the sun's influence upon the earth (SVF I 502). [1] We may conclude that Wisdom's theory of miracle is based primarily on the work of Cleanthes, perhaps through Posidonius. Given the basic assumption that the stories of the Exodus are history rather than legend, the explanation, as Goodrick remarks, is "not unscientific".

The greatest philosopher of Hellenistic Judaism, Philo of Alexandria, takes over this theory and expresses it in almost identical terms. [2] His attitude toward miracle is essentially affirmative, as Wolfson has shown. [3] He states as an axiom that everything is possible to God. [4] And most of his explanations or allegorizations are not intended to deny the historical actuality of the events of the Old Testament, even though for him the inward and spiritual meaning of the events is the true one.

In his *Life of Moses* Philo displays no hesitation whatever in retelling the startling nature miracles of the book of Exodus. When God promised that the river would turn into blood, this appeared credible not only because of God's truthfulness but because of the two marvels which had already been worked (*Mos.* i. 82). After Aaron's serpent ate the serpents of the magicians, the people no longer regarded these miracles as sophistries or tricks intended to deceive, but ascribed a "more divine power as their cause", for God can do everything with ease (i. 94). At the Red Sea, "to find a track in the trackless is characteristic of God; for what is impossible for every created being is possible to him alone" (i. 174). Philo's description of the division of the sea stresses the strangeness of it (i. 177). In the desert the people who had experienced countless strange happenings "contrary to ordinary practice" ought to have believed "him of whose unfailing truthfulness they had received the clearest proofs"; but they were hungry and therefore complained (i. 196). They then received manna —an "incredible sight" (i. 200), but for Philo unquestionably real. In fact, the double portion of manna on Sabbath eve made it possible for the Israelites to check their calendar, which had gone awry (i. 207):

---

[1] Compare also the astronomical interests of Wisdom 7 : 17–19 (chapter 7, p. 88).  [2] *Mos.* i. 96ff., 103.  [3] H. A. Wolfson, *Philo* (Cambridge, 1947), I 122–26, 347–56.  [4] *Opif.* 46, *Abr.* 112, 175, etc.

> If anyone disbelieves these things, he neither knows God nor has ever
> sought to know him. For if he did he would at once have comprehended
> and would have known firmly that these paradoxical and irrational events
> are child's play for God.

Consider the created world, which is a greater marvel than any of
these. But the wonders of the created world are overlooked because
of their frequency. We are impressed by the unusual, even though
it is much less remarkable (i. 212–13). The only explanation Philo
gives for these events is God's alteration of some of the elements
(ii. 267)[1].

We can hardly say that Philo has dealt here with the credibility of
miracle. He simply asserts that the events of the Exodus are remarkable
and that they took place. On the other hand, his whole philosophical
system is in a way an attempt to create an environment in which
the question of credibility will not arise. And the allegorical method
serves the same purpose.

Wolfson points out that Philo not only could insist upon the reality
of miracles but also could admit that the creation narrative was a
special case.[2] Philo did not claim literal factuality for the stories of
creation but held that they contained a spiritual meaning. They
consisted[3]

> not of mythical fictions in which poets delight, but of typical examples
> which demand allegorization according to the correspondences of hidden
> things.

Even in his soberly literal *Quaestiones in Genesim* (i. 32), Philo has to
give not one explanation of the speech of the serpent but three.
Perhaps it was characteristic of "the beginning", the golden age of
Eden. Alternatively, one may simply ascribe it to God's power. Or
perhaps it could be perceived by primitive man's keener senses—a
theme derived from Posidonius.[4]

But when we have encountered difficulties even in Eden, we shall
expect to find problems in insisting on the factuality of later miracles.
The *Life of Moses*, after all, is an encomium; and the encomium form
does not require absolute adherence to literal fact (this point is
elaborately developed by Lucian[5]). And even in the *Life of Moses*

---

[1] Cf. Wolfson, *op. cit.*, I 349–54; Posidonius, p. 129 above; cf. Pyrrho in Diog.
L. ix. 87. [2] *Op. cit.* 349; cf. 120–21. [3] *Gig.* 58–60. [4] Sext. Emp. *Adv. math.*
ix. 28; cf. G. Rudberg, *Forschungen zu Poseidonios* (Uppsala, 1918), 54. [5] *Quomodo
hist. conscr. sit* 7–14.

(i. 269–72) Philo tells the story of Balaam and his ass but does not mention that it spoke. In *Cher.* 32–35 he vigorously allegorizes the story; he does not say that the ass spoke but the allegorization implies that it did. Irrational actions (the ass) have "a voice clearer than that through the tongue"; they lack vocal organs. Does Philo think that the ass spoke? It is hard to tell.

We may also observe that since the universe is governed by immutable laws of order (chapter 2 above), we can hardly expect to find Philo favoring cosmic miracles. In fact, he never refers to the sun's standing still for Joshua or moving backward for Hezekiah. He does not discuss the startling careers of Elijah or Elisha. And we may suppose that he did not regard the stories about them as literally true.

What Philo is trying to avoid is the application to himself or to his people of a common epithet for Jews in antiquity: "superstitious". Many Graeco-Roman writers use this word. [1] The best illustration is Horace's phrase, *Credat Iudaeus Apella*. After telling the story of a flame without fuel, he remarks, "The Jew Apella may believe this; I don't", and proceeds to set forth the Epicurean view of the gods' lack of interest in mankind. [2]

The anti-Jewish writer Apion tells an amusing story to portray Jewish credulity. [3] A certain Zabid informed the Jews that he would steal for them the Apollo of Dora, an Idumaean town. He made a machine with lights which gave the appearance of a traveling star, and got into it to terrorize the Jews. They were overcome by "the paradoxical nature of the sight" and Zabid was able to steal the golden ass's head from the Jewish temple!

Josephus' sober-minded horror at this story leads him to apply a somewhat literalistic historical criticism to it. [4] There is no town of Dora in Idumaea; it is a Phoenician town near Mount Carmel. Jews would never want an Apollo in their temple. There is no such machine as Zabid's. The Jewish city would have had guards in war time (assumed because they must be fighting Dora) and at any time the temple is heavily guarded. Thus Apion's story is "idiotic falsehood". Josephus' one humorous note arises when he says that the only ass connected with this whole story is Apion himself.

---

[1] Apollonius Molo, Cicero, Diodorus Siculus, Quintilian, Tacitus, Plutarch, Apuleius; cf. P. J. Koets, *Deisidaimonia* (Purmerend, 1929), 64–66. [2] *Sat.* i. 5. 99–103. [3] Jos. *C. Apionem* ii. 112–14. [4] *Ibid.*, 115–20. The ass's head story also was commonly accepted.

The earliest evidence we possess of discussions of credibility among Christians is to be found in the first epistle of Paul to the community at Corinth. This letter was written around the middle of the first century A. D., and clearly reflects the difficulty of presenting Hebrew conceptions to Greeks with even a modicum of education. To them the idea of a crucified "messiah" is "foolishness" (1 Cor. 1 : 23), and the idea of resurrection is thoroughly incredible (15 : 12). We shall later consider the ways in which the apostle endeavors to prove that resurrection is analogous to natural processes (chapter 15). We mention resurrection now only to observe that it was the most significant point on which Greek and Hebrew thought-forms differed.

Our oldest witness to the argument from miracles is concerned with resurrection, not the resurrection of Jesus but the raisings of dead men which he accomplished. This is the apologist Quadratus, who wrote early in the second century. I have elsewhere [1] attempted to reconstruct his argument, of which only a fragment remains, and I present the reconstruction here. The fragment itself is printed in italics. [2]

> You may say that Jesus was simply human and was regarded as a god only after his death. His career was like that of Heracles or Asclepius or the Dioscuri. "But the deeds of leaders—especially those which are false—remain unaltered only while the leaders are alive, and are done away after their death" (Sext. Emp. *Adv. math.* ix. 35). On the other hand, *our Savior's works were permanent, for they were true—those who had been healed and had risen from the dead did not merely appear healed and risen, but they endured not only during the Savior's stay on earth, and after his departure they continued for a considerable time, so that some of them reached our own times.*

Here Quadratus is arguing for the divine nature of Jesus on the grounds of the reality and permanence of the healings and resurrections which he worked. The debate is conducted in a semi-philosophical environment, but one in which historical questions were not very critically examined. It may be noted that Quadratus, at least in this fragment, does not state that he himself had seen any of these witnesses to the power of Jesus. Presumably Eusebius, who quotes the fragment, would have included such a statement had there been any.

Like Quadratus, Marcion of Pontus laid great emphasis on the miracles of Jesus. His emphasis was severely criticized by both

[1] *JR* 30 (1950), 114.  [2] Eus. *H. E.* iv. 3. 2.

Tertullian and Origen. Marcion said that Jesus proved himself to be the Son and the Messenger and the Christ of God by the "evidences of the miracles" (*documenta virtutum*). To this statement Tertullian replied that false Christs, according to the New Testament (Matt. 24 : 24) can perform signs and wonders; Origen observed that over a period of time miracle stories become less credible. [1]

Marcion held that Jesus proved himself to be a new Lord and Possessor of the elements when he commanded the wind and the waves and when he fed the five thousand. Tertullian replies by pointing to Old Testament parallels which show that the God of the Old Testament could also work such miracles. [2]

The case of Marcion is interesting because he seems to have rested the whole case for the divinity of Christ on the miracles. More orthodox theologians saw the dangers of such a method and were unwilling to follow him. Like Marcion, Hilary of Poitiers (p. 212 *infra*) lays great stress on miracles; like Marcion he comes close to docetism.

A little later in the second century we find the apologist Justin arguing on the subject of the virginal conception. His opponents regard it as "incredible and impossible". Justin, who believes that "everything is possible for God", replies that such things are made credible by God, who informs men in advance that they are going to happen. This information is given by the prophetic Spirit. [3] In this instance the proof is provided by Isaiah 7 : 14, "Behold, a virgin shall conceive and bear a son". When his Jewish opponent Trypho argues that the correct text is "Behold a young woman shall conceive", and that this text refers to king Hezekiah, Justin replies that the Septuagint translation is inspired, and that if other Greek translations do not mention a "virgin" it is because Jews have deleted the word. [4] We seem to be dealing with side issues, but since Justin's argument is based on prophetic prediction these side issues become central.

At one point Justin comes close to the main problem. He argues that since Trypho will admit that God can cause sterile women to conceive—the examples provided are the mother of Samuel, the wife of Abraham, and Elisabeth, the mother of John the Baptist—he must believe that God can do whatever he chooses to do, and therefore he cannot question the virginal conception. [5] Trypho, on the other

---

[1] Tert. *Marc.* iii. 2–3; cf. Orig. *Ioh.* ii. 34.   [2] Tert. *Marc.* iv. 20–21.   [3] *Apol.* i. 33. 2.   [4] *Dial.* 71, 254–56 Otto.   [5] *Dial.* 84, 304.

hand, compares the story to the myth of the birth of Perseus, brought about when Zeus appeared to Danae as a shower of gold. He also argues that for God to be born as a man is incredible and impossible. [1] Trypho's arguments thus arise primarily within a Hellenistic rather than a Jewish context, and Justin's replies cannot touch his underlying presuppositions.

Finally, Justin is aware that both Greek and Jewish critics ascribe the deeds of Jesus to magic. [2] The Jewish critics say that those who saw him at work said he was employing "magical phantasy". In other words, his tricks were simply deceptions. Against this charge an argument like that of Quadratus could have been used, but Justin prefers to rely once more upon prophecy. He believes, as he says, that this argument will seem the strongest and the most reliable proof even to Greek opponents. Presumably the reason he thinks so is that his own conversion was brought about through the reading of the prophets. His statement clearly shows that his philosophical environment was not one in which critical scepticism flourished. It was the Middle Platonism of a Maximus of Tyre or an Aelius Aristides.

Three later apologists lay no stress whatever on miracles. There is no mention of them in the apologies of Tatian and Athenagoras, while Theophilus [3] admits that if he were to provide an example of a man raised from the dead and alive his adversary would not believe it. Athenagoras' treatise on the resurrection of corpses carefully avoids the question of evidence in order to conduct the debate on more philosophical grounds. He discusses the questions of God's power and purpose, arguing that what is impossible with man is possible with God. These silences do not suggest that the apologists themselves did not believe in miracles. They only show that their opponents were somewhat more sceptical and critical than those faced by Quadratus and Justin.

Toward the end of the second century we find miracles discussed in the work against heresies by Irenaeus, bishop of Lyons. From Justin he takes over the proof from prophecy, [4] but he also goes on to examine the relation of miracle to the order of nature. He argues that God is greater than nature. God has the wish to alter nature,

---

[1] *Dial.* 67–68, 236–40.   [2] *Apol.* i. 30; *Dial.* 69, 250; cf. A. Fridrichsen, *Le problème du miracle dans le christianisme primitif* (Paris, 1925), 59–64. This charge was brought against others who worked miracles; cf. L. Bieler, ΘΕΙΟΣ ΑΝΗΡ I (Vienna, 1935), 84.   [3] *Aut.* i. 13.   [4] *Adv. haer.* ii. 32. 3.

for he is good; he has the power, for he is mighty; and he can accomplish this work, for he is resourceful. [1] The principal proof Irenaeus offers for these statements is God's creation of the universe out of nothing.

When he comes to discuss various wonders of the biblical tradition his attitude is one of firm acceptance. The blindness of the Egyptians, a symbol of the blindness of all who do not accept the gospel, is shown by their belief that the Exodus took place by magic and that the Red Sea was opened for the people not by the power of God but simply "naturally". [2] Here Irenaeus obviously has in mind not the Egyptians of antiquity but critics of his own day who question the miracles of God. The sea monster swallowed Jonah but later vomited him forth in order to prove that "God's power is made perfect in weakness" (2 Cor. 12 : 9). [3] The Lord changed water into wine at Cana, substituting a simple word of power for the ordinary process of nature. He could have used no matter at all, both in this instance and in the feeding of the five thousand; but he used matter in order to show that he was the Son of the God who created the world. [4] Similarly he healed the man born blind with his hand rather than with a word in order to manifest the Hand of God which formed man at creation. [5]

These statements are directed primarily at Marcionites, who denied that the God of the Old Testament was the Father of Jesus. They have a secondary reference, however, to all critics of miracle stories who might question various details of the stories. Irenaeus uses the examples of Elijah in the chariot of fire, Jonah in the sea monster, and the three children in the fiery furnace to show that God is more powerful than nature. [6] This fundamental principle, in turn, makes all the stories credible.

We may expect to find much more stress on the miraculous and on its actuality in writings which circulated among simpler believers during the second century. This expectation is fulfilled in the apocryphal gospels and acts. While we must avoid reading theological implications into works composed primarily to entertain, we must recall that these apocryphal writings were also intended to instruct and edify. The deadly seriousness with which they were sometimes taken is illustrated by the fact that a presbyter who confessed that

---

[1] *Ibid.*, ii. 29. 1, 360.  [2] *Ibid.*, iv. 29. 2, 247.  [3] *Ibid.*, iii. 20. 1, 105.  [4] *Ibid.*, iii. 11. 9, 43–44.  [5] *Ibid.*, v. 15. 2, 365.  [6] *Ibid.*, v. 5. 2–3, 331–32.

he had written the *Acts of Paul* was deposed. [1] And it is interesting to observe even Hippolytus of Rome arguing from the ground that a story in the *Acts of Paul* is literally true.

The story he uses is the description of Paul's encounter with a lion in the arena at Ephesus. [2] The fierce animal comes up to Paul and in a human voice says, "Grace be with you". Paul then recognizes him as a lion which he had previously baptized. What is this pretty story? Nothing but a Christianized version of Androcles and the lion, a story told both by Aulus Gellius [3] and by Aelian, [4] writers of approximately the same period as the author of the *Acts of Paul*. In these acts, as in the *Acts of John*, great emphasis is laid upon the wonder-working power of Jesus. [5] The naiveté of Hippolytus is all the more obvious when one recalls that many of the episodes in these acts come directly from the Hellenistic romance. An even better example is provided in the *Acts of Peter* and the *Clementine Recognitions*, where several chapters are devoted to a contest between Peter and Simon Magus to see which one's magic is the more efficacious. [6]

The baptized lion is the basis of Hippolytus' argument. Now we shall observe what he does with it. In two places in his *Commentary on Daniel* he is dealing with the problem of credibility. [7] The first example concerns the story of Hezekiah's sundial and the shadow which moved backwards. Someone may doubt this and call it impossible. But what is impossible for God? He created the cosmos out of nothing. Moreover, a proof can be given for this story—the miracle of the sun's standing still for Joshua. Thus Hippolytus, like Josephus (whose works he knew), uses a miracle to prove a miracle. This is what Lucian (p. 72 *supra*) called "driving in a nail with a nail".

Hippolytus' second example brings us to the lion. He loves the story of Daniel in the den. According to him the lions wagged their tails, licked Daniel's "holy feet", and rolled in his tracks so he could pat them.

> If we believe that when Paul was condemned to the beasts, the lion which was loosed against him lay down at his feet and licked him, how shall we not believe in these events in the case of Daniel?

---

[1] Tert. *Bapt.* 17 : 5.   [2] C. Schmidt, *Praxeis Paulou* (Hamburg, 1936), 44.
[3] A. Gell. *Noct. att.* v. 14.   [4] *N. A.* vii. 48.   [5] P. Mich. 3788v, identified by W. D. McHardy, *Expos. Times* 58 (1947), 279. For another example cf. F. Blatt, *Die lateinischen Bearbeitungen der Acta Andreae et Matthiae apud anthropophagos* (Giessen, 1930), 52–53.   [6] Note that Simon's crash after a brief flight is paralleled by the fate of a would-be Icarus (Suetonius, *Nero* 12).   [7] *Comm. in Dan.* i. 8; iii. 29. 3–4.

Hippolytus appeals to the records of the Persians and Medes; but his real authority is the story from the *Acts of Paul*.

Hippolytus is not so stupid as is often believed. He does not mention the lion's conversation with Paul, and the parallel which he is trying to establish between the two stories is only that of the friendliness of the lions involved in each case. We may admit that he should not have used the *Acts of Paul* in a theological argument. But Origen, although with more hesitation, also used them. [1]

The examples of the discussion of credibility we have given are based largely on one premise: that you can prove a miracle by either a miracle or by something rather like miracle. This premise was not very convincing to outsiders. On the other hand, it was an advance over the simple statement that although these stories might seem impossible, or indeed were impossible in the framework of nature, nevertheless God had worked them.

Christian theology was waiting for a new approach to the credibility of miracles. Two ways seemed to be available for use. On the one hand, the miracles could be taken literally and proclaimed vigorously. The seeming tyranny of natural law could be shattered. This thoroughgoing and sceptical attitude is found in Tertullian. On the other hand, the miracles could be taken symbolically and their inner meaning could be investigated. This is the method of Origen. At the same time, neither method was followed exclusively, for at times Tertullian allegorizes, and Origen insists on the factual reality of the virginal conception and the resurrection of Christ. But these writers' emphases are quite different. Tertullian stresses the absolute omnipotence of God, while Origen emphasizes the elements of order in the universe. Tertullian is usually scornful of the achievements of philosophy, which Origen regards as the foundation of theological study.

Philosophically Tertullian is close to scepticism, but everything he writes is so individual that he cannot really be identified with any school. He is primarily a rhetorician rather than a philosopher or theologian. When it suits his purpose he can argue that the resurrection is natural because of various parallels, including the phoenix; [2] on another occasion he can argue that the very strangeness of virginal conception proves that it comes from God. [3] For God nothing is impossible except what he does not will, and whatever is written in

[1] *Princ.* i. 2. 3; *Ioh.* xx. 12.  [2] *Res. carn.* 13.  [3] *Marc.* iii. 13.

13

scripture records what he did will. Therefore the physical resurrection of Jesus is "certain because it is impossible". [1] This sentence has become famous. It has been regarded as evidence of Tertullian's completely irrational attitude.

Is it really irrational? We must observe that just before this sentence Tertullian looks back to Paul's words in 1 Corinthians 1 : 23–24 about Christ crucified, foolishness to the gentiles but to us the power and wisdom of God. "The foolishness of God is wiser than men" (1 Corinthians 1 : 25); so the crucifixion of the Son of God, says Tertullian, is credible because it is foolish. His statement is simply a rhetorical development of Pauline thought. Moreover, James Moffatt has pointed out what the rhetorical basis of the statement was. [2] Aristotle had observed [3] that the rhetorician ought to use examples from things "which are thought to happen but are incredible". He argued that such examples were very likely to be true.

> We believe only in those things which actually exist or are probable. If then a thing is incredible and not probable, it will be true.

The premise which makes this reasoning possible is that "it would never have been thought that something happened if it had not happened or almost happened". Tertullian is able to accept this premise because of his principle of the inerrancy of scripture.

Tertullian's idea is related to rhetoric; it is also related to philosophical debates. Against the Epicurean method of empirical inference the Stoics were accustomed to appeal to unique cases within human experience. They gave examples of unusual phenomena and argued that since these examples were not similar to things "in our experience", therefore any phenomenon from which inferences are made may be abnormal. [4] The Epicureans replied that there are constant peculiarities in every class of objects, and that on the basis of this constant variation inferences could be drawn. [5] They also suggested that the unusual examples were often invented by the Stoics. [6] It is obvious that at this point, as at many others, Tertullian is following Stoic arguments.

What of the relation of such events to "laws of nature"? Tertullian bluntly denies the validity of such objections. Philosophers can demon-

---

[1] *Carn. Christ.* 5.   [2] *JTS* 17 (1915–16), 170–71.   [3] *Rhet.* ii. 23. 22; cf. also Quintilian, *Inst.* iv. 2. 34; sunt enim plurima vera quidem sed parum credibilia.   [4] Philodemus, Περὶ Σημειώσεων i. 19–ii. 25, 24–26 De Lacy.   [5] *Ibid.*, xiv. 28–xvi. 1, 54–58; xxiv. 10–xxv. 23, 78–80.   [6] *Ibid.*, xvi. 3, 58; xxvi. 9–12, 82; viii. 7–13, 110.

strate anything they like. They "overawe their audience by eloquence rather than convincing it by sound arguments; without taking account of the properties of things, they subsume them to general or specific rules, do not leave any room for the omnipotence of God, and make their personal opinions appear as natural laws". [1] As Waszink observes in his commentary on this passage, Tertullian nowhere else makes clearer the grounds for his distrust of philosophy. It makes generalizations from concrete instances, while for him only the concrete realities are meaningful. Moreover, philosophy does not take into account the omnipotence of God. Only the faith of the church, based on the tradition of prophets and apostles, adequately understands this, For faith there are no laws of nature to impede the working of the omnipotent God.

Suppose someone were to ask Tertullian, "How can you prove your points from scripture? Do not the scriptures require philosophical interpretation? Do not they themselves contain the saying, Seek and ye shall find?" In his *De praescriptione haereticorum* Tertullian denounces all philosophy as the mother of heresy. A famous passage denies that Athens and Jerusalem have anything in common. "We need no critical investigation after Christ Jesus nor inquiry after the gospel. When we have believed, we need believe nothing further. For we have held this prior belief, that there is nothing which we ought further to believe." [2] Perhaps some heretic, influenced by philosophical considerations, will suggest that there are ambiguous or contradictory passages in scripture. The rule of faith, shared by the African churches with Rome, provides the sole standard of belief. It was instituted by Christ himself. Therefore "let critical investigation yield to faith, let (desire for) fame yield to salvation". No questions can be asked.

Tertullian's epigrammatic formulation of his basic principle owes much to the sceptical Academy which imagined that it was following Socrates. According to the Sceptics Socrates had actually insisted that he knew only one thing, that he knew nothing. Following them, Cicero [3] claims that this belief was the basis of Socrates' philosophy. Tertullian simply uses scepticism to uphold the absolute demand of authority. "To know nothing—contrary to the rule of faith—is to know everything." [4] The only standard of all knowledge is the teaching of the church.

[1] *An.* ii. 2.   [2] *Praesc.* 9.   [3] *Acad.* 16, *Luc.* 74.   [4] *Praesc.* 14.

At the end of his treatise he reveals how closely the question of miracle is related to his theme. [1] He represents Christ as saying with deep irony:

> I had promised resurrection, even of the flesh; but I reconsidered, lest I should not be able to accomplish it. I had shown myself born of a virgin; but later this seemed shameful to me.

To uphold the rule of faith means to guarantee the miracle stories of the Bible. The scriptures must be interpreted in the light of the rule.

At the same time, we must admit that Tertullian's credulity has its limits. He does not mean to say that anything can happen. He holds, however, that whatever is written in scripture did happen (although he rightly recognizes the use of figurative language by the prophets [2]), and he rejects what is not written. Two examples illustrate this attitude. Tertullian rejects the view that Mary remained a virgin after bearing Jesus, contrasting the saying of the apocryphal Ezekiel, "the cow bore and did not bear", [3] with the prophecy of Isaiah 7 : 14, "She will conceive and bear". [4] Mary was a virgin in the conception of Jesus; she was not a virgin in bearing him. Again, Tertullian agrees with the Monarchians that nothing is difficult for God. [5] But when they go on to argue that therefore God could make himself both Father and Son, he points out that the principle of God's omnipotence can be abused.

> Just because God can do everything we do not have to believe that he did do what he did not do. We must ask whether he actually did it or not. If he had wished to do so, God could have equipped man with wings for flying, as he did kites. [6] But just because he could, he did not straightway do so.

Tertullian concludes by demanding scriptural proof of Monarchianism, and quotes many texts to prove the fact that Father and Son are distinct. His fundamental axiom is the inerrancy and completeness of scripture and the rule of faith.

The other approach to miracles which we have mentioned is to be found in the school of Alexandria. Before turning to Origen, we must

---

[1] *Ibid.* 44 : 10.  [2] *Marc.* iii. 5.  [3] This verse is quoted by Clement of Alexandria (*Str.* vii. 94. 2).  [4] *Carn. Christ.* 23.  [5] *Prax.* 10.  [6] Aelius Aristides (*Or.* xli. 7, 331 : 23 Keil) says that the power of Dionysus is such that he could give wings to asses as well as to horses. On the other hand, Palaephatus rejects the wings of Daedalus as "impracticable" (*Incred.* 12, 20 Festa) and those of the horse Pegasus as contrary to present experience (28, 37). For Porphyry's view see p. 131.

briefly consider his master Clement, head of the school at the end of the second century. Clement argues vigorously for God's omnipotence. His handling of some of the miracles, however, is somewhat ambiguous. We recall that he frequently states that he writes his *Stromata* in order to mislead the simple—he may be making a virtue of necessity—and therefore we cannot be altogether sure that he means exactly what he says. [1] The whole double truth theory of Alexandria is intended to keep literalists from discovering the writers' thoughts (cf. p. 204 *infra*).

Clement asks how the Greeks can regard the marvelous stories about Moses as incredible. [2] The chief example is the "divine epiphany" on Sinai. Now, says Clement, the so-called descent of God is simply an expression of the divine power. It is an allegory. In saying this, Clement is following Philo, word by word. [3] But he goes on to provide three parallels of his own. From historians, perhaps paradoxographers, he gives the story of a mountain cave in Britain where the wind makes strange sounds. [4] The rustling of leaves in the woods might come from personal experience, but more probably, as my father has suggested, refers to the oak leaves of Apollo at Dodona. [5] From writers on Persian affairs he describes three mountains on a great plain which emit sounds like human voices.

> I think the causes of all these sounds were the smoothness and hollowness of the places.

Clement is not denying the actuality of the event, but he is explaining away what makes it miraculous. [6]

An even more interesting example is found in Clement's rejection of erroneous natural history, even in what he regards as scripture. We know that Clement ascribes the Epistle of Barnabas to an apostle (*Str.* ii. 31. 2) and uses it as if it had the same authority as the books in our New Testament (*Str.* v. 63. 1). But when Barnabas speaks of the hyaena's annual change of sex, [7] Clement does not hesitate to correct what seems to him an error, bringing against it Aristotle's explanation of the phenomenon. [8] It is significant that Clement mentions neither Barnabas nor Aristotle by name. But it is quite clear that he is correcting the one by the other.

---

[1] E. Molland, *The Conception of the Gospel in the Alexandrian Theology* (Oslo, 1938), 5–14.  [2] *Str.* vi. 28–33.  [3] *Dec.* 33–35.  [4] Cf. Plut. *Def. orac.* 18, p. 419 e–f.  [5] Strabo vii. 329, frag. 1.  [6] The same theory is found in Lucr. iv. 595–614.  [7] Barn. 10 : 6.  [8] *De anim. gen.* iii. 6.

Of course Clement has no really clear or unified theory of miracle. He seems to have been a gnostic before he became a more orthodoy Christian, [1] and clouds of gnostic anthropology trail behind him throughout his career. We may recall his theory that Mary had no milk because she remained a virgin [2]. The same docetic strain is present in his Christology. He quotes Valentinus to the effect that Jesus was so continent that he never digested his food; [3] Clement does not criticize this statement, but draws the conclusion that we too should be continent. Elsewhere [4] he says that Jesus did not eat for nourishment but in order not to disturb witnesses. And in his commentary on 1 John [5] he says that sometimes when the beloved disciple reclined on the bosom of Jesus, nothing was there! From this picture to the statement in the *Acts of John* [6] that Jesus never left footprints is not a great distance.

Indeed the whole ancient "alternating current" Christology may be viewed as a form of docetism within the Christian church. Melito of Sardis says that Jesus showed his human nature during the thirty years before his baptism, and his divine nature through his later miracles. [7] From this view to the *Tome* of Leo is not far. Jesus was hungry and thirsty as man; he multiplied bread and changed water into wine as God. [8]

In the theology of Origen we pass beyond many of these difficulties, although at the same time we encounter new ones. Origen is a genuinely subtle theologian. His thought is extraordinarily difficult to analyze, as we shall see. The problems which concern him are ordinarily quite unlike the problems which concern us, and we must avoid reading our own ideas into his mind. He is a Christian and a Platonist at the same time. Therefore his attitude toward historical events is not that of a Tertullian. He is not concerned with facts as Tertullian was. Indeed, he rejects the Stoic idea that sense perception is the source of all knowledge. Objects of sense perception can have an analogy to the true intelligible realities, but they are not true in themselves. [9] Nevertheless, when Origen comes to argue with Celsus over the credibility of miracles he is forced to use sense perception as the basis of our knowledge of them, for it is just their

---

[1] W. Bauer, *Rechtgläubigkeit und Ketzerei* (Tübingen, 1934), 60–61.    [2] *Paed.* i. 42. 1. [3] *Str.* iii. 59. 3.    [4] *Str.* vi. 71. 2.    [5] *Hypot.*, iii. 210 Stählin.    [6] C. 93, p. 197 Bonnet.    [7] Frag. 6 Otto (p. 415).    [8] C. 4, p. 30 Blakeney; cf. Tert. *Marc.* ii. 27; SVF II 1070.    [9] *C. Cels.* vii. 37; *Ioh.* i. 26.

factual reality which Celsus denies. At this point Origen uses the "clarity" or perspicuity of the miracle to prove that it happened. This ground had already been used by Epicureans, Stoics, and Middle Platonists. [1] Thus Celsus, who is a Middle Platonist, refers to the responses of oracles as "clear" and rejects Christian stories as "marvels and mythical fictions". Origen replies that the miracles of the Bible are so "clear" that even Democritus, Epicurus, and the followers of Aristotle would have accepted them if they had witnessed them. [2]

Another kind of argument he uses is based on historical probabilities. Celsus had said that the gospels were fictions. Origen replies that their accuracy is guaranteed by prophecy, which they describe as fulfilled. Since this argument is not likely to convince his opponent he goes on to psychological proofs. If they had been fictions they would not have contained the stories of Peter's denial of Jesus and the falling away of the disciples after Jesus' arrest. The very difficulty of the Gethsemane story proves its accuracy. If the gospels were fictitious they would have included more stories of resurrections of dead men who had spent a longer time in tombs. All these arguments have one foundation—the character of the disciples proves that their stories are true. [3]

The psychological character of Origen's approach to this problem is shown by a significant passage in *Contra Celsum*. [4] This is Origen's clearest statement on the question of credibility, although it also reflects the ambiguity of his attitude. He is arguing for the objective factuality of an event which he elsewhere describes as purely subjective. [5] Here he observes that to establish the truth of almost any event by an "assured sense impression" (the Stoic term for reliable knowledge) is very difficult and in some cases impossible. For instance, in the *Iliad* we find heroes who were called sons of gods or goddesses. Because of these fictions someone may deny the actuality of the Trojan war. In fact, however, there was a real war into which poets introduced these fictions. Similarly the story of Oedipus and Jocasta is true while the Sphinx is fiction. The problem is very complex. Some stories are true; others are fictions, and must be taken allegorically; still others must be rejected altogether. At this point,

---

[1] R. E. Witt, *Albinus and the History of Middle Platonism* (Cambridge, 1937), 51–52. [2] *C. Cels.* viii. 45. [3] *C. Cels.* ii. 10; cf. 13, 15, 26, 48. [4] *C. Cels.* i. 42–43. [5] *C. Cels.* i. 48; *Ioh.* frag. 20 Preuschen.

as in his discussion of biblical exegesis which we shall presently consider, Origen is simply insisting on the ordinary methods of grammarians and rhetoricians. He wants them applied not only to Greek history and mythology but also to the Bible.

We should of course avoid reading modern psychological ideas into Origen's analysis of this problem. All he is doing is repeating the techniques of Graeco-Roman rhetoric (cf. pp. 59–60) by which myth or history was refuted or confirmed. Thus Dio Chrysostom devotes his eleventh oration to the proof that Troy was not actually captured by the Greeks; in passing (*Or.* xi. 8) he argues that the story of Oedipus and Jocasta, like the Sphinx, was fictitious. Similarly Origen's classification of literary types is based on rhetorical teaching, where true stories are called "history"; then there are "fictions"; and finally there are stories to be rejected altogether, which are "myths".

From grammar he goes on to philosophy. He believes that basic presuppositions are exceedingly important. Followers of Epicurus or Democritus or Aristotle will be sceptical of Christian miracle stories. (We may recall that Lucian had also observed their lack of credulity, p. 73). On the other hand, a Jew whose own prophetic writings are full of paradoxical accounts, will not find it difficult to believe more stories of the same kind. This argument is aimed at Celsus' use of the figure of a Jew for attacking Christianity. Again, many philosophical writers, not generally regarded as inventors of myths, relate such stories. Origen gives the examples of Chrysippus, Pythagoras, Plutarch and Numenius. We know that this argument is accurate: Cicero tells us that Chrysippus collected examples to prove the truth of divination; the life of Pythagoras is full of marvels; Plutarch tells many miracle stories; and Origen himself describes Numenius' interest in the Egyptian magicians who competed with Moses. [1] The soundness of the argument is another matter. It assumes that credulous writers deserve more credit than sceptics do, and does not bother to ask which group had the greater critical acumen.

On the other hand, when Origen is dealing with the relations of God and nature in his treatise on prayer, he vehemently attacks three classes of simple believers: (1) those who would pray for the sun to rise; (2) those who would think the sun rose because of their prayer; and (3) those who would pray for the course of the sun to be

---

[1] *C. Cels.* v. 67; Cic. *Div.* i. 37, ii. 115 (cf. SVF III 642); *C. Cels.* iv. 51.

changed. [1] "It is probable that God not only foreknows the future but also foreordains it, and that nothing takes place for him contrary to his foreordinances." What then of Joshua and Isaiah and the alteration of the sun's course?

Again, he criticizes Marcion for his exaggerated emphasis on the miracles of Jesus. "The phenomenal miracles were able to produce belief in those who lived in the Lord's time, but with the passage of time they have not preserved their vividness and are supposed to be myths." [2] Obviously this is the reverse of Quadratus' earlier apologetic argument (p. 188). Origen agrees with Stoics and Sceptics that mythological stories lose credibility with the passage of time. [3] He might not agree with them that such stories as those in the gospels are mythical. He does not insist, however, that everything in the Bible is a record of historical fact.

His attitude toward the stories of the Old and New Testaments is most clearly set forth in his *De principiis*, the first Christian work of systematic theology. There he observes that the divine Logos, intending to convey spiritual or mystical meanings to those hearers who could understand them, used historical events when they were capable of bearing the higher meaning. When they were not usable, the scripture "wove" into the history two other types of narratives which were not historical. These are (1) what could not happen, and (2) what could have happened but in fact did not. [4] In contemporary rhetoric and grammar these two types of narratives are ordinarily called "myth" and "fiction". [5]

Origen goes on to prove his case by examples taken from scripture. There could not have been three "days" of creation without sun, moon, and stars. This example had already been used by Philo, [6] as well as by the anti-Christian writer Celsus. [7] Origen says that there are "countless" similar examples in the Old Testament and in the gospels. The example he uses from the gospels is the story of the devil's taking Jesus up into a high mountain to see "the kingdoms of the whole world and their glory" (Matt. 4 : 8). In order to prove

---

[1] *Orat.* v. 3; cf. the views on prayer of Maximus Tyrius; G. Soury, *Aperçus de philosophie religieuse chez Maxime de Tyr* (Paris, 1942), 15–38; H. Schmidt, *Veteres philosophi quomodo iudicaverint de precibus* (Giessen, 1908), 42.   [2] *Ioh.* ii. 34.   [3] Cic. *N. D.* ii. 5; Sext. Emp. *Adv. math.* ix. 35 (cf. p. 188); all stories lose credibility: Dio Chrys. *Or.* xi. 5.   [4] *Princ.* iv. 2. 9.   [5] See p. 59 above.   [6] *Leg. alleg.* i. 2, *Opif.* 13.   [7]. P. 166 Bader (Orig. *C. Cels.* vi. 60).

the impossibility of this story Origen has to explain "their glory" as "the way in which their rulers are glorified by men". From a mountain high enough to see the kingdoms of the Persians, Scythians, Indians, and Parthians one could not observe procedure at the royal court. [1]

Origen also attacks food laws in the Old Testament which mention nonexistent animals, such as the "goat-stag" or the griffin (Deut. 14 : 5, 12). Plato and Aristotle had denied the goat-stag's existence, and Herodotus had regarded the griffin as mythical. On this minor point Origen's attitude later changed. As we have said (p. 108), in the *Contra Celsum* (iv. 24) he speaks of the griffins [2] and elephants which are larger than man but not rational. [3] Presumably he has simply been reading different books on natural history.

Where did he get his basic ideas of possibility? Two modern scholars have examined his use of a grammatical-rhetorical dictionary. [4] Three of the definitions which seem to come from such a book are related to the question of credibility. These are the definitions of "enigma", "parable", and "hyperbole". Enigma is defined [5] as "a narrative concerning things which did not take place and cannot take place, which describes them as if they did take place and signifies something secret and hidden". Parable is defined [6] as "an account of something which does not take place but is literally possible, which describes it as if it took place and signifies figuratively the matters spoken of in the parable by the use of one word for another". And hyperbole is defined "by the Greeks" as an expression which goes beyond the truth for the sake of emphasis. [7] "They use as an example the expression 'whiter than snow'—not that it is possible for anything to be whiter than snow, but it is said hyperbolically; and again, 'certain horses run like the wind'—not that such a thing is possible, but for the sake of emphasis to set forth the speed of the horses...." All these definitions are closely paralleled in contemporary handbooks.

[1] Origen may also be criticizing the dream of Severus (Dio Cass. lxxiv. 3). [2] Cf. Ael. *N. A.* iv. 27. [3] A commonplace: cf. Sen. *Ben.* ii. 29. [4] R. Cadiou, *La jeunesse d'Origène* (Paris, 1936), 28; E. Klostermann in *ZNW* 37 (1938), 54–61. [5] *Fragm. in Prov.* 1 : 6 (Klostermann, *op. cit.*, 58); cf. Trypho, *De modis* i. 4, 193 : 14 Spengel. [6] *Ibid.* (Klostermann, *op. cit.*, 61); cf. Herodian, *De schematis* 104 : 1 Spengel. [7] *Hom. in I Cor.* 13 : 1 (C. Jenkins, *JTS* 10 [1908–9], 32f. = Cramer, *Cat.* v. 249); cf. Trypho, *De modis*, ii. 1, 198 : 31 Spengel. The examples are from Homer, *Iliad* x. 436.

Thus for the more common term "myth" Origen prefers to substitute "enigma" or "hyperbole"; for "fiction" he would use "parable". Presumably this preference is based on two causes: these expressions are biblical (Proverbs 1 : 6, 1 Corinthians 12 : 31), and they had been used at Alexandria by Clement. [1] The meaning of the terms he derives from contemporary rhetoric.

The influence of rhetorical analysis can also be perceived in Origen's clearest criticism of literal exegesis of the Bible. In his *Commentary on John* [2] Origen deals with disagreements among the gospels, and urges that the existence of such disagreements proves that "their truth lies not in their outward and visible features". He then goes on to argue that the essence of the evangelists' disagreement consists of their discordant statements that God appeared to such and such a person at such and such a time in such and such a place, that he performed such and such an action, appeared in such and such a form, and then went away to such and such a place. [3] This analysis is based on contemporary rhetoricians' analyses of "myth"; the critic is expected to examine the persons, the places, the times, the modes of such stories. [4] Origen uses the analysis for a theological conclusion; God cannot be in any fixed place or fixed time; in short, his actions cannot be described in the language of history. Then Origen proceeds to state explicitly that his remarks apply to the miracles of Jesus. The evangelists "wove" such stories into their writing—the same phrase as in *De principiis* (p. 201 above)—describing what was clear to them through the mind alone as if it were perceptible to the senses. [5] Do miracles literally and historically take place? They do not. The spiritual truth is preserved in something like a "bodily falsehood". [6]

What then shall we say of a fragment of his exegesis of Galatians, preserved by Pamphilus, [7] in which he emphatically states that the miracles of Jesus did literally take place? Another passage from Pamphilus [8] is also difficult. Here too Origen is represented as upholding an entirely literal interpretation of miracle stories. The true

---

[1] *Paed.* iii. 97. 3; *Str.* v. 32. 1. The definition of parable in *Str.* vi. 126. 4 is in part exactly paralleled in Trypho, *De modis* ii. 5, 201 : 12 Spengel. [2] *Ioh.* x. 1–3, 171–73. [3] *Ibid.*, x. 4, 174. [4] Theon, *Progymn.* 3, 76–77 Spengel; see p. 59 *supra*. [5] *Ioh.* x. 5, 175 : 7. [6] *Ioh.* x. 5, 175 : 18. For this view of myth cf. A. D. Nock, *Sallustius Concerning the Gods and the Universe* (Cambridge, 1926), xliv–xlv. [7] *Apol.* v. 4. [8] *Ibid.*, vi. 2.

believer in God believes that Adam was formed as the first man, that Eve was fashioned out of one of his ribs, that Joshua, heard by God, made the sun and moon stand still....

How can this passage be reconciled with others in which Origen rejects the literal historicity of Eve's creation? [1] How can he say of simple believers that "they move the universe with great simplicity"? [2] In his treatise *On Prayer*, as we have said, he describes as "surpassing all madness" one who would pray for the sun's course to be changed, and he devotes several pages of his *Commentary on Matthew* [3] to explaining away the idea of an eclipse at the time of the full moon. Indeed, he claims that the reference in Luke to an eclipse, accepted by simple believers, was inserted by insidious enemies of the church. The simple believers try to demonstrate the greatness of a miracle and thus arouse more incredulity than faith. [4]

There are several ways in which these contrasting viewpoints may be explained. One explanation can be based on the fact that like Clement Origen adheres to the double truth theory for the purpose of education. Only the more intelligent Christians ought to ask questions concerning causes. [5] Such questions are to be "hidden" when dealing with simpler believers. [6] Perhaps Origen thought that in preaching to simple believers in Caesarea he ought to make use of the medicinal lie. [7] This explanation seems to be broken on the rock of fact. Origen's *Commentary on Matthew* is one of his latest works, and it is clearly not addressed to the simple believer. But in it he explains the feeding of the five thousand as an historical event. Jesus looked up to heaven, "with the rays of his eyes, so to speak, bringing down power from there which was to be mingled with the loaves and fishes". When he blessed the elements he "increased and multiplied" them. [8] In dealing with the healing of a lunatic Origen explicitly rejects the idea of "physicians" who would say that there was no unclean spirit but some bodily symptom. They might say that the moist elements in the patient's head ebbed and flowed by "sympathy" with the moon. Origen holds that "we who believe in the gospel" must hold that the man had an unclean spirit. [9] In the same commentary, however, he compares the working of faith on divine power

---

[1] *C. Cels.* iv. 38; cf. Philo, *Leg. alleg.* ii. 19.   [2] *C. Cels.* i. 48.   [3] Pp. 272–73 Klostermann.   [4] P. 275 : 15 Klostermann.   [5] *Princ.* i. praef. 3.   [6] *C. Cels.* iii. 52.   [7] On Plato, p. 45 above. Platonists: Xen. *Mem.* iv. 2. 17, Max. Tyr. *Diss.* xiii. 3, 161 Hobein.   [8] *Tom.* xi. 2.   [9] xiii. 6.

to the physical attraction of a magnet for iron or of naphtha for fire. [1]
The magnet is a classical example of "sympathy".

It may also be argued that in his later writings Origen came to
accept miracles more readily than in his youth. To say this, however,
would be to neglect passages in which he still insists on the incom-
petence of the simple believer to pass beyond history, and above all,
the passage in which he criticizes the story of the eclipse at the crucifixion.

Perhaps, we shall simply have to neglect these passages and emphasize Origen's epistemology. All nature, all history exists for the
education of the children of God. The knowledge they acquire is
spiritual, not subject to sense-perception. The simple believer begins
by marveling at the mighty acts of God, but if he can he must pass
on to higher knowledge. [2] The question of fact is secondary. Origen
speaks more boldly in his earlier works concerning the literal impossibility and irrationality of miracles than he does when he is older.
It is possible, though not certain, that his basic attitude changed.

One more solution remains to be considered. Does he accept only
those miracles which he regards as philosophically or historically
defensible? In other words, is Greek philosophy his criterion rather
than the Bible? Certain passages which we have discussed might seem
to imply this conclusion. On the other hand, we have already seen
that on the basic question of creation he disagrees with the philosophical schools. Let us examine his attitude toward nature. He
explicitly refuses to say without qualifications that everything is
possible for God. [3] He agrees with Celsus that God does not act
"contrary to nature". He therefore insists on greater precision in
defining the relation between God and nature. In the first place,
following Aristotle, Chrysippus and other Stoic teachers he holds
that whatever takes place "according to the reason of God and his
will" is necessarily not "contrary to nature". God's workings are
therefore not contrary to nature, even if they are paradoxical or seem
paradoxical. In the second place, if we speak of the ordinary course
of nature, there are events which lie outside it. Origen refuses to call
these events "contrary to nature". He agrees with the Stoic-Academic
teaching that "events which are contrary to nature do not take place
but seem to take place". [4] He therefore says that God produces some

[1] x. 19. [2] *Luc.* frag. xv, p. 239 Rauer. [3] *Princ.* ii. 9. 1, *C. Cels.* v. 23.
[4] SVF II 938.

effects "beyond nature", ὑπὲρ τὴν φύσιν. This is the first example in Christian literature of the philosophical idea of the supernatural. [1]

With his avoidance of stress on God's omnipotence, he carefully distinguishes "wonders", which go beyond what is customary and are simply marvels, from "signs", which point toward God and need not be marvels. He also distinguishes faith based on marvels from the higher kind of faith based on signs alone. [2]

How, then, shall we describe Origen's attitude toward miracles? Logically considered it is self-contradictory and confusing as well as confused. The Neoplatonist Porphyry [3] suggested that he was outwardly a Christian but inwardly a Greek, trying to introduce Greek philosophy into foreign myths. Many modern critics have accepted Porphyry's theory without question. For example, Mme. Miura-Stange has devoted her *Celsus und Origenes* (Giessen, 1926) to arguing that the basic presuppositions of both Celsus and Origen are the same. This thesis is hard to prove, since Origen differs from Celsus on the basic questions of creation, miracles of Jesus, and resurrection. Moreover, it is obvious that *Contra Celsum* is essentially an appeal to the Greeks. It is an apology, not a theological treatise. A view opposite that of Porphyry seems more tenable. Origen is basically a Christian. Born a Christian, he feels free to express the faith in various ways in order to meet the contemporary situation. As Nock says of the apostle Paul, [4] externally he hellenizes. Inwardly Origen's thought is unhellenic and Christian, at least for the most part.

Porphyry also tells us [5] that some time after 244, Origen was in Rome and attended a lecture of Plotinus. The Neoplatonist brought his discourse abruptly to an end, saying that he could not lecture to one who knew what he was going to say. The reason for this knowledge is to be found in the fact that both Origen and Plotinus had been pupils of Ammonius Saccas at Alexandria. But Origen, as we have seen, insists on the actuality of the unclean spirits of the gospels. Plotinus, on the contrary, rejects "gnostic" use of formulae to expel "demons"; the cause of the diseases is external, not internal. [6] Here it is plain that Origen's attitude is based on the Bible rather

---

[1] Cf. H. de Lubac, *Surnaturel* (Paris, 1946), 355–73.   [2] *Ioh.* xiii. 64.   [3] Eusebius, *H. E.* vi. 19. 7.   [4] *St. Paul* (London, 1938), 167; on Origen cf. E. Molland, *The Conception of the Gospel in the Alexandrian Theology* (Oslo, 1938); J. Daniélou, *Origène* (Paris, 1948).   [5] *Plot.* 14; cf. R. Cadiou, *La jeunesse d'Origène* (Paris, 1936), 257; perhaps another Origen; cf. Beutler, *RE XXI* 480.   [6] *Enn.* ii. 9. 14.

than on philosophy. He is not really in sympathy with Plotinus.

We have said that logically considered, Origen's attitude is confusing. If we do not consider it logically, but remember that we are dealing with a living person who is not always concerned with logic, we may be able to understand his attitude with greater clarity. He himself has pointed out how subjective the standards of credibility were in his day. He frequently accepts miracles we might explain away, or explains away miracles we might reject. But we cannot impose upon him either our ideas of credibility or a logical rigor which he would not have accepted. For him God can worksometimes beyond nature and sometimes in nature, and it does not make much difference which method God employs. Origen is willing to compare the virginal conception with parthenogenesis in vultures, with the origin of the first men from "seminal principles" in the earth, with the birth of Plato, and with Greek mythology. He also compares it with the spontaneous generation of worms, relying on the phrase of Psalm 22, "I am a worm and no man". [1] He will argue that the dimensions of Noah's ark as given in the Old Testament need to be cubed in order to provide room for all the animals. [2] His primary interest, however, is always in the spiritual truths which lie behind these stories. Sometimes he denies the literal meaning in order to pass to the spiritual; sometimes he finds the spiritual built upon the literal. The spiritual is always the essential meaning.

We may observe with de Lubac that part of his stress upon allegory is due to an inadequate understanding of metaphor. Origen would hold that the literal meaning of anthropomorphisms is that God has hands and feet. [3] He thus wrongly agrees with the simple believers he attacks. With all his grammatical analysis, he does not seem to understand that the literal meaning of a metaphor is metaphorical. But this observation does not change the fact that no simple formula will explain his attitude toward the credibility of miracle stories. Sometimes he accepts them; sometimes he rejects them. In spite of his statements in the fourth book *De principiis* and the *Commentary on John*, he accepts them more often than he rejects.

Tertullian gave us a relatively simple formula: the literal statements of scripture are inerrant because God can do anything and it is the record of his acts. Origen's thought is more complicated. Some of

[1] *C. Cels.* i. 37; *Luc. hom.* xiv, 101 Rauer.  [2] *Gen. hom.* ii. 2, *C. Cels.* iv. 41.
[3] *Origène Homélies sur la Genèse* (Paris, 1943), 44.

the statements are literally true while others are not; God cannot do absolutely anything, and not everything in scripture is the record of God's acts. In it there are stumbling blocks [1] to direct us to higher truths.

[1] Cf. A. D. Nock, *Sallustius Concerning the Gods and the Universe* (Cambridge, 1926), xliv–xlv.

# NATURE MIRACLES IN LATER PATRISTIC THOUGHT

After Tertullian and Origen little novelty enters patristic discussions of credibility until the time of Augustine. The old arguments are repeated and occasionally refined. But the refinements do not touch the main point, the fact that no common standard of credibility exists. Moreover, both inside and outside the church, controversialists are busy treating the objective as if it were subjective—the allegorical method—and treating the subjective as if it were subject to sense perception. The result is what Johannes Geffcken [1] called the debate over allegorization: "a genuine chaos of inconsequential polemic".

Arnobius is an interesting example of an apologist whose reach exceeded his grasp, at least as far as the question of miracles was concerned. He is very enthusiastic about the healings of Jesus, which he reckons as "a hundred or more", and describes Jesus' walking on water as performed with dry feet. Unfortunately he goes on to describe the disciples' talking with tongues at Pentecost as if Jesus himself spoke in foreign languages in his ministry. [2] If we compare his cures with those performed by others, we find that Jesus employed no material means. [3] Here Arnobius forgets the application of mud or spittle in two synoptic healing miracles. Fundamental to Arnobius is the delegation of Jesus' powers to his disciples, and the belief that "magicians" were unable to perform such feats.

How is Arnobius to prove that the accounts of the miracles are true? Here his argument is more interesting. [4] The human race, he says, is naturally sceptical. Yet the men who told these stories went out of their way to incur hatred and to be held in contempt because of their views. Therefore the stories must be true. And if they are false, how does it happen that the whole world has come to believe them? Opponents may call these stories exaggerated, but if the whole

[1] *Zwei griechische Apologeten* (Leipzig, 1907), 82.  [2] *Adv. nat.* i. 46, with the notes of G. E. McCracken.  [3] *Ibid.*, i. 48.  [4] *Ibid.*, i. 54–57.

truth about Christ were known it would be even more wonderful, for he was God and came down from heaven. The antiquity of pagan myths suggests that they are simply based on opinions (Arnobius reveals no acquaintance with the Old Testament), while the Christian story is told by witnesses. Here Arnobius drops the old apologetic argument that the Old Testament is older than Greek philosophy and religion, and simply attacks the old from the standpoint of the new. His argument reminds us somewhat of Tertullian.

His pupil Lactantius discusses miracles in a more apologetic context. If animals can conceive from wind, as everyone knows, why is the spirit-conception of Jesus remarkable?[1] Of the feeding of the five thousand he asks,

> What more marvelous thing could either be described or take place?[2]

It could not have been worked by sleight of hand because of the material proof of its happening. And Jesus' walking on water is more remarkable than that of Orion (Vergil, *Aen.* x. 764), who is falsely described as having his shoulders above the surface. Jesus, coming on to the sea with his feet, followed the disciples just as if he were walking on solid ground.[3]

A generation later, the catechetical lectures of Cyril of Jerusalem reflect a more vigorous attack on the problem, as well as on his opponents. When outsiders question the virginal conception, catechumens should attack with parallels from Greek mythology.[4] If the opponents are Jews, the Christians should cite miracle stories from the Old Testament, beginning with Sarah's conception and continuing with Moses' hand which became white as snow and his rod which turned into a snake. The catechumen should emphasize the fact that the snake had teeth and eyes. Finally he should point out that Eve was made from Adam and Adam from mud.[5] In dealing with the resurrection, Cyril recommends the use of the parallel of the phoenix. Unfortunately the phoenix itself may be questioned; in this case one should compare it with the development of bees from larvae and birds from eggs![6]

In his *Oratio catechetica* (c. 13) Gregory of Nyssa uses the relation of miracle to nature for an apologetic purpose. The person who regards the miracles of virginal conception and resurrection as "beyond

---

[1] *Div. inst.* iv. 12. 2.  [2] *Ibid.,* iv. 15. 17.  [3] *Ibid.,* iv. 15. 21.  [4] *Catech.* xii. 27.
[5] *Ibid.,* 28–29.  [6] *Ibid.,* xviii. 8.

belief" implicitly admits that they are "beyond nature". When he claims that the Christian preaching is not in harmony with natural laws, he should accept this fact as a proof of the divinity of Christ. For if the narratives about Christ were within the limits of nature, where would the divine be? When the story goes beyond nature its incredible elements prove the divinity of the one who is proclaimed. Here we find the language of Origen used in support of a theory much like that of Tertullian. Origen had used "supernature" to avoid the expression "contrary to nature"; Gregory comes close to regarding the supernatural as contrary to nature, and employs its unnaturalness as a proof of its divine origin. Elsewhere (c. 23) he again appeals to the absolute novelty of the miracles of Christ. Nothing similar ever took place or was described. Gregory lists the miracles, stressing their remarkable character. The walking on water was not like the miracle of Moses, for the surface of the water hardened under Jesus' feet and by a certain secure resistance held them up. He could do without food as long as he wanted, but he could also provide banquets in the desert for thousands of people. For them the bread was ready in the hands of the servants and multiplied the more they ate. It is obvious that Gregory regards the miracles as literal and physical events which have value as proofs of the divinity of Christ. [1]

Hilary of Poitiers, on the other hand, is not concerned with parallels from nature or mythology. His point of departure is the absolute omnipotence of God and the superiority of faith to reason. [2] The power of God is above natural laws, [3] and men should not ask how miracles are performed. Hilary constantly stresses the factual nature of the miracles, which took place even though they cannot be explained. [4]

If an explanation of virginal conception is requested, Hilary believes that a parallel miracle will suffice. The corporeal body of Jesus passed through solid walls. The nature of wood and stone is not such as to admit bodies, and the body of the Lord did not disappear and come into existence again ex nihilo. Sense-perception and reason must yield before this miracle; the truth of the actual event is outside human reason. [5]

Again, at Cana the water became wine by a new creation, not out of nothing but out of matter already existing; it was not the result

---

[1] A similar use of these miracles is found in Athanasius, *De incarnatione* 18; cf. J. H. Srawley, *The Catechetical Oration of Gregory of Nyssa* (Cambridge, 1903), 28. [2] *Trin.* iii. 5. [3] *Ibid.*, iii. 26, ix. 72 (see p. 26). [4] *Ibid.*, iii. 18. [5] *Ibid.*, iii. 19.

of mixture; the fact defeats both vision and tasting. [1] Similarly when
the bread was multiplied the understanding of the event escapes the
eyes of our sense-perception. There is something which did not exist
before, something is seen which is not understood, and there remains
only the belief in God's omnipotence. [2] This miracle, Hilary says in
his *Commentary on Matthew*, "passes human understanding". It cannot
be explained. Unfortunately he proceeds to explain it. The five
loaves were not simply divided among the crowd, for there were
first fragments, then eating, and then more fragments. Where did
the material increase? Either in the place where tables were, or in
the hands of those who took it (he favors this explanation in writing
*De trinitate*), or in the mouths of those who ate,

> There can only be admiration for the divine power. [3]

The closest Hilary comes to a theoretical justification of these
miracles is in his teaching on the body of Christ. Insisting against
the Arians on the omnipotence of Christ, [4] he goes so far as to teach
that Christ had a "heavenly body", and that for such a body to walk
on the surface of water and to enter a closed house was in accordance
with its nature. [5] From this point of view the miracles were not
miracles but natural expressions of the divine nature. Hilary's theory
is not unlike the docetism of Marcion and the semi-docetism of
Clement (see p. 198).

Like many of the fathers before Augustine, John Chrysostom (first
of Antioch, then of Constantinople) stresses the importance of contemporary miracles to prove the credibility of those in scripture. [6]
He also compares the changes in nature which, according to Amos
5 : 8, God can accomplish: "He makes everything and transforms
everything". Thus God altered the working of the fire in the furnace
and of the sea at the Exodus. Similarly snow regularly turns into
water. [7] Therefore one would expect the effecting of such changes,
which were inevitable when such a person as Jesus was present.
For him it was as easy to perform a sign as it is for us to speak. [8] The
Hellenistic Jewish explanation of miracles has overcome the mystery
of the work of Jesus.

Chrysostom uses this theory to explain the changing of water into

[1] *Ibid.*, iii. 5. [2] *Ibid.*, iii. 6. [3] *Comm.* xiv. 12; cf. *Trin.* iii. 6. [4] *Trin.* ix. 72.
[5] *Trin.* x. 23, *Comm.* xiv. 6. [6] F. H. Chase, *Chrysostom* (Cambridge, 1887), 127–28.
[7] *Expos. in Psalmos* 147, PG 55, 480. [8] *In Ioh. hom.* 88, 2, PG 59, 481.

wine. [1] This miracle has clearly been under attack. Chrysostom's answers are not very satisfactory. People ask why Jesus did not work the sign before the jars were filled, so that the miracle might have been greater. He replies that this method was used so that the sign would be credible and because Jesus would have been considered a magician had not other witnesses brought the water. Moreover, the disciples did not at first (i.e. in the synoptic gospels) describe this sign because without other miracles to back it up it might have been incredible. This argument reads Chrysostom's fourth-century problems into the apostolic age. Some opponents say that at the feast everyone was drunk and could not distinguish water from wine. Chrysostom replies that the master of the feast, who testifies to the miracle, had not drunk any wine previously. For a positive explanation he offers the idea that the normal process of conversion of water into wine was simply speeded up. The miracles are not contrary to nature; they are

> much more beautiful and beneficial than those which take place through nature.

The difficulty with Chrysostom's application of his theory is obvious. The transformation is not simply speeded up. The means by which the transformation takes place are removed.

On the other hand, Chrysostom is sometimes hesitant about these problems. Psalm 113 : 4 states that "the mountains skipped". This, he says, presents us with a genuine problem. [2] There is no historical record of mountains skipping, and we must conclude that the psalmist is prophetically and hyperbolically setting forth the future delight and greatness of marvels. As a modern critic would say, his statement is eschatological. This sensible conclusion is balanced by Chrysostom's exegesis of "moving mountains" in the New Testament, where he suggests that the apostles probably did move mountains, since not all their miracles are recorded. [3] But ancient exegetes generally deal more freely with the Old Testament than with the New.

In a work probably written by Chrysostom's contemporary Theodoret, the *Quaestiones et responsiones ad orthodoxos*, the same theory is set forth. Events "above nature" (see p. 206 *supra*) take place in nature because of divine power. The interesting conclusion which the author draws from this statement is that the credibility of miracles cannot be demonstrated from nature itself. [4] On the basis of his faith

---

[1] *In Ioh. hom.* 22, 2, PG 59, 135–36.  [2] PG 55, 307.  [3] PG 58, 562.  [4] C. 117, p. 192 Otto.

he is therefore forced to deny the miracles of non-Christians. No one has ever seen rain-makers bring rain. Hearsay reports of their activity is not proof. [1] Apollonius of Tyana did not work miracles, but ingeniously made use of the "sympathies and antipathies" of nature. Like Arnobius, Theodoret observes or rather argues that Christ did not need to use any "matter" for his miracles. He spoke and they took place. The argument has advanced a stage, however, for Theodoret says that if anyone claims that the stories themselves do not convey this impression, we must reply that the miracles of Christ are not set forth in the literal language of the stories. [2] Here theology, and a rather unsound theology, has overcome historical exegesis. Surely the stories are the sources of any judgments to be made on what they describe!

We have now come as close to a theory of credibility as the church fathers came in the period before Augustine. If we attempt to summarize their conclusions, we shall find that they are uncritical of miracle stories because of their belief in the inerrance of the Bible. Origen provides the only exception to this rule, and in his case it is a partial exception. At the same time, he is the church father who best understands the inward and spiritual meaning of scripture, although we must not forget or deny Tertullian's insistence on the omnipotence and freedom of God. One of the rare variations from biblical literalism is found in Chrysostom's view that the disciples thought that Jesus cursed the fig tree, while in fact he did not. [3] Chrysostom here goes so far as to say that the gospels generally give us only the opinions of the disciples. Jesus over the heads of his reporters!

In the first five centuries there is a tendency to explain God's working of miracles as beyond or above nature but coordinated with nature rather than contrary to it. The extremism of Tertullian seems to have lost much of its attractiveness as the dogmatism and the vitality of ancient science steadily faded. Men were no longer so sure what was credible and what was not. In a world where the philosophy of Iamblichus and later Neoplatonists could flourish, problems of credibility were not regarded as relevant. The real difficulty came to be the differentiation of Christian miracles from magic. The criticisms of Celsus, Porphyry, and to a certain extent of Julian, are the expressions of philosophers who were fighting a losing battle. Since

[1] C. 31, p. 48.  [2] C. 24, pp. 36–38.  [3] PG 58, 633; H. Schlingensiepen, *Die Wunder des Neuen Testaments* (Gütersloh, 1933), 70 n. 2.

their criticisms had no genuine epistemological foundation they were destined to failure.

Symptomatic of the age is the appearance and gradual growth and popularization of the *Physiologus*. This compilation of animal lore was probably made between the time of Origen and the year 380, when it is utilized by Greek and Latin exegetes. [1] We have already discussed the collection in some detail in dealing with the relation of science to theology cf. pp. 117–18. It is significant for the allegorical meanings which the author finds in the characteristics of animals, and for the characteristics which he invents in order to confirm his theological ideas. Thus the lion cub is born dead, but on the third day its father breathes on its face and it becomes alive (*Phys.* 1, p. 6). No other ancient author confirms this "fact" of zoology. The pelican feeds its offspring with its own blood (*Phys.* 4, p. 16). This seems to be a confusion of the vulture, which drinks its own blood according to Horapollo, and the pelican which carries food for its young in its throat! Naturally the *Physiologus* includes the story of the phoenix (*Phys.* 7, pp. 25–28).

This work was frequently used by Rufinus, who introduced allusions to it into his translations of Origen, and also by Ambrose. Augustine made extensive use of the *Physiologus* and of Pliny's *Natural History*, both of which he employed uncritically. We have already discussed his attitude to nature. For the present we must bear in mind that when Augustine speaks of science or of natural law he relies on books like these for his knowledge of the world about him. [2]

This point is important when we deal with credibility, for Augustine can use an example from the *Physiologus*—the pelican—and comment on it:

> Perhaps this is true, perhaps it is not.

For him the religious purpose of the example is all-important. [3] And when in his *De doctrina christiana* (ii. 24) he recommends books on natural history to the Christian exegete, the example he uses to prove

[1] The homilies of Basil on the *Hexaemeron* reflect a similar combination of folklore and science; cf. p. 115 and the remarks of S. Giet, *op. cit.* (p. 115, n. 1), 68. But, as A. Rey observes (*L'apogée de la science technique grecque* I, Paris, 1946, 165–70) "botanical folklore" is already found in Theophrastus. [2] H. Marrou, *Saint Augustin et la fin de la culture antique* (Paris, 1949), c. vi. [3] M. Pontet, *L'exégèse de saint Augustin prédicateur* (Paris, 1945), 203.

their value is taken from the *Physiologus* (11, p. 43)! Moreover, as Marrou reminds us, we must always consider the fact of Augustine's own temperament, which inevitably determined the use he made of these stories of the wonders of nature.

> His memory was especially retentive of extraordinary facts, while his reason was unable to guard itself against their generally fantastic character. He speaks without too much hesitation about all sorts of fabulous animals: salamander, dragon, unicorn, "goat-stag"; it is true that for most of them he can add the superior authority of scripture to that of the tradition of the learned! [1]

Thus for Augustine scripture and uncritical reading about nature combine to provide an uncritical picture of the world. He absolutely insists that in Moses' day water was actually changed into blood. To question this miracle is to insult God's power. [2]

In an appendix to his book on Augustine and the end of ancient culture, Marrou has recently modified his earlier criticisms of Augustine. He now reminds us that Augustine's contemporary, the historian Ammianus Marcellinus, was very fond of extravagant wonder stories, and admits that had Augustine quoted more opinions of ancient scientists his theology would not have gained a great deal. At the same time, he still maintains that Augustine's interest in the world around him was inadequate; too much in the manner of Tertullian, Augustine condemned interest in scientific questions. For this reason, Augustine is genuinely credulous. To Marrou's examples we can add a really startling one. Augustine cannot definitely state whether the novel of Apuleius, in which he describes his metamorphosis into an ass and his later return to human form, is fiction or simply a narrative of something unusual! Perhaps demons change phantoms of men into phantoms of animals. [3]

Thus Augustine can justify strange and unnatural phenomena by others more unnatural. For example, if Adam and Eve had not sinned, they could have produced offspring without intercourse. How is Augustine to prove this? By the examples of Mary's miraculous conception and—to use the examples of unbelievers—of bees. [4]

---

[1] Marrou, *op. cit.*, 140.  [2] A sermon edited by Frangipane, quoted in M. Pontet, *op. cit.*, 170.  [3] *Civ. dei* xviii. 17–18; cf. Marrou, *op. cit.*, 662 n. 7, 681, 683–84, 707 n. on 157.  [4] *Bon. coniug.* 2; cf. *Gen. ad Litt.* ix. 4, where he uses the renewal of the Israelites' clothing in the desert (Deut. 29 : 5) to show the possibility of a strange miracle in the case of Adam and Eve.

Again, when Moses turned his rod into a serpent this was simply a speeding up of the natural process by which snakes are produced spontaneously from rotting wood. [1] Of course, we must admit at once that belief in spontaneous generation was universal in antiquity, and that Augustine could have proved both his points from Pliny's *Natural History*. [2] But he is "driving in a nail with a nail". Similarly he tells us that the changing of water into wine was simply the acceleration of a natural process. We may say that Augustine's view is not so much that miracles are natural as that nature is miraculous. To view nature from this point of view alone is to abandon any attempt to explain its workings. To Augustine such attempts are essentially irrelevant.

With his attitude toward nature in mind, we may turn to examine his theory of miracle. [3] In the *De utilitate credendi* [4] he gives a subjective and sceptical definition. Miracle is simply an extraordinary event. Similarly in a letter [5] he holds that it is essentially something un-known. The origin of a miracle, as far as the witness to it is concerned, is the ignorance of causation in nature. What are these definitions? They are nothing but the traditional remarks of Greek sceptics, presumably known to Augustine through the *De divinatione* of Cicero. In Cicero's work we read that "ignorance of causes creates admiration in the case of something novel, while the same ignorance does not arouse wonder in ordinary events". [6] For Augustine nothing is ordinary, and in the *City of God* he speaks of the world itself as more marvelous than anything in it. [7] Similarly he says that "a miracle is not contrary to nature but to what is known of nature". [8] The dif-ference between Cicero and Augustine is that Cicero ascribed such events to chance, while Augustine, who emphasizes providence rather than chance, ascribed them to God.

This point deserves somewhat fuller discussion, since so much of Augustine's thought on this matter is related to the classical debates on the relation of fate or necessity to chance and the relation of both to providence. According to the Stoics, fate or necessity was simply the chain of causation which governed all events, [9] while chance was

---

[1] *Gen. ad litt.* vi. 13. [2] *N. H.* xi. 46, x. 188. [3] Cf. P. de Vooght in *RTAM* 10 (1938), 317–43. [4] *Util. cred.* 34. [5] *Ep.* 162 : 9; de Vooght, *RTAM* 11 (1939), 206. [6] *Div.* ii. 49. [7] *Civ. dei* x. 12; cf. Cic. *N. D.* ii. 115. [8] *Civ. dei* xxi. 8; cf. *Con. Faust. manich.* xxvi. 3. [9] Cf. Cic. *Acad.* i. 29, with Reid's note, p. 134; see chapter 2, p. 21.

"a cause unclear to human reasoning". [1] According to some Stoics and other writers, God can use either fate or chance (fortune) to accomplish his purposes. Precisely the same ideas are expressed by Augustine when he tells us that God is the source of the whole succession of causes, and that the causes which are called fortuitous actually exist although in their working hidden from us. [2] He goes on to interpret these causes from a Christian point of view when he insists that all causes are voluntary since they depend upon the will of God. There is nothing which happens apart from the "laws of his providence". [3]

Thus Augustine combines Stoic faith in natural law and providence with sceptical insistence on the limitations of human knowledge. The result is his insistence upon revelation and—with the Stoics—on *exempla* [4] and his refusal to accept the possibility of a science based on nature. But he does not simply remain within the framework of scepticism. If he had done so, he would have been less a Christian theologian than was Origen, who insisted that God can work beyond nature. We therefore find further attempts to explain the miraculous in two of his works.

In the treatise *De trinitate* [5] he explains miracle as due to the *semina seminum* implanted in the world at creation. These "seeds" ultimately produce the miracle in nature. It is thus unusual but not strictly supernatural, although it is due to the work of God. In the commentary *De Genesi ad litteram* [6] he goes into the question much more thoroughly. Here he stresses the part played by these "seeds", which he calls *causales rationes*. The example of changing water into wine has a strong influence on his mind. He explains that in the first place there is an order in nature which has its "natural laws", while in the second place there is another order above this, a potential order given by the Creator with *quasi seminales rationes*. The examples he provides for this order are the flowering of Aaron's rod (Numbers 17 : 8), the childbearing of an old woman formerly sterile (Sarah), and the speech of Balaam's ass (Numbers 22 : 28). He does not actually identify any of these examples but mentions the miracles as general cases. It is clear, however, that he has the biblical stories in mind. In any event, the only difference between miracle and non-miracle is that the miracle, being unusual, is assigned to a different

---

[1] *Ibid.*, with note on p. 135.   [2] *Civ. dei* v. 9.   [3] *Ibid.*, v. 11.   [4] See p. 194 above.   [5] *Trin.* iii. 5–10.   [6] *Gen. ad litt.* vi. 14, ix. 16–18.

mode of causation from that of ordinary events. Both classes of events are natural and both have their origin in God.

The origin of the theory of "seeds" implanted by God in the universe can be traced back through Philo to the Stoics. It was Philo who took the immanent seminal principles of the Stoics and asserted that they were placed in nature by the transcendent God, and his thought is echoed by the later church fathers. [1] The prior assumption of both Philo and Augustine is that the miracle stories of the Bible are literally true.

Augustine's position was widely influential in later Christian thought. In the first place, it treated miracles as facts of history along with other facts. This view was widespread in ancient Christian thought, and to it are due many difficulties of patristic apologetics. In the second place, it was a position based on the fact that natural science was moribund. Thus it reiterates the position of ancient Academic scepticism. While thoroughly justified by the state of learning in the fourth and fifth centuries, it is not a position which would have been tenable in other periods. In the third place, it enshrines an optimistic belief that nothing new will be discovered which scepticism cannot attack. It holds that Greek science is really dead and will not resemble the phoenix by rising from its ashes. It wrongly places paradoxography on the same level as exact knowledge. And its belief in the death of science was eventually doomed to failure, as is any theological position which is based on nothing but negative criticism.

Toward the end of his life Augustine convinced himself that miracles were actually taking place in his own times. In 424 or 425 relics of Stephen the martyr were brought from Jerusalem to Hippo with immediate miraculous results. [2] These miracles did not change Augustine's view of miracles; they simply intensified it and made it more prominent in his mind. This is why the *De civitate dei* ends with a tremendous emphasis on the miraculous. This emphasis is a portent of the mediaeval attitude of receptivity to nature miracles.[3]

[1] Cf. H. A. Wolfson, *Philo* (Cambridge, 1947), I 351–52, 357–58. See pp. 27f.
[2] Cf. de Vooght in *RTAM* 11 (1939), 5–16. P. Courcelle, *Recherches sur les Confessions de saint Augustin* (Paris, 1950), 139–53. A list of miracles, *Civ. dei* xxii. 8.
[3] Examples in C. Grant Loomis, *White Magic* (Cambridge, Mass., 1948), cf. also H. Delehaye, *Les légendes hagiographiques* (ed. 2, Brussels, 1906), 56–60. On Jerome and Augustine cf. E. Pickman, *The Mind of Latin Christendom* (New York, 1937), 210–28; on some incredulity among Christians, *ibid.*, 193–96.

It marks the end of ancient science and indeed of ancient civilization.

This significance of Augustine's altered point of view cannot be overemphasized. It not only produced the last books of the *City of God* but also was responsible for the introduction of a new literary form into the church. This is the *libellus miraculorum*. Augustine was so strongly impressed by the miracles produced by Stephen's relics that he began to collect narratives of miracles for public reading in church. [1] They were to be read in the offices and preserved in the church archives. Gradually these stories were united in collections, and thus the way was prepared for the hagiography of the Middle Ages.

As Delehaye points out in discussing this development, they were not utilized by theologians; Augustine himself admits that the people could not remember them very well; but their general success was due to their appeal to the rank and file. [2] For the development Augustine himself is primarily responsible.

[1] *Serm.* 322 (PL 38, 1443); cf. H. Delehaye, "Les premiers 'libelli miraculorum'," *Analecta Bollandiana* 29 (1910), 427–34. [2] *Ibid.*, 434 cf. Delehaye, "Les receuils antiques de miracles des saints", *Analecta Bollandiana* 43 (1925), 5–85, 305–25; on Augustine and Stephen's relics, 74–85. On pagan collections cf. p. 70 *supra* and A. D. Nock, *Conversion* (Oxford 1933), 90–93.

# 14

# RESURRECTION IN THE BIBLE

The doctrine of resurrection is one of the most important and most controversial of Christian beliefs. Like the doctrine of creation and the faith in miracles, it expresses the Christian's confidence in the providential power and goodness of God, who is not bound by matter, which he created, or by nature, which he controls. It is not the same as the Greek belief in the immortality of the soul, with which it was gradually combined. For the early Christians man was not a soul entombed in a body but a complex being consisting of both body and soul. If God's judgment of man was to be complete, it would be made at the last day on body and soul alike.

For Greek critics of Christianity, as we shall see, such a belief was absurd. It represented a return to the stories of mythology and failed to account for the spiritual nature of man. Within Christianity there were those who tried to reinterpret it by using isolated biblical passages. In general, however, the church insisted upon the resurrection of the body, which was understood to be a physical body of "flesh and blood". This insistence involved not only the future resurrection of believers but also the resurrection of Jesus.

In the Bible itself the idea of resurrection was developed only gradually. Clear expressions of the belief are to be found only after the Persian exile in the sixth century B. C. This fact has led many writers to ascribe the origin of the belief among the Hebrews to Zoroastrian influence. Even in the Greek world it was well known that the Persian magi believed in resurrection, although clear evidence for Greek knowledge is found only in the fourth century. Theopompus [1] tells us that according to the magi "men will live again and will be immortal". They will not need food or cast shadows. The last statement suggests that in Persian belief men will have something like the "spiritual body" later described by the apostle Paul.

[1] Fr. 64–65 Jacoby; cf. J. Bidez–F. Cumont, *Les mages hellénisés* (Paris, 1938), II 67–69. On resurrection in Plato's myth of Er cf. J. Bidez, *Eos ou Platon et l'orient* (Brussels, 1945), 45.

We may readily admit that the Persian environment of Jewish
leaders at the time of the exile may have given impetus to the formation
of belief in resurrection, but a factor of greater importance was
probably the inner development of Jewish theology. This development
was based on faith in God, whose judgments cannot be limited by
human death and whose providential care must go beyond the grave.
It is this belief which we see reflected in the resurrection of individuals [1] and of the righteous as a group [2] and finally of the people as
a whole. [3]

A plain testimony to the belief in resurrection is to be found in
Isaiah 26 : 19 ("thy dead shall live; my dead bodies shall rise") but
not in Job 19 : 25–27 ("though worms destroy this body, yet without
the flesh shall I see God"). In these passages we encounter the
cleavage present even within Hebrew thought. Most writers speak of
a physical resurrection, but there are always a few who regard it as
spiritual rather than physical.

Before the time of the Maccabees we even find resurrection rejected,
as well as life after death of any kind. In the sceptical book of
Ecclesiastes a question is asked. "Who knows whether the spirit of
man goes upward and whether the spirit of the beast goes downward
to the earth?" [4] The answer is given in another passage. "He who
is joined with all the living has hope, for a living dog is better than
a dead lion. For the living know that they will die, but the dead do
not know anything." [5] At a later date three incongruous passages
predicting future judgement had to be added to Ecclesiastes before
it could be admitted to the Old Testament canon. [6] Similarly, though
less sceptically, the sage Jesus ben Sira looks forward only to an
immortality of influence; he regards death as an eternal sleep. [7]
Among the conservative Sadducees and Samaritans resurrection was
rejected, for it was not to be found in the Pentateuch. [8]

At the time of the Maccabaean crisis, however, the faith of the
martyrs who died rather than accept the foreign gods of Antiochus
Epiphanes intensified belief in resurrection. In the apocalyptic book
of Daniel [9] we read that

---

[1] Is. 53 : 10, 26 : 19? [2] Dan. 12 : 2. [3] Hos. 6 : 1–2, Ezek. 37 : 1–14; cf. F.
Nötscher, *Altorientalischer und alttestamentlicher Auferstehungsglauben* (Würzburg, 1926).
[4] Eccl. 3 : 21. [5] Eccl. 9 : 4–5. [6] C. F. Burney, *Israel's Hope of Immortality*
(Oxford, 1909), 58–59. [7] *Ibid.*, 62–69; cf. Ecclus. 44. [8] A. Oepke in *RAC* I
934. [9] Dan. 12 : 2–3.

> Many of those who sleep in the land of dust shall awake, some to ever-lasting life and some to reproaches and everlasting abhorrence. And those who are wise will shine forth as the brightness of the firmament, and those who make many righteous as the stars forever and ever.

Similarly the miracle-loving 2 Maccabees speaks of the "resurrection of the flesh". [1]

Under Pharisaic influence this belief became practically a dogma of Judaism, although the Sadducees were still resisting it in the first century of our era. The apostle Paul was able to bring about a riot in Jerusalem by claiming to be a Pharisee unjustly judged by the Sanhedrin because he believed in the resurrection of the dead. [2] After the destruction of Jerusalem in the year 70 the Pharisaic teaching became normative. In the Mishnah [3] it is stated that

> All Israelites have a share in the world to come.... And these are they who have no share in the world to come: he who says that there is no resurrection of the dead prescribed in the Law....

The same doctrine is expressed in some of the peudepigraphical literature; thus Enoch 61 : 5 states that God will raise the bodies even of those who have been eaten by animals, and the fourth book of the *Sibylline Oracles* mentions physical resurrection. [4]

In Hellenistic Judaism, on the other hand, there is no trace of belief in resurrection. The book of Wisdom says that the souls of the righteous are in the hand of God and that "their hope is full of im-mortality". [5] It mentions the pre-existence of the soul. [6] And although it apparently refers to Daniel in saying of the righteous that "in the time of their visitation they will shine forth", [7] we cannot be sure that he accepts Daniel's idea of physical resurrection. Neither Philo nor Josephus mentions resurrection, and Josephus explains the faith of the Pharisees as belief in immortality. [8]

A kind of compromise between the two extremes is found in the Apocalypse of Baruch, where we find a resurrection of the spirit which is to be clothed in a new body of glory and light. [9]

In early Christianity the predominant doctrine seems to be that of the Pharisees. The teaching of Jesus generally takes belief in resurrection for granted, and only at one point is the subject explicitly discussed. This point is a pericope of controversy with the Sadducees. [10]

---

[1] 2 Macc. 7 : 11, 14 : 46.  [2] Acts 23 : 6–9.  [3] Sanh. 10 : 1.  [4] *Or. Sib.* iv. 179–90.  [5] Sap. 3 : 1, 4; cf. 8 : 1.  [6] Sap. 8 : 19–20.  [7] Sap. 3 : 7.  [8] *Bell.* ii. 165.  [9] 2 Bar. 50–51.  [10] Mark 12 : 18–27, Matt. 22 : 23–33, Luke 20 : 27–38.

The Sadducees bring forward a typical test question. Under circumstances in which the law compels a woman to have had seven successive husbands, whose wife is she at the resurrection? The Sadducees obviously infer that the teaching of the law is quite clear and cannot lead to such an absurdity as this example, while it does not mention resurrection.

Jesus' answer, on the other hand, implies that the resurrection is not to be understood so materialistically, and he goes on to argue that resurrection is found, at least implicitly, in the law. He accuses his opponents of knowing "neither the scriptures nor the power of God"—a phrase which may refer to one of the Eighteen Benedictions called "Power", a blessing of God for the resurrection. [1] The risen dead neither are married nor marry; they are like angels in heaven. This statement resembles Enoch 15 : 6–7, where God says to the angels: "You will become immortal spirits.... therefore I have created no wives for you". The second part of the argument proves from Exodus 3 : 6, a reference to the God of Abraham, Isaac, and Jacob, that the patriarchs did not die but live to God. The same proof is found in 4 Maccabees 7 : 19. Presumably it was a stock reply to a stock question.

From this pericope of controversy we should assume that Jesus believed in a resurrection which was not only physical but spiritual. In the early tradition of his teaching there are a few references to resurrection, which seem to suggest that he believed that it would be physical. These are such verses as Mark 9 : 43–47 (Matt. 5 : 29–30) which seem to show that physical defects continue in "life" or "the reign of God". These expressions may be metaphorical. The basic text for discovering the attitude of Jesus, which we have already discussed, shows that he regarded the resurrection body as an earthly body transformed.

Paul's teaching on this subject is by no means uniform, and isolated proof texts could serve those who upheld the resurrection of the flesh as well as those who taught that the flesh was not raised. For example, in 1 Thessalonians 4 : 13–18 it certainly appears that those who are raised "to meet the Lord in the air" are not significantly changed, although it may be said that in writing to the Thessalonian church Paul was strongly influenced by Jewish apocalyptic. The same criticism cannot be made of Philippians 3 : 21, where it would appear

[1] Cf. C. K. Barrett, *The Holy Spirit and the Gospel Tradition* (London, 1947), 74.

that the "body of our humiliation" which, though transformed, is to be raised is the same as our body of flesh and blood.

In view of the apparently different emphases in his thought, we must ask to what extent he is really concerned with the question of the kind of body which can rise. Does he think in terms which sharply distinguish spirit from body? Or is it not the case that he believes firmly in resurrection, but can express his ideas sometimes in more Jewish forms and sometimes in forms which are more Greek? Thus the Corinthian epistles may represent his attempt to make resurrection comprehensible to Greek readers. The details of expression in them do not necessarily represent basic axioms in the apostle's thought.

With this qualification in mind we must next examine the controversy at Corinth which was the occasion for his teaching in 1 Corinthians 15. There were Christians—apparently gentile converts—who denied the resurrection of the dead. They asked sceptically, "How are the dead raised? In what sort of body do they come?" To the more general objection Paul replies by adducing the example of Christ's resurrection, which we shall presently discuss. "If the dead are not raised, neither was Christ raised; and if Christ was not raised, your faith is groundless." As for the kind of body which will rise, Paul contrasts perishable, dishonored corpses with imperishable, gloriously radiant spiritual bodies. The physical body is buried; it is raised as a spiritual body. [1]

Paul sums up his teaching with these words: [2]

> I mean this, brethren, that flesh and blood cannot inherit the kingdom of God, nor will corruption inherit incorruptibility.

The second half of the verse repeats in Greek terms the more Jewish thought of the first half. Does Paul intend to exclude the idea of physical resurrection, as Lietzmann, [3] for example, states? Does he reject the idea of the resurrection of the flesh? We can at least say with Origen [4] that "neither we nor the sacred scriptures say that 'those who died long ago rise from the earth and will live in the same flesh' without that flesh having undergone a change for the better". "Flesh" does not rise as "flesh"; the whole human being is to be transformed. "We shall all be changed." The present corruptible

[1] 1 Cor. 15 : 42–44.  [2] 1 Cor. 15 : 50.  [3] *An die Korinther* I–II (ed. 3, Tübingen, 1931), 86.  [4] *C. Cels.* v. 18.

15

body will acquire incorruption and the mortal body will acquire immortality. [1]

The Corinthians seem to have understood resurrection as a crudely materialistic reiteration of physical life. The apostle, on the other hand, is arguing that the resurrection life will not be physical but spiritual, although there will be complete continuity between the present "body" of man and the "spiritual body" which he will receive from God.

In his second letter to the Corinthians he further stresses the spiritual nature of the risen body. [2]

> We know that if our earthly tabernacle be destroyed, we have a dwelling-place from God, a house not made with hands, eternal in the heavens.

This eternal temple, which corresponds to our present body, also a temple of the Holy Spirit, [3] will not replace the body we have now but will be added to it. "We desire not to be unclothed but to be clothed upon, that the mortal may be swallowed up by life." [4]

Moreover, while Paul strongly stresses the warfare between "flesh" and "spirit" (see chapter 7), the warfare is to end not in the annihilation of the flesh but in its control by the Spirit.

> You are not in the flesh but in the spirit, since the Spirit of God dwells in you.... If Christ is in you, your body is dead because of sin, but your spirit is life because of righteousness. If the Spirit of him who raised Jesus from the dead dwells in you, then he who raised Jesus from the dead will also make your mortal bodies live by his Spirit which dwells in you. [5]

The Pauline doctrine is not purely spiritual but involves the resurrection and transformation of men's physical bodies. [6]

Throughout Christian history the resurrection of Christ and the future resurrection of believers are intimately associated. The kind of belief held concerning one has been the kind held concerning the other, for when Christ rose he rose "as the first-fruits of those who have slept". [7] In the early church those who held that Christ's risen body was spirit held that they too would be spirit. Those who held that he rose in the flesh held that they would rise in the flesh. As Origen [8] says,

[1] 1 Cor. 15 : 53.  [2] 2 Cor. 5 : 1; cf. Lietzmann, *op. cit.*, 119–21; W. L.Knox, *St Paul and the Church of the Gentiles* (Cambridge, 1939), 125–45.  [3] 1 Cor. 6:19, 2 Cor. 6:16.  [4] 2 Cor. 5:4.  [5] Rom. 8:9—11.  [6] Against C. H. Dodd, *Romans* (London, 1932), 125, and my own article in *JR* 28 (1948), 120–30.  [7] 1 Cor. 15 : 20; cf. 1 Clem. 24 : 1.  [8] J. Scherer, *Entretien d'Origène avec Héraclide* (*Publ. de la soc. Fouad I de papyrol.*, *Textes et Documents* IX, Cairo, 1949), 132:4; cf. Method. *Res.* i. 26. 1.

> The church.... professes the resurrection of the dead body, for as a conse-
> quence of the resurrection of the first-fruits from the dead it follows thas
> the dead must rise.

Exceedingly important, therefore, is the oldest account of the resurrection, which Paul provides in 1 Corinthians 15 : 3–8.

> I handed over to you among the essentials a tradition which I received,
> that Christ died for our sins according to the scriptures, and that he was
> buried, and that he was raised the third day according to the scriptures;
> and that he appeared to Cephas, then to the twelve, then he appeared to
> more than five hundred brethren all at once, most of whom are still alive,
> though some have died; then he appeared to James, then to all the apostles;
> last of all, as to an abortion, he appeared even to me.

No word in this account suggests that the appearances of Jesus were
other than "spiritual"; it was not the "flesh and blood" of Jesus
which the witnesses saw. This interpretation is confirmed by the
expression employed in 1 Corinthians 15 : 45: "The first Adam
became a living soul; the last Adam, a life-giving spirit". [1] What Paul
saw, and what he believes other Christians saw, was the "spiritual
body" of Jesus. It shone in his heart to illuminate it with the knowledge of the glory of God in the face of Christ. [2]

Unfortunately for our knowledge of the primitive tradition, Mark,
the earliest gospel, ends before any resurrection appearance is
described, and the theory of some scholars that the transfiguration
story is misplaced in tradition and really is an account of the resurrection seems highly uncertain. We may assume, however, that the
resurrection as Mark conceived it cannot have been very different
from the transfiguration. [3] Jesus' resurrection body would have been
regarded as brilliantly white and like the spiritual body of angels. It
would have been an earthly body transformed.

The gospel of Matthew, which is very largely a revision of Mark,
is in part close to the primitive tradition. After our gospel of Mark
ends, Matthew continues with the matter-of-fact "and behold, Jesus
encountered them" with a greeting and an order to proceed to
Galilee. They go to Galilee; they see him; and the gospel concludes
with his promise to be with them until the end of the world. [4] Nothing
is explicitly said of the nature of the resurrected body, and although

---

[1] Cf. 2 Cor. 3 : 17, Rom. 8 : 9–11.  [2] 2 Cor. 4 : 6, a comparison with the first
creation; cf. Phil. 3 : 21.  [3] Mark 9 : 2–8.  [4] This promise is replaced in Acts
by the promise of the Spirit (1 : 8) and in John by the coming of the Paraclete.

obviously the whole personality of Jesus is thought of as alive, his body is not a body of flesh. Another aspect of Matthew's attitude toward the resurrection of Jesus' flesh is made clear in a series of controversies with Jews, near the end of his gospel. These controversies are certainly not primitive. [1] The first passage (Matt. 27 : 62–66) argues that, since the tomb was well guarded, the disciples could not have stolen the body; the second (Matt. 28 : 11–16) answers the objection that the guards were asleep by claiming that they were paid to say so. "And this story is widespread among Jews to this day." There is not necessarily any close relation to fact in this account; but it reflects the idea of the resurrection of a physical body. It is the sort of narrative which might be handed down among Jewish Christians.

The gentile evangelist Luke, on the other hand, tells the mysterious story of the stranger on the road to Emmaus. It may reasonably be assumed that Luke is here suggesting that Jesus is known to his disciples in the Eucharist; "he was known to them in the breaking of the bread" (Luke 24 : 35). [2] As in Justin's description of a second-century Eucharist, [3] so here the apostolic preaching, the messianic texts of the Old Testament, and the broken bread are joined together. [4] But what kind of body does Jesus have? Both resurrection appearances are concluded with his disappearance; and the second one includes elements which are intended to avoid the suspicion that he was simply spirit. He tells his disciples to handle him and see that he has flesh and bones, and in their presence he eats a piece of fish. [5] Possibly in the tradition this appearance was also eucharistic and contained no mention of his flesh and bones; but in any event the evangelist believes that Jesus' flesh is risen, and in Acts 1 : 19 it is taken up into heaven somewhat as Elijah's was in 2 Kings 2 : 11. [6]

A more profound treatment of the meaning of Jesus' resurrection is found in the Fourth Gospel. In the author's time the Christian understanding of the Eucharist and of baptism has greatly deepened. Like Luke, he associates the resurrection of Jesus with the sacraments. Baptism is the efficacious sign of rebirth, and, as in Romans 6 : 3–4,

---

[1] H. J. Cadbury in *Quantulacumque: Studies Presented to K. Lake* (London, 1937), 99–108. [2] Cf. Acts 2 : 42; cf. G. D. Kilpatrick in *JTS* (1946), 52–53. [3] Justin, *Apol.* i. 66–67. [4] Luke 24 : 19–30, 44–46. [5] Angels merely seem to eat (Tob. 12 : 19, Philo, *Abr.* 118; Josephus, *Ant.* i 197; Justin, *Dial.* 57) or else they eat manna (Ps. 77 : 25, etc.). [6] F. J. F. Jackson–K. Lake–H. J. Cadbury, *The Beginnings of Christianity* IV (London, 1933), 9.

it is a rebirth through a death of the flesh (John 3 : 12–15). But "that which is begotten of the flesh is flesh, and that which is begotten of the spirit is spirit" (John 3 : 6). Similarly the Eucharist, the means of attaining eternal life, is described in John 6 : 53 as eating the flesh and drinking the blood of the Son of Man. And yet—with a reference in John 6 : 62 to the resurrection and ascension of Jesus— "the Spirit is the life-creating one; [1] the flesh is of no avail" (John 6 : 63). In such a sacrament-centered gospel as John's, where the eucharistic flesh and blood of the risen Jesus are not only material, physical, but also "spiritual", we may expect to find that this is also the case with his risen body. And so it is. Details about the grave-clothes (John 20 : 6–7) make plain the evangelist's belief that the corpse of Jesus was revived, as in the prophetic example of Lazarus in chapter 11. On the other hand, Mary Magdalene at first thinks the risen Lord is the gardener, and he orders her not to touch him because he has not yet ascended to the Father (John 20 : 15, 17). Again, in the first Sunday's worship of the disciples Jesus appears (though the doors are closed), [2] shows them his hands and his wounded side, imparts the Spirit to them, and presumably disappears (John 20 : 19–23). A week later the spiritual flesh of Jesus is made still more evident to the sceptical Thomas. Jesus tests him by appearing and inviting him to put his finger on his hand and his hand on Jesus' side. Thomas, like the disciples in Luke's narrative, does not make the test but is convinced, and Jesus points the moral of the story by saying, "Because you saw me you believed; blessed are those who do not see, yet believe" (John 20 : 24–29). The flesh of Jesus is strongly stressed. As Hoskyns puts it, "the purpose of the Fourth Gospel is .... to make known the faith of the Church and the meaning of the history or 'flesh' of Jesus". [3] Yet it is no ordinary flesh, for at the same time it is spirit. In John 21 : 13, somewhat as in Luke 24 : 42–43, Jesus takes bread and fish and gives it to the disciples. But while in Luke's story he eats with them, in John he does not himself eat.

John's idea of a "spiritual body" may be derived from Paul. In any event, it is clear that he stresses (as later writers do not stress) the

---

[1] Probably a reference to 1 Cor. 15:45. [2] The miracle involved may be that of doors opening spontaneously; cf. O. Weinreich in *Genethliakon W. Schmid* (Stuttgart, 1929), 200–464. [3] E. Hoskyns–F. N. Davey, *The Fourth Gospel* (London, 1940), I, 175.

spiritual nature of the risen body of Christ. After his time the two elements in the paradoxical resurrection faith were split asunder, and the half-truth that was called docetism was recognized as unorthodox. The emphasis on the flesh of Jesus (as in the view of Luke) remained alone in the church. To some extent this was inevitable. If Christians were to proclaim the historical reality of the rising of their Lord, they had to insist on a somewhat crude understanding of it in order to reach a wider audience. If they were to defend their faith from critical opponents, they had to insist on the novelty of the resurrection. Other gods died and rose; only Jesus rose in the flesh.

The "tension" between flesh and spirit is strikingly relaxed in the letters of Ignatius, bishop of Antioch early in the second century. In the stress of his struggle with docetism he abandons anything like the restraint which the gospels reflect. This is most clearly shown in the third chapter of his letter to the church of Smyrna:

> For I know and believe that he was in the flesh even after the resurrection. And when he came to those about Peter he said to them, "Take, handle me and see that I am not a bodiless demon". And they immediately touched him and believed, being mingled with both his flesh and his spirit.... After his resurrection he ate and drank with them as a being of flesh, though spiritually he was united to the Father.

This passage is important because it is the first clear statement of the resurrection of Jesus' flesh outside the New Testament. It is therefore equally important to determine on what it is based. Origen [1] states that "I am not a bodiless demon" comes from the *Teaching of Peter*, an apocryphal book, while Eusebius [2] does not know where the saying comes from. The most obvious explanation of the saying is that it is a paraphrase of Luke 24 : 39, "Handle me and see, for a spirit does not have flesh and bones such as you see me having". Ignatius alters the saying because he believes that the disciples were united not simply with Jesus' flesh but also with his spirit, as he says. He knows from Acts 10 : 41 that the disciples ate and drank with Jesus after the resurrection. He probably substitutes "demon" for "spirit" because in the gospel proof text for Jesus' eating and drinking (Matt. 11 : 19, Luke 7 : 34) [3] the first part of the saying speaks of John the Baptist, who neither ate nor drank and was said to have a demon, or because "demon" is better Greek.

What Ignatius has done is to choose from among the various

[1] *Princ.* i. praef. 8.   [2] *H. E.* iii. 3. 2.   [3] Cf. *Trall.* 9 : 1.

accounts of the risen body of Jesus in the New Testament the one which gives most support to him in his struggle with the docetists. At this point he might have quoted the story of doubting Thomas, but as we have seen, it is not absolutely antidocetic. Ignatius cannot use it to prove his point.

What contact Ignatius has with any of the sciences is apparently with astrology, and the possibility or impossibility of such a resurrection does not seem to have entered his mind. Had he discussed it, he would undoubtedly have said as he says in regard to the star of Bethlehem that something new had happened in the history of the universe. The old kingdom had been destroyed and everything was disturbed. [1] Hence no statements about credibility or possibility are valid any more. Purely religious and mythological conceptions alone have weight.

These are the conceptions which were of primary importance among most Christian believers during the second century. To them philosophical considerations were largely irrelevant. We know that the resurrection of the flesh was regarded, even by outsiders, as characteristic of Christians. Inside the church, Justin [2] tells us that it is the orthodox view. Outside, the persecutors of the church at Lyons in 177 burned the bodies of martyrs to ashes and swept them into the river Rhone, "in order that they may not even have hope of a resurrection". [3] Tatian has to argue [4] that even if his body is burned the universe retains the matter in the form of ashes.

In the faith of these Christian martyrs and of such leaders of the church as Ignatius, Justin, Irenaeus, and Tertullian, a future life would be impossible without the physical body. In part this faith is supported by considerations of morality. Extreme asceticism and its complement, libertinism, were common dangers of Christianity in the second century. Belief in a future resurrection of the flesh was regarded by ordinary Christians as a deterrent to such practices.

The resurrection faith was also defended by sacramental considerations. As we have already seen, there is a strong connection between the resurrection and the Eucharist, for both are regarded as mediations of the risen flesh of Jesus. [5] This connection seems to lie at the heart of ancient Christianity. As Irenaeus says:

[1] *Eph.* 19 : 3.   [2] *Dial.* 80.   [3] Eusebius, *H. E.* v. 1. 62–63; cf. A. D. Nock in *HTR* 25 (1932), 334.   [4] *Or.* 6, 6 : 31 Schwartz; cf. Min. Fel. *Oct.* xi. 4.   [5] Ignatius, *Philad.* 4, *Rom.* 7 : 3, *Smyrn.* 7 : 1.

> If this flesh is not saved, neither did the Lord redeem us by his blood, nor is the cup of the Eucharist communion in his blood, nor is the bread which we break communion in his body (1 Cor. 10 : 16). For blood comes only from veins and flesh.... As the blessed apostle says in the epistle to the Ephesians (5 : 30), "Since we are members of his body, from his flesh and from his bones"; not saying these things of some spiritual and invisible man ("For a spirit has neither bones nor flesh" [Luke 24 : 39]), but of the dispensation of the true man, which consists of flesh and sinews and bones, and is nourished by the cup, which is his blood, and by the bread, which is his body. [1]

We are members of the risen body of Christ; and since we are still flesh and blood, the body which we compose must be flesh and blood too. In Ephesians 5 : 30, which Irenaeus quotes, we see the literalism with which some Christians interpreted the Pauline concept of the church as the body of Christ. [2] The reading "from his flesh and from his bones" is not found in Alexandrian manuscripts but only in those classified by von Soden as Caesarean and Antiochene. This realistic symbol, based on Gen. 2 : 23, is very much like the sacramental realism of John 6 : 53–56, where the believer who eats the flesh and drinks the blood of the Son of Man abides in him, that is, in the church, which is his body. Christology and ecclesiology are very closely related in the New Testament. And as he so often does, Irenaeus tries to set forth, in the light of second-century Christianity, a biblical theology.

Similarly Methodius, while making use of philosophical arguments, is essentially a defender of the traditional faith. He is indebted to no one else as much as he is to Irenaeus. [3] And when in opposition to Origen he writes his dialogue called *Aglaophon*, in spite of its philosophical-romantic form it is ultimately based only on scripture. For Methodius scripture is the source of all knowledge. [4] Moreover, scripture must be interpreted according to the rule of faith. When he discusses Origen's exegesis of Psalm 66, he comments on it that "in it there is absurdity rather than orthodoxy". [5]

On the Origenist view (see p. 254) our present bodies are nothing but the "coats of skin" which, according to Genesis 3 : 21, God gave Adam and Eve after the Fall. This idea is ultimately based, as we shall see, on the Orphic-Platonic concept of the body as the tomb of

[1] Iren., *Adv. haer.* v. 2. 1–2.  [2] See W. L. Knox in *JTS* 39 (1938), 243–46.
[3] N. Bonwetsch, *Die Theologie des Methodius von Olympus* (Göttingen, 1903), 164.
[4] *Ibid.*, 140, 153–54.  [5] *Res.* i. 54. 1.

the soul. It was also gnostic, and Irenaeus had rejected it. [1] To Methodius, as to ancient Christianity generally, man's nature consists of both body and soul, and it is the whole man who must finally be raised.

For Methodius the traditional doctrine of the church is the criterion of truth; he stands in the succession of Irenaeus. Though he sometimes makes use of philosophical arguments to prove the possibility of the resurrection of the flesh and discusses the theory of exegesis, he is fundamentally the son of Mother Church. [2] The faith has priority over natural reason; and the exegete is guided by God, to whom he prays. His treatise on the resurrection ends with a prayer. "Thou hast sent thy Word from heaven to us to teach us the truth; who being impassible, through thy will assumed this much-suffering body, in order that through passions the impassible might become a passion for passions, in this struggle, freed from passions; and through the death of the deathless one a death for death might be found, with death extinguished, since the mortal was changed into immortality and the passible into impassibility, because of thy compassion." [1] The wearisomely rhetorical style should not conceal from us the fact that Methodius is convinced of the truth of resurrection because of his firmly orthodox faith and theological considerations are discussed, but they are secondary. What is fundamental is faith in God and in his purpose for mankind.

The religious meaning of resurrection is also set forth in the creeds. As early as the old rules of faith underlying much of the writing of Irenaeus and Tertullian, the resurrection of the flesh is set forth as authoritative Christian teaching. In that period no essential distinction was yet made between the resurrection of the flesh, of the body, and of the dead. [3] Yet the phrase "resurrection of the flesh" is not scriptural; and it may have been an attempt to conform to biblical usage which caused the substitution of "resurrection of the dead" in creeds and baptismal confessions after the middle of the fourth century.

The Christian belief is reflected in a brief but significant episode in the life of Augustine, just after his mother's death. His son Adeodatus lamented bitterly, but the father checked his grief. "For she did not die in sorrow, nor did she entirely die. We held this because of the

---

[1] Iren. *Adv. haer.* i. 10. 1. Cf. Clement, *Excerpta ex Theodoto* 55. 1; Philo, *Quaest. in Gen.* i. 53.   [2] J. C. Plumpe, *Mater Ecclesia* (Washington, 1943), 109–22.   [3] H. B. Swete in *JTS* 18 (1916–17), 139.

evidencies of her character and because of an unfeigned faith and
convincing reasons." [1] These words express the Christian hope. But
what were the convincing reasons? And what was their relation to
the unfeigned faith? Why did opponents of Christianity find them
unconvincing?

[1] *Conf.* ix. 29.

# RESURRECTION IN APOLOGETIC

From a very early date the Christian idea of resurrection aroused opposition. In the Acts of the Apostles (17 : 31–32) we read that Paul's mention of the resurrection of the dead produced two kinds of response in his audience, which consisted of Epicureans and Stoics. Some—presumably the Epicureans—mocked, while others—Stoics—said that they would listen to him at another time. We shall presently examine the Stoics' more receptive attitude. Now we must consider the more common mockery.

Plato had defended the immortality of the soul, and with the Orphics had regarded the body as an evil, a fetter, a tomb. [1] The ideal for man is to escape from the body. The Hellenistic Jew Philo derives his attitude toward the body from Plato. "The body is wicked and a plotter against the soul, and is always a corpse and a dead thing. For you must understand that each of us does nothing but carry a corpse about, since the soul lifts up and bears without effort the body which is in itself a corpse." [2] Naturally such writers rejected the idea of resurrection. The Middle Platonist Celsus tells us that God cannot perform shameful acts and therefore would not arise corpses which consist of flesh full of unspeakable things. [3] Neoplatonists also attacked the idea. Plotinus declares that the true "awakening" is that which takes place from the body, not an awakening of the body, whose nature is opposite to that of the soul. The body comes into existence, changes, and decays; it does not possess true being. [4] His disciple Porphyry vigorously attacks the Christians for their idea of resurrection. [5]

On the other hand, there was one philosophical school which found something like resurrection comprehensible. The old Stoa, following an idea of Heraclitus, expected the periodic destruction

---

[1] *Phaedo* 66 b–67 d, *Cratyl.* 400 c; cf. E. Rohde *Psyche* (New York, 1925), 467–68. [2] *Leg. alleg.* iii. 69; cf. E. R. Goodenough in *HTR* 39 (1946), 85–108. [3] Orig. *C. Cels.* v. 14. [4] *Enn.* iii. 6. 6. [5] Fr. 34 (cf. 92).

of the world by fire and its periodic renewal. Chrysippus explicitly said that it was not impossible for human beings to be restored to the form in which they now are. [1] In the cyclical renewal Socrates and Plato, for example, would relive their former lives. [2] Christian descriptions of Stoic views include the word "rise again", but this may be Christian interpretation. [3]

In speaking of this cosmic "regeneration" [4] the Stoics compared the fire of the cosmic conflagration to a seed from which the new world would arise and develop. [5] And in the Roman Stoic Seneca we find analogies used to show that in the ordinary course of nature there is change rather than decay. Summer goes away, but another year brings it back; winter comes to an end, but the months make it return. Night overcomes the sun and then is overcome. The course of the stars remains the same. [6]

The cyclical theory was held by most Stoics, as Origen tells us. While Panaetius rejected it and taught that the world is eternal, [7] Posidonius returned to the traditional Stoic view and we hear of no further rebels from orthodoxy. [8] We shall see that Christian writers found the Stoic analogies very useful in developing their "proofs" of resurrection. Christians could not, however, accept the Stoic idea of predetermined cycles, endlessly repeated and controlled by the positions of the stars. [9]

Outside philosophical schools there was occasional acceptance of individual "resurrection". A fragment of Aelian [10] tells us that just as the Dioscuri, Heracles, and Glaucus lived again because they were "friends of God", so the fabulist Aesop received resurrection. Some people accepted the stories of the resurrections of Pythagoras and Epimenides. [11] Apuleius says that the physician Asclepiades of Prusa raised a man from the dead; but the medical writer Celsus notes that he recognized that a man about to be buried was actually alive. [12]

The general attitude to this problem is best represented by the elder Pliny, who discusses the topic of death in some detail. He relates the stock stories about Hermotimus, Aristeas, and Epimenides,

[1] SVF II 623, cited approvingly by Lactantius. [2] SVF II 625–27. [3] SVF, I 109 (Tatian), II 630 (Clement of Alexandria). [4] H. Leisegang in *RE* XVIII 3, 139–48. [5] SVF II 596, 618. [6] *Ep.* 36 : 11. [7] Arius Didymus, *Epit. fr. phys.* 36 (p. 468 Diels). [8] D. L. vii. 142 (cf. M. Pohlenz, *Die Stoa* I 219). [9] Tat. *Or.* 5-6; Orig. *C. Cels.* iv. 12. [10] Fr. 203. [11] L. Bieler, ΘΕΙΟΣ ΑΝΗΡ I (Vienna, 1935), 48. [12] Apul. *Flor.* 19; Cels. *Med.* ii. 6, 38 : 15 Daremberg (cf. Plin. *N. H.* vii. 124).

and says that they are mythical; with considerable scepticism he tells two tales of death-bed predictions; and he concludes with these words: [1]

> there are also cases of persons who were seen after burial; but we are concerned with the works of Nature, not with miracles (*prodigia*).

He severely criticizes the view of Democritus that because the signs of death were not absolutely certain, life after death was possible. [2] Such ideas are illusions and are based on credulity; they destroy the principal benefit of nature, which is death, by tormenting mankind with ideas of a future life. After death man ceases to exist, just as before birth he had no existence. [3] Resurrection and immortality cannot be effected even by God. [4]

In answering such objections, Christian apologists tried to prove that the order of nature did not exclude the possibility of resurrection. Their arguments were based on two closely related ideas: first, something like resurrection is found in the ordinary course of nature; second, something like resurrection is found in unusual, paradoxical events. The first idea is based on Stoic arguments for the renewal of the universe; the second is the Christians' own contribution.

The earliest example of arguments from the ordinary course of nature are to be found in 1 Corinthians, where the apostle is debating with Greek opponents largely on their own grounds.

(1)  A seed apparently dies when it is placed in the ground; its shell disappears and something which looks very different comes up. The comparison of human life to that of a seed, buried and hidden, is found in Epictetus (*Diss.* iv. 8. 36); and the Pauline parallel is repeated in John 12 : 24, 1 Clement 24, and many later writers. [5]

(2)  Another parallel is derived from current doxographical tradition. The apostle argues that not all flesh is the same; it differs in the cases of men, beasts, birds, and fish. He goes on to point out that heavenly bodies differ from earthly bodies. This argument seems to be based on the common Platonic-Aristotelian teaching that there are four kinds of "animals". These are land animals, marine, winged, and heavenly; "for the stars are also called animals". [6] With this

[1] Plin. *N. H.* vii. 179.  [2] *Ibid.* 189; cf. Cels. *Med.* ii. 6, 38 : 10; Waszink on Tert. *An.* 51 : 2 (p. 528).  [3] *Ibid.* 188, 190.  [4] *Ibid.* ii. 27; cf. p. 129; for the general Graeco-Roman view cf. A. Oepke in *RAC* I 931–32.  [5] Cf. *Carmen ad Flavium Felicem de resurrectione* (ed. J. H. Waszink, *Flor. Patr.* Suppl. I, Bonn, 1937), 121–25.  [6] *Plac.* v. 20. 1, p. 432 : 4 Diels.

point Paul combines another based on a philosophical commonplace, that of the magnitudes of stars. The relative brightness of sun, moon, and stars was obvious, but the expression, "One star exceeds another star in brightness", may be related to the idea of Posidonius that only the planets could be called *asteres*. These *asteres* exceed or differ from the *astra*, stars in general. [1]

This argument does not go beyond the idea of the ordinary course of nature. But it prepares the way for the later use of paradoxography by its insistence on the wide variety to be found within nature. We see, therefore, that both elements of the later arguments can be traced back to the apostle Paul. By the end of the first century we meet another argument based on the orderly course of nature. This is in the Roman writer Clement (24).

(3) "Day and night manifest a resurrection to us; night dies, day rises; day goes away, night returns." This analogy is identical with that used by the Roman Stoic Seneca to commend the idea of cosmic renewal (p. 236). Like the analogy of the seed, it won widespread favor.

Other analogies derived from the Stoics and based on the cycles of seasons included (4) the flowering of plants in the spring (Minucius Felix), and (5) the "resurrection" of the moon after its monthly waning (Theophilus). [2]

In the middle of the second century we meet another kind of argument. It is based not on the life of nature in general but on human life as it now is (5). Athenagoras compares death and resurrection to loss of consciousness in sleep followed by awakening. This analogy could be widely accepted because of the commonplace, as old as Homer (*Il.* xvi. 672), that "death is the brother of sleep". Again (6), Theophilus compares resurrection to the recovery of strength after sickness.

Another argument starts from the natural and proceeds to treat it as something amazing. This is (7) the analogy of birth to rebirth, or rather of conception to resurrection. The comparison of human life to that of an embryo is found in Seneca and in Marcus Aurelius, as well as in Megasthenes' description of Hindu thought. [3] This

---

[1] Ar. Did. *phys.* fr. 32, p. 466 : 18 Diels; cf. E. Maass, *Comm. in Arat. reliq.* (Berlin, 1898), 41 : 13, 42 : 3; Macrob. *Somn. Scip.* i. 14. 21; cf. F. Boll in *ZNW* 18 (1917–18), 41–43. [2] Cf. F. Cumont, *Recherches sur le symbolisme funéraire des romains* (Paris, 1942), 211 n. 6, 218. [3] Sen. *Ep.* 102 : 23–26; M. Aurel. ix. 3. 4; Meg. in Strab. c. 712; cf. F. Cumont, *Lux Perpetua* (Paris, 1949), 399.

thought is further developed in the *Apology* of Justin. "What would be more incredible, if we were not in a body, and someone said that it was possible for those bones and sinews and that flesh which we see to be formed from some tiny drop of human seed?" [1] Athenagoras tries to explain why he finds this example so satisfactory. He points out (*Res.* 17) that the seed did not have "written in it" the life or form of men; no one could have predicted that it would produce a man. Nevertheless, this actually happened and continues to happen; it is a "natural sequence". Therefore reason, relying on the natural sequence, can proceed to prove the truth of resurrection, for reason is safer and more valid than experience in confirming the truth." Once more we encounter the great weakness of ancient philosophy and science, its preference for argument rather than observation, for deduction rather than induction. We shall presently see the absurdity to which Athenagoras' rationalism leads him.

Finally we must mention the famous proof from paradoxography, (8) the example of the phoenix. The first time we meet it is in the letter of Clement (25), who probably derives it from Roman historians.

> Let us look at the strange sign which takes place in the east, that is, in the neighborhood of Arabia. There is a bird called phoenix. It is the only one of its species and lives 500 years. And when the time of departure comes, for it to die, it makes for itself a bier of incense and myrrh and other spices, which when the time is fulfilled it enters, and dies. As its flesh decays a worm is produced, which is nourished by the juices of the dead creature and grows wings. Then, grown strong, it takes up the bier on which lie the bones of its predecessor and flies with them from Arabia to Egypt, to the city called Heliopolis. And by day, in the sight of all, it flies to the altar of the sun and lays them there and then flies back again. The priests then consult the records of the past and find that it has come after an interval of 500 years.

This story was very popular, but many writers were quite sceptical about it. Herodotus (ii. 73) strongly questioned it; the elder Pliny said that it might be mythical (x. 3); and Tacitus says (*Ann.* vi. 28): "All this is full of doubt and legendary exaggeration". [2] Unfortunately he believes that it was actually, though of course only occasionally, seen.

Many later Christian writers overlooked the doubt and legendary

---

[1] *Apol.* i. 19.    [2] Cf. A. Wiedemann, *Herodots zweites Buch* (Leipzig, 1890), 314; J. Hubaux–M. Leroy, *Le mythe du phénix* (Liège, 1939). On the phoenix as a symbol of *aeternitas* cf. Türk in Roscher, *Ausf. Lex. f. griech. u. röm. Mythol.* III 3466–69.

exaggeration in their delight at finding such a prophetic bird. [1] As we might expect, Origen was somewhat sceptical, but Tertullian was immensely pleased. He devotes the thirteenth chapter of his *De resurrectione carnis* to a discussion of its wonders:

> Consider a very complete and reliable example of this hope.... What proof could be found more clearly and strikingly intended for this case? For what other matter is there such a proof? For in his scriptures [Ps. 92 : 12] God says: "And he will flourish like a phoenix", that is, from death.... The Lord declared that we are of more value than many sparrows [Matt. 10 : 31]; this would mean little if it did not also apply to phoenixes. And will men die, once and for all, when Arabian birds are sure of resurrection?

This argument is vitiated by the fact that the word "phoenix" in the Greek Old Testament means "palm tree"—although the palm tree was also a symbol of resurrection; a more satisfactory allusion could have been found in Job 29 : 18, where the Greek version has inserted a reference to the bird.

A further method of rational proof consisted of outlining the disagreements of philosophers and arguing on the basis of their least common denominator. As we have seen, this task was made easy by the existence of doxographical collections in which the opinions (*doxai*) of the schools were listed under subjects. It is undertaken in a work on the resurrection mistakenly attributed to Justin but apparently written early in the third century. In the sixth chapter the opinions of philosophers of nature are discussed. The author notices only Plato, Epicurus, and the Stoics, for, he says, "it is sufficient to mention the especially prevalent opinions". They disagree in details but agree on one point: "that which exists is not created from non-existence, nor is it dissolved and destroyed into non-existence, and the elements are imperishable; everything is produced from them". Then, if matter is imperishable, the restoration of the flesh is obviously possible. Pseudo-Justin considers this a proof made in gentile fashion. Tertullian also uses it. [2]

Finally, there are rational arguments directed against the objections of pagan critics. Two examples will suffice, the first a "natural" one, the second derived from paradoxography. As might be expected,

---

[1] We also find the phoenix in a second-century anthology, published by A. Vogliano, *Papiri della R. Università di Milano* I (Milan, 1937), no. 20, pp. 175–83.
[2] *Res. carn.* 11. But the body would not be the same as the one which perished; see Lucretius iii. 847–60, and Varro in Augustine, *Civ. dei* XXII. 28, with Augustine's comment.

Athenagoras provides us with what he considers a thoroughly reasonable answer to a strong pagan criticism. The criticism is this: "Now these people say that many bodies of those who meet death in shipwrecks and rivers become food for fishes, and many of those who die in battles, or lack burial from some worse cause and the circumstances of the situation, remain as meat for passing animals." [1] The result is that these bodies become part of the animals which eat them, and then, when men eat the animals, the original bodies are hopelessly mixed. The opponents back up this attack on resurrection with many examples of cannibalism from tragedy and paradoxography. Athenagoras makes his reply on their grounds. "To me such people seem to be ignorant of the power and wisdom of the Creator and Sustainer of all, who adapted suitable and convenient food to the nature and species of each animal.... For they surely would have known that not everything which one takes in under the pressure of need from without becomes suitable food for the animal." [2] And according to Greek medicine there are three processes of digestion: in the stomach, in the liver, and in the members and parts to be nourished. In one or another of these, unsuitable foods are rejected. Now, human flesh is not the "natural and convenient" food of man. Therefore it cannot be digested into the members and parts of the body itself, even though it may pass through the stomach and into the liver. Unnatural or harmful food is entirely rejected during digestion.

Athenagoras takes over this argument from medical and philosophical writers who describe the process of digestion and explain the wonderful naturalness of the process. For example, his contemporary Galen writes: [3]

> Nature acts throughout in an artistic and equitable manner, having certain faculties, by virtue of which each part of the body draws to itself the juice which is proper to it, and having done so, attaches it to every portion of itself, and completely assimilates it; while such part of the juice as is not capable of undergoing complete alteration and assimilation to the part which is being nourished is got rid of by yet another (an expulsive) faculty.

But why is it unnatural to eat human flesh? Why would such flesh be rejected in the process of digestion? The reason Athenagoras else-

[1] Ath. *Res.* 4; cf. Tat. *Or.* 6. On Origen's use of this argument see p. 252 above. Jewish writers had already asserted that such bodies would rise again (Enoch 61 : 5).
[2] Athenagoras, *Res.* 5. [3] *On the Natural Faculties* i. 12 (trans. A. J. Brock); cf. Cicero, *N. D.* ii. 137–38; Nemesius of Emesa, *Nat. hom.* 23, pp. 236–40 Matthaei.

16

where adduces for this argument [1] is that animals do not molest other animals of the same species. They are guided in their behavior by the "law of nature". Similarly Pliny tells us in his *Natural History* [2] that nature shows us that animals do not eat their own kind.

Of course Athenagoras is also aware that fish eat fish. [3] This is a commonplace of ancient observation and moralizing. But men are not like fish; they are like other animals, and therefore they should not eat their own kind. Since in his mind the moral law is equivalent to the law of nature, he proceeds to argue that men not only should not, but actually cannot eat human flesh. The process of digestion is guided by nature; therefore it is impossible to digest unnatural foods. Therefore.... Athenagoras' contemporaries agreed with him on both points but were not so rationalistic as to deny the edibility of their fellows. Indeed, the founders of the Stoa had taught that cannibalism was permissible in case of need; it was the natural thing to do, since animals eat their own kind. [4] Petronius amusingly discusses the problem in his story of a Roman in whose will most of the bequests are contingent upon the heirs' cutting up his corpse and publicly eating it. No meat, he observes, is naturally attractive; it has to be made so by a certain art. In this case consideration of the legacies will take the place of cooking in rendering the meat palatable. [5] Moreover, in the course of their education Greeks became aware that in Homer and in Herodotus, not to mention such lost tragedies as the *Thyestes* of Euripides, cannibalism is portrayed. [6] To eat human flesh is shocking, as we see from Porphyry's reaction to John 6 : 53; [7] it is not impossible.

In this example we see the rationalistic tendency of apologetic leading it to an absurd conclusion. Athenagoras is thoroughly unrealistic. It is not as a Christian, however, that he goes astray; it is as an amateur philosopher convinced of the validity of his concept of "nature" and of his deductive method. Methodius, who uses medical information and in fact sets the scene of his *De resurrectione* in the clinic of a physician, avoids such an argument and is content

---

[1] *Leg.* 3 : 1; parallels in J. Geffcken, *Zwei griechische Apologeten* (Leipzig, 1907), 168. [2] *N. H.* vii, praef. 5. [3] *Leg.* 34 : 4; cf. W. Parsons in *Traditio* 3 (1945), 380–88. [4] *SVF* III 753. [5] Petronius, *Sat.* 141. He adds historical examples of cannibalism. [6] *Iliad* xiv. 114; Herodotus i. 119, 216, iii. 99; Sext. Emp. *Pyrrh.* iii. 207; Bardaisan in W. Cureton, *Spicilegium Syriacum* (London, 1855), 18. [7] Fr. 69 Harnack.

to demonstrate the essential continuity of the body and the necessity of God's judging a body which remains identical. [1]

The "argument from digestion" was used for a long time by opponents of Christianity. It was clear and convincing, and it could be made even more interesting by elaboration. Porphyry expresses it thus: "A man is shipwrecked and eaten by fish. The fish are then caught and eaten by fishermen. For some reason the fishermen die and their bodies are eaten by dogs. The dogs thereupon die and are eaten by vultures. Where is the sailor?" [2] Ambrose states that this problem greatly disturbs Gentiles, and Augustine admits that it is a very difficult question. [3] But his answer is quite different from that of Athenagoras. It is based not on rationalism but on experience and faith. From "the unhappy experiences of our times"—in the sack of Rome in 410—he knows that cannibalism is a fact. "Would anyone hold with right reason that the whole had been digested through the deepest movements, and that from there nothing had been changed and converted into his flesh, when that emaciated state which formerly existed and now does not, sufficiently proves that the needs have been supplied by that food?" Augustine admits the truth in his adversaries' argument. But he claims that eventually this cycle of carnivorousness will come to an end. Death will be succeeded by decomposition, and from the air the omnipotent God will recall his own. Unfortunately in his proof of this statement he relies on the text, "Not a hair of your head will perish". [4] But the tone of his answer is as realistic as that of Petronius. The "natural" argument of Athenagoras has been abandoned.

The other argument directed against the objections of pagan critics is based on paradoxography and is also found in Augustine. Ultimately it turns on the question of miracle, and it comes from the period late in his life when he was willing to accept contemporary evidence for the miraculous. [5]

The opponents of Augustine, relying on a commonplace of antiquity, [6] claim that perpetual punishment of the resurrected body is impossible, since punishment involves pain and pain eventually brings death. They reject the example of the salamander which

[1] *Res.* ii. 9–14. [2] Fr. 94; this illustration may come from *Odyss.* xv. 133–35 (cf. *VC* 3 [1949], 225). [3] Ambrose, *Fid. res.* 58; Aug. *Civ. dei* xxii. 20. [4] *Civ. dei* xxii. 12, 20. [5] See p. 219. [6] Cic. *N. D.* iii. 32, with Mayor's note; so Sen. *Ep.* 79 : 2, Tert. *Paen.* 12 : 3.

Christians advance, pointing out that salamanders do not live forever and, moreover, that when they are living in the flames they do suffer pain. Augustine's argument, however, is only that the salamander lives in fire, and he relies on another parallel to prove the possibility of burning without being consumed. The volcanic mountains of Sicily have burned for a long time but remain as high as ever. [1] Another example, which he claims to have seen at Carthage, is that of a peacock whose flesh was preserved for a year (more than a month, anyway) after cooking. Other paradoxical marvels are to be found in fire itself, in quicklime, in the diamond, and in the magnet. Some of these Augustine himself has seen; the power of the magnet he knows from a thoroughly reliable witness. [2]

His opponents ask him to give a natural explanation of the resurrection of the body. "If you want us to believe in these events", they say, "give us an explanation of each point." [3] His reply is to the effect that they themselves know of many natural phenomena which they cannot explain. He gives ten examples, nine from the *Natural History* of Pliny. They answer: "But those neither exist nor are credible; they are incorrectly reported and written down". [4] Undoubtedly, Augustine admits, this is often true. But there are some genuine examples which are really "contrary to nature" or at any rate contrary to what they regard as nature. These examples include some which he himself has experienced. [5]

Augustine believes as thoroughly as do his opponents in the orderly course of nature. But his view of nature is broader than theirs, since it allows for the activity of an omnipotent God who reveals himself through nature. Of his paradoxical examples he writes: "We say that all portents are contrary to nature, but they are not. For how is that contrary to nature which is done by the will of God, when the will of so great a creator is itself the nature of every created thing? A portent, therefore, takes place not contrary to nature, but contrary to nature as it is understood". [6] As he elsewhere states the principle, "The will of God is the necessity of things". [7] Miracles such as resurrection are no more remarkable than the ordinary events of life, and

[1] On the other hand, Ael. *V. H.* viii. 11 and Ovid, *Metam.* xv. 340–41, state that Aetna is declining. [2] *Civ. dei* xxi. 4. [3] *Ibid.*, xxi. 5. [4] *Ibid.*, xxi. 6. [5] *Ibid.*, xxi. 7; examples are given in xxii. 8. See p. 220 *supra*. [6] *Civ. dei* xxi. 8. [7] *Gen. ad litt.* vi. 26; cf. C. N. Cochrane, *Christianity and Classical Culture* (New York, 1949), 442–43.

for God there is no difficulty in bringing them about. Thus he is able to say that the resurrection of the flesh is "according to nature", and he shifts the whole setting of the argument. He endeavors to cut the ground from under pagan objections to resurrection which are based on classical conceptions of nature and rationality, although he rejects irrationalist arguments based on faith without reason. Theology, based firmly on the revelation of God in scripture, is not only the queen of the sciences but their judge. We must therefore consider the theological and exegetical arguments which the fathers use in supporting the resurrection of the body.

16

# RESURRECTION IN THEOLOGY

Philosophical apologetic, as we have seen, was quite inadequate for the task of defending the Christian belief in the resurrection of the body. For this reason Christian theologians turned to revelation to support their arguments. By revelation they understood the whole course of God's plan for the history of mankind; and this revelation was contained in scripture as interpreted in the light of tradition. Scripture was thought to back up tradition, and tradition was the means by which scripture was understood. Thus the theologian could turn his back on the inconclusive arguments of philosophers and rely upon the word of God.

This rejection and acceptance had a certain logical warrant; for if the world owes its existence solely to the will of God—and Hermas states that this is the primary point of Christian belief [1]—the arguments of natural philosophers who do not take God's working into account cannot explain nature, and those who believe in such a God can properly disregard natural philosophy and go behind it. When Paul sets forth Christian teaching in 1 Corinthians 15, he eventually proclaims to the church a truth of revelation, a "mystery". Unless the dead are raised incorruptible and we are changed, the Old Testament saying, "Death shall be swallowed up in victory" (Is. 25 : 8), cannot be realized (1 Cor. 15 : 51–52, 54–55).

Tatian, who explicitly rejects Greek philosophical views and points out their difference from Christian faith, discusses the doctrine of creation before turning to the resurrection. Then he continues:

> Before I was born I did not exist and did not know who I was, but only existed in the substance of fleshly matter. Then I came to be what I was not before, and believed in my existence because I came to be. Just so, I who came into existence and through death no longer exist and am no longer seen shall again exist, just as I once was not and then was born. [2]

[1] Hermas, *Mand.* i. 1.  [2] *Or.* 6. Tatian seems to be working over the funerary formula discussed by F. Cumont, „Non fui, fui, non sum", *Musée belge*, 32 (1928), 73–85.

No matter what happens to the believer, he belongs to God, who will care for him.

The earliest extant Christian treatise on the resurrection is that of Athenagoras. In his first ten chapters he gives arguments, some of which we have already discussed, for the possibility of resurrection. Another significant argument also concerns its possibility (*Res.* 2). Athenagoras tells us that a person may be unable to perform some act either because he does not know what to do or because he does not have enough power to act. God is omniscient and omnipotent. Therefore resurrection is not impossible. This argument is Posidonius' reply to the sceptical attack on providence. To be gods, the gods must be omniscient and omnipotent (Cic. *N. D.* ii. 77).

In the last fifteen chapters he endeavors to prove its necessity. He himself analyzes his arguments as follows: proof (1) from the end and design of the creation of the first man and his descendants, (2) from the common nature of all men as men, and (3) from their future judgment at the hands of their creator. [1] His first argument leads to the conclusion that "if God created man for the enjoyment of a rational life, and for the contemplation of his magnificence, wisdom and power in all the works of the creation, then his existence according to God's purpose and his own nature must last as long as there is matter for wonder and admiration in the universe". [2] He then proceeds to examine the nature of man as "a mortal body and an immortal soul united", thus confirming his first argument, with which, as he says, it is closely bound. Finally, if God is just, his judgments must take place hereafter, since they evidently do not take place now. And if man is both soul and body, judgment must be made upon both elements of his nature. Therefore there must be a resurrection of the flesh.

Clearly Athenagoras is not producing proofs which will convince outsiders that they must believe in a resurrection. In discussing the nature of rational proof he claims that he relies not on opinions or philosophical dogmas but on "the common and natural notion or the sequence between premises and conclusions". [3] But when he speaks of the world and man as created beings and defines man as soul plus body, his opinions would seem neither common nor natural

[1] *Res.* 11.   [2] This seems to imply the idea of the eternity of the universe; compare Platonists in Diels, *Dox.* 330 b 18–331 b 4.   [3] *Res.* 14; the „natural notion" was the Stoic criterion of truth: *SVF* II 473 (p. 154 : 29 Arnim).

to outsiders. They are based on revelation, and his arguments are theological.

Still more theological are the teachings of Irenaeus, who as Audet has observed was born a Christian and did not have to become one by conversion. [1] Arguments based on natural science seem irrelevant to him. We should not bother to find out the causes of obscure natural phenomena, for God alone knows them. Therefore he comes directly to the heart of the problem, arguing against Marcion and other docetists. [2] The Lord redeemed us with his own blood and gave his flesh for our flesh, not in appearance but in true substance. How then can docetists say that the flesh is incapable of receiving the gift of God, eternal life, when it is nourished by the body and blood of the Lord and is a member of him? Irenaeus stands in the succession of John, Ignatius, and Justin, in whose writings the physical and the spiritual are inextricably bound together.

If God does not give life to the mortal and does not lead the corruptible to incorruption (the Pauline conception), it must be because he is unable to do so. But he is able to do so, for in the beginning he created man from the earth. The flesh is capable of receiving life; otherwise the docetists would be corpses (as Ignatius had suggested). And God not only creates living bodies but also preserves them; consider the examples of the long-lived antediluvian patriarchs and of Enoch and Elijah, who were taken up bodily into heaven. If anyone thinks that such longevity is impossible or that Elijah was burned up in the chariot of fire, let him consider the examples of Jonah and of the three holy children: "Since the hand of God was with them and in their case accomplished things paradoxical and impossible for human nature, why is it remarkable if in the cases of translation something paradoxical took place by the will of God?.... For God is not subject to things that take place, but things that take place are subject to God, and everything serves his will". [3] In Irenaeus we find a Christian theologian who does not subject God to the limitations imposed by human knowledge but emphasizes his dominion over nature. Irenaeus' theological outlook was eventually to find its clearest expression in Augustine.

Other arguments which Irenaeus provides are similar to those which we have mentioned. Christ's resurrection, especially as described

[1] T.–A. Audet, „Orientations théologiques chez Saint Irénée", *Traditio* 1 (1943) 15ff.  [2] *Adv. haer.* v. 1–16.  [3] *Ibid.*, 5.

in the gospel of John, is a proof of ours, since "the God who raised the Lord will also raise us by his power" (1 Cor. 6 : 14), and "he who raised Christ Jesus from the dead will also make alive your mortal bodies" (Rom. 8 : 11). Those whom Jesus raised during his ministry obviously retained a body of flesh. And if the flesh was not to be saved, Irenaeus concludes, the Word of God became flesh to no purpose. [1]

In all these arguments the givenness of revelation is primary. Flesh can recover life, and God can again give it life, because according to the Old Testament he gave it life in the beginning. The resurrection of Christ (Paul) and the Eucharist (John) are the great New Testament proofs of resurrection. And both Old and New Testaments proclaim the same doctrine, since "all scripture was given us by God". [2] Irenaeus is a genuinely biblical theologian.

A more philosophical approach is found in the work *On the Resurrection* once mistakenly attributed to Justin. [3] Its author is aware, however, of the difference between philosophical and theological proofs. The first six chapters of his book are devoted to philosophical proof, "after the fashion of the gentiles", and from these he turns to proofs "after the fashion of the faithful". These theological proofs begin with a description of his opponents' views. They claim that the flesh is unworthy of resurrection, since its substance is earth (Gen. 2 : 7) and it is full of sin and forces the soul to sin. [4] There are other opponents who say that even if the flesh is dear to God, there is in scripture no promise of its resurrection. [5]

In reply to his first group of adversaries Pseudo-Justin says that they ignore the whole creative working of God, especially the creation and the formation of man in God's image (Gen. 1 : 26). Furthermore, how could the flesh alone sin unless the soul led the way and encouraged it? They are bound together like a yoke of oxen. [6] Surely the Savior called the flesh when he said, "I came not to call the righteous but sinners" (Matt. 9 : 13). Against the second group of opponents, who cannot find proofs of resurrection in scripture, Pseudo-Justin

[1] He adds a few Old Testament examples: Is. 26 : 19, 66 : 13–14, Ezek. 37. [2] *Adv. haer.* ii. 28. 3, an echo of 2 Tim. 3 : 16. [3] For its date see F. R. M. Hitchcock in *ZNW* 36 (1937), 35–60. [4] Cf. Epict. *Diss.* i. 3. 5–7; E. V. Arnold, *Roman Stoicism* (London, 1911), 258. [5] Cf. Origen in Epiph., *Pan. haer.* lxvi. 10. 1; Cyril, of Jerusalem; *Catech.* xviii. 14. [6] Cf. the yoked horses of Plato in *Phaedr.* 246*A* (Ath. *Res.* 15). Presumably they are guided by the spirit; cf. Pseudo-Justin 10. On the soul's leading the flesh to sin cf. Tert. *An.* 40 : 2, 58 : 7.

first directs the general consideration that God surely does not desire to annihilate his most valuable work. A sculptor or a painter does not destroy his creations but wants them to endure. We cannot accuse God of laboring in vain. And the salvation which the Savior offered must have been for bodies as well as for souls, because by definition man is "that rational animal consisting of soul and body". [1]

Additional arguments are based on the works of the Savior, who raised bodies as well as souls, and whose own resurrection was not merely spiritual but corporeal. "Why did he rise in the flesh which suffered, if not to prove the fleshly resurrection?" This proof was made not only by the resurrection but also by the ascension. Again, since the body is the house of the soul, and the soul the house of the spirit, all three elements of the man must rise. [2] Finally, if the Savior had proclaimed only the salvation of the soul, he would have taught nothing more than what Pythagoras and Plato had already said. [3] He actually prescribes a sober and continent life for us because our flesh has hope of salvation. Otherwise, our physician might as well have treated us as incurably ill and said, "Serve your desires".

Pseudo-Justin synthesizes moral arguments, based on the Christian understanding of human nature, with more purely theological arguments, based on the creation of the world and the resurrection of Christ. He is not primarily a biblical theologian but one who works over the inferences already made from the Bible in the tradition. Like Athenagoras he believes that philosophy can prove only the possibility of resurrection; theology must go on to make it probable or certain.

Within the church, however, there were some who denied the resurrection of the flesh. Marcion of Pontus, who upheld the existence of two gods, the higher of whom had nothing to do with the world and human affairs, while the lower creator-god made an evil world out of evil matter, naturally rejected any idea of fleshly resurrection. He understood the saying of Jesus, "like angels", to mean that the bodies of risen men will be of "angelic substance". [4]

Strangely enough, in Marcion's version of the gospel of Luke he

---

[1] Pseudo-Justin 8; cf. Nemesius, *Nat. hom.* 1 (pp. 35ff. Matthaei); other definitions in E. Schwartz, *Tatiani oratio ad Graecos* (Leipzig, 1888), 64–65; Philo, *Leg. alleg.* iii. 161.   [2] Threefold division: Plato, *Tim.* 30*B*; 1 Thess. 5 : 23.   [3] Cf. Diels, *Dox.*, 392 : 12–13, 205; Tert. *An.* 54.   [4] A. von Harnack, *Marcion: Das Evangelium vom fremden Gott* (2d ed.; Leipzig, 1924), 136–37; cf. 103–6, 139 n. 2, 273*.

retained the stories of physical resurrection. Luke 24 : 30 proved too difficult to accept as it stood; he found it necessary to omit the words which we bracket here. "See my hands and my feet, that it is I; [handle me and see,] for a spirit does not have [flesh and] bones such as you see me having." [1] Tertullian ridicules the nonsensical text and ironically asks why Marcion did not remove this section entirely. Instead, he preferred to explain it away by exegesis. His attempt to do so is fantastic. "A spirit, such as you see me having, does not have bones." As Tertullian correctly observes, as a proof of the physical reality of Christ's resurrection there would be no point to such a saying. But as Tertullian fails to see, it would set forth the theory that Jesus rose only in the spirit; and this idea is primitive, as we have already pointed out.

Still more strangely, later Marcionites retained the description in Luke 24 : 42–43 of Jesus' eating fish, for they explained their own eating of fish and not flesh as done in imitation of Christ after his resurrection. [2] This may not have seemed to them as contradictory as it does to us, for Valentinus held that while Jesus ate and drank, there was such a degree of continence in him that the food was not corrupted. [3]

This general tendency to docetism was very pronounced in the second century and was connected with the rising flood of asceticism in the same period. Even Clement of Alexandria did not rid himself entirely of survivals from his gnostic days. But the greatest exponent of such views within the church was Origen. In his thought we are able to see that the difficulties with the idea of a fleshly resurrection are not only importations from the world of philosophy but also stem from scripture itself. The doctrine of the resurrection of the flesh was not yet firmly established among theologians as a part of the rule of faith.

Origen intended to uphold the traditional doctrine of the church while avoiding the errors of simple believers. Often he has been represented as a boldly philosophical critic who desired to subvert the Christian faith. Admittedly, he does not stand close to what later became the central stream of Christianity. But in his time most of his views were by no means as horrifying as Jerome later found them. [4]

---

[1] *Ibid.*, 239\*; Epiph. *Pan. haer.* 42. 11. 6.   [2] Harnack, *op. cit.*, 240\*.   [3] Clem. *Str.* iii. 59; see p. 198 *supra*.   [4] *Ep.* 84 : 7.

In his *De principiis* (ii. 10) he admits that his work on the resurrection has drawn attacks from heretics and at the same time has astonished simple believers. The heretics cannot believe that the body will rise at all. To them he replies that there will be a resurrection of the body. But his greatest difficulties arise with more simple believers, "who have a really low and debased conception of the resurrection of the body". In a long fragment of his commentary on the first psalm [1] he sets forth and answers their arguments.

The simple believers say that the body which we now wear will rise. If we ask whether complete in substance or not, they say it will be complete. We ask whether along with it will rise the blood which flowed out in blood-lettings and the flesh and hairs which formerly existed, or only those which existed at the time of death. They can maintain their argument only with difficulty and take refuge in the maxim that God can do whatever he desires. The more intelligent among them, however, say that it will be the body in existence at the time of death which will rise. If we argue that animals sometimes eat the bodies of men and then are eaten by men or other animals, and the original flesh obviously becomes a part of the bodies of other men or other animals; and if we ask whose the body will be in the resurrection; then they simply retreat to the expression, "All things are possible for God". Then they bring forward such scriptural texts as can be used for their purpose, such as the vision of the valley of dry bones in Ezekiel 37. They cite the gospel: "weeping and gnashing of teeth shall be there" (Matt. 8 : 12) and "fear him who can destroy soul and body in Gehenna" (Matt. 10 : 28), as well as a Pauline expression: "He will make alive your mortal bodies through his Spirit indwelling in you" (Rom. 8 : 11).

Origen's reply is that of a theologian of the church who is nevertheless determined to avoid irrationalism. "It is absolutely necessary for the lover of truth .... to preserve the tradition of the ancients and to keep from falling into the nonsense of beggarly concepts which are at once impossible and unworthy of God." From this sentence we can see that he was close to the outlook of his philosophical antagonist Celsus, who also wanted to avoid ascribing impossibilities and unworthy deeds to God. But his argument, as it

[1] In Method. *Res.* i. 20–24; Epiph. *Pan. Haer.* 64. 12–16. Origen favors the view of the heretics as against that of literalists; cf. *Comm. in Matt.* xvii. 29. On his work see R. Cadiou, *La Jeunesse d'Origène* (Paris, 1936), 117–29.

develops, reaches conclusions very different from those of Celsus. Since the body changes all the time even from day to day [1] (though the soul remains the same) and apparently fits itself to its environment, after the resurrection the soul must have a suitable body. "Just as if we had to be aquatic animals and live in the sea we should certainly need to have gills and the other equipment of fishes, so we who are going to inherit the kingdom of heaven and be in places above must use spiritual bodies—though the former appearance will not pass away, even if its change should be into something more glorious, as was the appearance of Jesus and Moses and Elijah in the transfiguration; it was not different from what it had been." [2] Origen insists, then, on the spiritual nature of the resurrection body, citing 1 Corinthians 15 : 50, and argues that the "character" of the person wearing the spiritual body will be the same as before. He will have a body, but not of flesh. In other words, his personal identity will remain constant.

Origen then turns to the texts cited by those who uphold a literal resurrection of the flesh. If they insist on the literal interpretation of scripture, such an interpretation they will receive. Look at the passage in Ezekiel 37; what does it prove? Taken literally, it proves not the resurrection of the flesh but the resurrection of bones, skin, and sinews. But, of course, parallel passages from the Psalms show that "bones" are not meant literally; the resurrection is one from their corpselike condition, after they had been handed over to enemies because of their sins. The Savior himself called sinners "tombs full of dead bones and all uncleanness" (Matt. 23 : 27). As for the "teeth" of Matthew 8 : 12, in this life God has provided us with members for special functions; the teeth are for chewing solid food. What need will there be for the tormented to have teeth? They will not be eating in Gehenna. Moreover, in Psalm 3 : 7 there is a reference to "breaking the teeth of sinners", and in Psalm 58 : 6 "the Lord broke the teeth of lions". It would be strange indeed if God were to break only the teeth of sinners and preserve their bodies! This passage must therefore not be taken literally. [3] Similarly, in the case

---

[1] Cf. Ovid, *Metam.* xv. 214–15, 165–72.  [2] Method. *Res.* i. 22. 5; Epiph. *Pan. Haer.* 64. 14. 8–9. Origen's arguments are strikingly similar to those of Porphyry. [3] A common observation of antiquity was that the teeth do not decay. Plin. *N. H.* vii. 79, says that the teeth are fireproof to such an extent that in cremation they are not destroyed. Dio Chrys. *Or.* iv. 32, compares the persistence of dogmas in the

of Matthew 10 : 28 the text simply shows that the incorporeal soul cannot be punished without a body; it says nothing of a resurrection of the flesh. The making alive of our mortal bodies mentioned in Romans 8 : 11 will be the change of the form of our bodies from what is mortal to something else; from being fleshly they will become spiritual. Origen's exegesis of these passages is actually closer to Pauline thought than that of his opponents is.

They are isolated passages, however, and Origen places them in a context which is due not to Paul but to Greek philosophy. When he uses the language of ordinary Christians to say, "The end will be like the beginning", [1] he is not referring to the return of the earth to its primitive state of goodness but to a future point at which "God will be all in all". [2] Originally there was a point at which God, the eternal creator, had not made man. Then God made him of spirit; next, because of moral deterioration, of soul; finally, as a consequence of the Fall, the soul was imprisoned in the "coat of skin", the body, for corrective punishment. The plan of redemption requires man to retrace his steps. His risen body, like the Lord's, will be spiritual, and eventually he will become completely incorporeal spirit. [3]

This doctrine naturally encountered sharp opposition. The most important attack on it was made by Methodius of Olympus, whose treatise *De resurrectione* is almost entirely directed against Origen. Methodius rejects Origen's idea that the body is the "coat of skin" received after the Fall. Certainly the soul sinned, but its sin was not related to its acquisition of a body. If it sinned before receiving a body, the body is ethically neutral. On the other hand, if it sinned while in a body, the body is not a coat of skin given because of sin. [4] If the soul itself is able to sin, it is not simply a prisoner of the body. [5] And man actually consists of body and soul united. [6] We know from sripture that the soul is immortal; therefore there must be a resurrection of the other essential part of man, the body. [7]

Methodius also provides a few parallels from nature to show that resurrection is possible. He gives the traditional example of human

wise man's soul to the continuing existence of teeth even of cremated persons. And Tert. *Res. carn.* 42 goes so far as to claim that the teeth remain undecayed and serve as seeds for the body which is to rise.

[1] *Princ.* i. 6. 2. [2] 1 Cor. 15 : 28. [3] H. Koch, *Pronoia und Paideusis* (Leipzig, 1932), 36–38; cf. H. Chadwick in *HTR* 41 (1948), 83–102. [4] *Res.* i. 29. 6. [5] *Ibid.*, i. 31. 6. [6] *Ibid.*, i. 34. 4. [7] *Ibid.*, i. 52. 1–2.

conception and—to prove that individual bodies will rise—the examples of the existence of differentiated elements and, in Tiberias in Judea, of a spring which gives forth five different kinds of water.

Against Origen's exaggerated "spirituality" Methodius provides a useful corrective. It may be asked, however, whether he does not incline too far toward the identification of the dead body with the risen body or, to express this question in another way, whether he does not exaggerate one side of the Pauline doctrine as Origen had exaggerated the other.

The resurrection doctrine of Gregory of Nyssa seems to reflect a compromise between Origen and Methodius. He emphatically denies that the body will rise as it was when it died, and provides a vivid description of various diseases and old age in order to support his denial. [1] If the risen life were to be just as it is now, "I should tell men that the hope of resurrection should be rejected". [2] With Origen he holds that the human body is like a river, not in moving from place to place but in its mutations. [3] His opponents will doubtless say that the body must rise just as it is, for no part of it was created in vain. [4] But the purpose of resurrection is the restoration of life as it was before the Fall; the future life is to be in God. [5] Man is to put off the "coat of skin" acquired after the Fall. In the risen life there will be no

> sexual intercourse, conception, childbirth, filth, nursing, nourishment, adoption, gradual growth, maturity, old age, disease, death. [6]

Like Origen, Gregory combines ascetic abhorrence of human sexuality with his resurrection teaching. Anyone who admits the possibility of such phenomena after the resurrection is really opposed to the resurrection doctrine. [7]

He elsewhere argues that divine power proves the possibility of resurrection, [8] and that the example of quicksilver shows that the dissolved elements of the human body can be restored. [9] His fundamental emphasis, however, is laid on the dissimilarity of the risen body to the body which dies.

In all these debates over the resurrection of the body appeals were constantly made to isolated passages in the New Testament. Defenders

---

[1] *De anima et res.*, PG 46, 137B–141A.   [2] *Ibid.*, 137B.   [3] *Ibid.*, 141A.   [4] *Ibid.*, 144B.   [5] *Ibid.*, 152A.   [6] *Ibid.*, 148C–149A.   [7] *Ibid.*, 149A.   [8] *Hex.*, PG 44, 213C.   [9] *Ibid.*, 228B.

of a physical resurrection claimed that various verses proved their case, while opponents of it also used proof texts. Their favorites were the words of Jesus concerning resurrection "like angels", and the Pauline sentence, "Flesh and blood cannot inherit the kingdom of God".

The former statement could more easily be explained by orthodox interpreters as a metaphor, but the latter remained a permanent embarrassment.

According to Irenaeus, all the heretics made use of 1 Corinthians 15 : 50. [1] He claims that they completely misunderstand the apostle's meaning, "suiting only the bare words to themselves, and fighting to the death over them, overturning, as far as they are able, the whole dispensation of God". They make the apostle's words self-contradictory, since he explicitly says that death will be swallowed up in victory. When will that take place but when the flesh leaves the power of death? Moreover, in Philippians 3 : 20–21 he says that the Lord Jesus will transform the body of our humiliation. What can this be if it is not the flesh, which humbly lies in the ground? According to Colossians 1 : 22 we are reconciled in the body of his flesh. But if the flesh of the Lord is something other than ours, reconciliation is meaningless. "In every epistle the apostle clearly testifies that we are saved through the flesh of our Lord and his blood." [2] Therefore Irenaeus allegorizes the difficult passage in 1 Corinthians: "If flesh and blood provide life for us, it is not literally said of flesh and blood that they cannot inherit the kingdom of God, but of carnal actions, which by perverting man to sin deprive him of life". He confirms this exegesis by referring to Romans 6 : 12–13, where sin is mentioned as reigning in the mortal body.

Thus Irenaeus attempts to destroy the force of a literal interpretation. But as he allegorized this passage, he opened the way for others, who were not bound by the rule of faith, to allegorize the Old Testament passages in which resurrection could be found. When Tertullian rewrites the work of Irenaeus, he finds himself in the same maze of devious turnings where allegorical and literal interpretation offer themselves as alternatives in every verse. There is no standard of interpretation but the faith of the church. Yet the faith of the church is to be proved from the documents in question. Tertullian takes flight into irrationalism when he finds heretics allegorizing

[1] *Adv. haer.* v. 13–14.   [2] *Ibid.*, v. 14. 3.

passages which he must take literally to prove his point. Resurrection, he says, would be incredible had it not been foretold by God. [1] But, as a heretic could observe, that statement begs the question. Was the kind of resurrection of which Tertullian speaks so foretold?

Tertullian approaches 1 Corinthians 15 : 50 very late in his work *De resurrectione carnis*. [2] As he admits, he does so in order to gain the benefit of many other arguments and passages from Scripture which he has placed ahead of it. In this whole passage, he observes, the apostle sets before us the example of Christ: "Is an example given for its unlikeness or its similarity? Obviously, you will reply, for its similarity. How then did Christ rise? In the flesh or not? No doubt, if you hear that he was 'dead and buried according to the scriptures', not otherwise than in the flesh. And so also you admit that he was resuscitated in the flesh". Paul was not discussing the question of substance when he said "flesh"; he meant the discipline of sins of the flesh. Then Tertullian introduces a new subtlety. It is impossible that the apostle so abruptly, "with closed eyes", without distinctions, without conditions, could have excluded all flesh and blood from the kingdom of God, when Jesus is sitting there at the right hand of the Father—man, even though God, and flesh and blood, even though purer than ours.

Moreover, as for the apostle's simile of seeds, they are clearly the same after they "rise"; they do not really die but grow. Finally, Tertullian allegorizes the Jewish distinctions between kinds of flesh (1 Cor. 15 : 39), concluding with a note of contempt: "If these are not figurative, he rather pointlessly compared the flesh of mules and mullets and the bodies of celestial lights with human affairs, since just as they are not relevant for the comparison of their condition, so they are not for the proof of resurrection". He concludes by rejecting explicitly the Pauline conception of a "natural" body and implicitly the higher "spiritual" body. As E. Aleith observes, Tertullian's whole personality and his experience of religion are entirely different from those of the apostle Paul; it is impossible for him to understand him. [3] The subtleties of Pauline theology have disappeared in the feverish materialism of a Montanist. "The flesh will rise", he cries at the end of his book, "just as it was, and entire." This is not the biblical doctrine.

[1] *Res. carn.* 18.   [2] *Ibid.*, 48–52.   [3] E. Aleith, *Paulusverständnis in der alten Kirche* (Berlin, 1937), 61.

17

He discusses another passage his opponents propose, the "like angels" verse (Matt. 22 : 30). Why should all the members of the body rise? If we are like angels, they will be unnecessary. Tertullian's answer is not impressive. Nothing, he says, will prove unnecessary with God. The mouth, for example, is not just for eating and drinking but for praising God as well. Present-day ascetics prove the uselessness of many parts of the body, even though they have them; Moses and Elijah fasted forty days, while Christ not only fasted but stated that man shall not live by bread but by the Word of God.

It is evident that Tertullian never takes his opponents' arguments really seriously. As a clever student of law and of court procedure, he knew that often it was more satisfactory to ridicule his adversary's claims than to answer them. In his view arguments were always conducted in order to win, never to discover new truth, for truth is the possession of the church. Indeed, it might be said that truth is whatever the church possesses. [1] Tertullian represents the irrationalist group within the church. They reject the complexity of secular thought in order to turn wholeheartedly to the revelation of God. But there were those, also within the church, who did not believe it necessary to practice isolationism. At Alexandria such men developed both the theory of exegesis and the doctrine of resurrection with a new subtlety. The pioneer work of Origen on the resurrection is lost, but many of his ideas can be recovered from other sources, especially his *De principiis*. [2]

We need not discuss Origen's exegetical methods in detail. [3] In dealing with the problem of resurrection his interpretation is both grammatical and "spiritual" and certainly comes closer to the meaning of Paul than does that of his opponents. In his handling of 1 Corinthians 15, we do not find the sense of strain that characterizes that of Irenaeus and Tertullian.

Origen's view is that there is a resurrection not of the "dead" or of the "flesh" (literally understood) but of the "body". The first book of his *De resurrectione* was apparently devoted to proving against Syrian Bardesanians that the risen man must have a body. [4] Here he took his stand with contemporary orthodoxy. It was his second book which drew the accusation of heresy, for in it he attacked the

[1] Cf. *The Bible in the Church* (New York, 1948), 85–90. [2] He says that he is using these materials: *Princ.* ii. 10. 1. [3] See pp. 202–3. [4] Bardaisan's views: Ephrem Syrus, *Opera* ii. (Rome, 1740), 438 *C*, 551–53.

"simple believers" for their faith in the resurrection of the flesh. [1] Here trouble arose, for the "simple believers" were the majority of orthodox Christians. [2]

Origen's learned exegesis takes its point of departure from 1 Corinthians 15 : 50, as we see not only from fragments of his commentary on the book [3] but also from *De principiis* [4] and from the commentary on the first psalm fragmentarily preserved by Methodius. [5] His position is rendered precarious by his insistence that the risen Jesus had a body which could eat. [6] He believes, however, that had the Lord appeared with his glorified body he could not have been seen. It was necessary for him to give at least the appearance of his wounds. [7] This essay in docetism is to some extent abandoned in *Contra Celsum* when he speaks of the "border line" between body and soul which Jesus' body held, according to John 20 : 26–27. [8] And the contradiction between a border line and a body which eats may be resolved if we recall that the fragments on 1 Corinthians are from popular homilies. In these Origen sometimes takes scripture more literally than in commentaries.

Origen's exegesis of 1 Corinthians 15, is somewhat allegorical, but it effectively reproduces the spirit of the apostle. He insists that the main question is whether Christ rose from the dead or not; every heresy consists of error on this point. If he rose, then he must have had a body. But it was not a body of flesh and blood. The apostle says, "We all shall be changed", and the "power" of the seed brings forth the new grain. Origen's opponents may say that the flesh must rise, if only to be burned in the fire of Gehenna. He replies that there is no corporeal fire to punish the body of flesh, for sinners arouse their own conscience to flame (Is. 50 : 11) ,and it consumes not them but—with an adroit allusion to 1 Corinthians 3 : 12—their sins. The judgment is one of conscience. God, the physician of our souls, is not going to burn us. He will burn our diseases. [9]

With this brief analysis Origen effectively removes the foundation for the literal interpretation of the bodily resurrection. Whether or

---

[1] Cf. Cadiou, *op. cit.*, pp. 117–29. [2] As Tertullian points out (*Adv. Prax.* 3): simplices.... ne dixerim imprudentes et idiotae, quae maior semper credentium pars est. [3] C. Jenkins, *JTS* 10 (1908–9), 44–46; cf. C. H. Turner, *ibid.*, 274–75. [4] *Princ.* ii. 10. 3. [5] *Res.* i. 20–24. [6] *JTS* 10, 46 = Cramer, *Cat.* v. 275; *Comm. in Matt.* xi. 2. [7] Method. *Res.* iii. 12; cf. *C. Cels.* ii. 61. [8] *C. Cels.* ii. 62. [9] *Princ.* ii. 10. 3–6.

not he fully understands the implications of the doctrine of resurrection is another question.

One of Origen's most formidable adversaries, as we have seen, was Methodius, who argues vigorously against Origenist quotation of the "like angels" passage. He explains it away by interpreting it to mean that as the angels are in heaven, so also men will be in paradise [1]—which will be a place on earth. [2] Again, when the apostle speaks of the destruction of "our earthly tabernacle we live in", he means not the tabernacle itself but life here on earth. The "dwelling-place from heaven" which we expect is not another body but immortality. [3] In dealing with 1 Corinthians 15 : 50 Methodius simply allegorizes it as Irenaeus had done before him. [4] We have given enough examples to show that Methodius contributes little novelty to the controversy.

With the unsettlement which preceded the collapse of Rome, the resurrection doctrine came to be taught with a militant literalism which goes far beyond the New Testament.

In writing against John of Jerusalem in 396 Jerome observes that there are Origenists who try to use the word "body" to deceive those who think they mean "flesh". But flesh is what is bound together by blood, veins, bones, and sinews. [5] Some Origenists even use the expression "resurrection of the flesh" but destroy the meaning by the way they use it. [6]

What this view of Jerome's involves is to be seen at its crudest in his letter 108 to Eustochium, written in 404 after the death of Paula. In it he insists that the resurrection body will rise with all its members and therefore will be either male or female (against Origen). He proves that it will be complete by using the resurrection narrative of John 20 : 26–29, which Origen had employed for his "borderline" theory. Jesus stood among his disciples; therefore he had feet. He said (hence a tongue, palate, and teeth): See my hands (hence arms) and touch my side (hence belly and chest "to hold the sides together"). Therefore he had a complete body. Suppose someone objects to this line of argument, asking if we are going to eat in the resurrection. "Do not for food's sake drag the resurrection faith into a false interpretation." After all, when Jairus' daughter was raised, she was given something to eat (Mark 5 : 43), and Jesus had supper with

[1] *Res.* i. 51. 2.   [2] *Ibid.*, 55. 2.   [3] *Ibid.*, ii. 15.   [4] *Ibid.*, ii. 18. 1ff.   [5] *C. Joann. Hieros.* 27.   [6] *Ep.* 84 : 7.

the risen Lazarus (John 12 : 2). [1] "But if you try to prove that he entered when the doors were closed and therefore had a spiritual body made of air, then before his passion he had a spiritual body, for contrary to the nature of weighty bodies he walked on the sea." And if that be so, Peter also had a spiritual body, for he walked on the sea to Jesus. And this is absurd, for Peter speaks of dying with Jesus (Mark 14 : 31), and Jesus had a visible body (John 20 : 27, Luke 24 : 34, 40). "You hear of bones and flesh and feet and hands, and you invent the spheres of the Stoics and certain fantastic imaginings made of air." [2] These arguments are obviously more clever than convincing. They are the random thoughts of a brilliant controversialist. Unfortunately such interpretations influenced Augustine, great theologian though he was, toward the end of his life.

As we have already seen Augustine gave fresh life to the philosophical defense of Christian faith in the resurrection. But in his exegetical work we find a definite retrogression. Two views are to be found in his writings. The earlier, more biblical view, sets forth the resurrection of the body but not of the flesh; the later, explicitly upheld in his *Retractationes* and *De civitate dei*, contradicts Paul while claiming to interpret his thought. We must hold that Augustine's earlier judgment was more nearly right than his later one.

The resurrection faith came to him as a traditional doctrine expressed in the creed. In 393 in his *De fide et symbolo*, Augustine explains the resurrection in Pauline terms. [3] If this doctrine seems incredible to anyone, he is considering only what the flesh now is, not what it will be. In that future time of angelic change it will no longer be flesh and blood but simply "body". For this statement Augustine relies on 1 Corinthians 15. Philosophers admit that any one element can be transmuted into the next one of the four; therefore by the will of God our bodies can be transmuted "in the wink of an eye, without any such stages, just as generally smoke is changed into flame with wonderful quickness". Similarly in the year 400 he refers in the *De catechizandis rudibus* only to the resurrection of the body. [4]

In 426, however, when he had completed his treatment of the doctrine in the last two books *De civitate dei*, he referred to his earlier view and maintained that the resurrection must be understood to

---

[1] *Ep.* 108: 23, cf. Methodius on Abraham, *Res.* iii. 17. 2.  [2] *Ep.* 108: 23.
[3] *Fide et symb.* 24.  [4] *Catech. rud.* 7. 11.

involve "limbs and substance of flesh". [1] After the resurrection the Lord's body

> appeared in the same members, not only to be seen by the eyes, but also to be handled by the hands, and even proved himself to have flesh by discourse, saying, Handle me and see, for a spirit does not have flesh and bones, such as you see me having (Luke 24 : 39). From this it is clear that the apostle did not deny that there will be the substance of flesh in the kingdom of God but either called men who were after the flesh "flesh and blood", or the corruption of the flesh itself, which then surely will be no more. For when he said, Flesh and blood cannot inherit the kingdom of God (1 Cor. 15 : 50), it is right to understand him as having added for explanation what follows directly, Neither shall corruption inherit incorruption. Of which point, on which it is so difficult to convince unbelievers, anyone who will read my last book on the City of God will see that I have treated it with all the pains I could bestow.

To the treatise *De civitate dei* we therefore turn. The resurrection is discussed in the last two books, xxi and xxii (as well as in xiii. 20–22). After citing the usual paradoxographical examples, Augustine comes to grips with the problem. Book xxi deals with the limitations of human knowledge and the possibility of apparent breaches in natural law. In Book xxii our author follows this analysis with an attack on the incredulity of the pagan world, rather in the manner of Tertullian. These things are credible because most people believe them. Here Augustine turns against his opponents the old Stoic argument from consensus of opinion. [2] It is we who represent the consensus, he says, not you. After these preliminaries he proceeds to the business of exegesis.

The subjects chosen for discussion (xxii. 12–20) are rather curious, but they were not chosen by Augustine. His opponents have asked questions. Will abortions rise? How large will children be? Will everyone be the same size as the Lord? What about all the hair and nails which are produced in a lifetime? Augustine is unwilling to say that the language of scripture is metaphorical. He takes Luke 21 : 18, "Not a hair of your head will perish", with full literalness. But it does not mean that all your hair but that all your hairs will be preserved. The body will have the appearance of "a perfect man" (Eph. 4 : 13), that is, of a man "about thirty years old" (Luke 3 : 23). [3] Women will be raised as women. The expression "like

---

[1] *Retract.* i. 17; cf. 29.   [2] Cic. *N. D.* ii. 5; *Tusc.* i. 12–13, 16.   [3] Age of maturity: cf. Diels, *Dox.*, 434 a 16; Censorinus, *Die nat.* 14; C. Taylor, *Sayings of the Jewish Fathers* (ed. 2, Cambridge, 1897), 97–98. Cf. J. H. Waszink on Tert. *An.* 56:7 (p. 572).

angels" does not mean that they will be incorporeal but that they will be like angels in immortality and felicity.

The fundamental belief which makes such a resurrection credible is one on which Augustine laid great emphasis, and one which lies at the center of Christian theology. God is the omnipotent creator of the universe. His freedom is limited only by his own nature, not by the physical universe and its order. Augustine rejects the classical conception of the world as either coeternal with God or in some way limiting God's power. There is no fixed system through which God has to break, for the will of God is the origin of the order in nature.

In Augustine's doctrine of resurrection we see summed up the whole early Christian world-view, with its stress on creation, miracle, and resurrection. These three notes are bound together in a common theme, the omnipotence of God. To each of the three notes, as well as to the theme, Greek scientists and philosophers were resolutely opposed. As regards these basic physical and metaphysical questions, Nestle rightly observes [1] that Christianity was in no way whatever the heir of Greek philosophy. At the same time, Christians knew enough about philosophy, and about science as mediated by philosophers, to use scientific and philosophical arguments in defence of their faith, and to treat its mythological-religious themes on the same level as natural phenomena. Augustine uses such arguments, but he reverses the ordinary treatment by regarding natural phenomena as miraculous. His fundamental belief, like that of ancient Christianity generally, is in the omnipotence of God.

[1] *ARW* 37 (1942), 51–53.

# THEOLOGY AND SCIENCE

At the heart of early Christianity lies its eschatological proclamation. After the arrest of John the Baptist Jesus came into Galilee proclaiming the gospel that the time of prophecy had been completed and that the reign of God was at hand. God would soon take up his power and reign; indeed, Jesus' expulsion of demons proved that God was already at work through him. For those who believed, all things were possible. Temporarily the powers of darkness won a victory, for Jesus was crucified by the rulers of this evil age when they failed to recognize him as the Son of God; but in his resurrection God turned human defeat into the triumph of his power. After the resurrection, the believer, who died and rose with Christ, was free from the bondage of the evil in the world.

The apostle Paul analyzes the human situation as enslavement to the creation instead of worship of the Creator (Romans 1 : 25). Through their idolatry men had been enslaved to "the elemental principles of the world", to gods who "by nature are no gods" (Galatians 4 : 3, 8). But the Christian has participated in the resurrection of Christ, which is a new act of creation, for

> Whoever is in Christ is a new creature. The old has passed away. Behold, the new has come (2 Corinthians 5 : 17).

The power of God is experienced anew in Christian life, and Christians describe it as manifested externally in miracles, acts of God in which the believer transcends his ordinary human capabilities. As the apostle says, "I can do all things through him who strengthens me" (Philippians 4 : 13).

With the passage of time Christians did not lose their faith in the marvelousness of God's acts. Speaking of the star of Bethelehem, Ignatius declares that

> by this all magic was dissolved and every bond of wickedness vanished away.... for God was manifest as man for the newness of eternal life, and that which had been prepared by God received its beginning; hence all things were disturbed, for the abolition of death was being planned (*Eph.* 19 : 3).

The old creation, subject to the iron laws of astrology—subject even to science—has been completely renovated. Human freedom, derived from the freedom of the omnipotent God, has been restored. In the second century the church firmly rejected the gnostic cosmology of Basilides, Valentinus and others, for they denied the freedom of God by postulating chains of aeons (shall we say chains of causation?) which separated God from evil matter but at the same time tied him to it. The church upheld the Old Testament, with its stories of the free creator and the free governor of human history. This faith was proclaimed in the first article of the church's creed: "I believe in God the Father Almighty, maker of heaven and earth".

Early Christians thus insisted upon the power and the freedom of God. This is the primary factor in all the miracle stories with which we have been concerned. These stories are intended to show not only that God can control nature and human history, but that he actually does so. At this point Christian apologists entered into conflict with contemporary historians and philosophers. Many historians had learned to question similar stories in Greek and Roman history, and philosophers had been accustomed to allegorize the myths about the gods in order to distill their own philosophies from them. A further difficulty was brought about by the fact that Christian apologists were often trained in the philosophy and history of those whom they were attacking. Their embarrassment over the question of miracle led them into partial scepticism, as in the case of Tertullian, or into partial acceptance of allegorization, as in the case of Origen. When Greek learning had lost most of its allure a new approach was taken by Augustine, who reinterpreted what science he knew in the light of miracle.

Only Origen seems to have come close to asking the question of the essential purpose of miracle stories. He contrasted their inner meaning with their outer form, and often—but not always—concluded that the inner meaning was more significant than the story itself taken as fact. In this way his thought comes close to the idea of a philosopher whom all early Christians detested. Epicurus, oppressed by Platonic star-mysticism, had already denied the truth of the myths about the gods. But in trying to save the freedom of mankind he looked back to mythology with nostalgic enthusiasm.

> It would be better to follow the myth about the gods than to be a slave of the Fate of natural philosophers; for the myth gives some hope for

relief through worship of the gods, but Fate contains inevitable necessity (Diogenes Laertius x. 134).

Though no early Christian would have agreed that the Bible contains mythology (as we have seen, Origen substitutes other terms for "myth" [1]), the apologist Tatian expresses a similar attitude toward philosophy and science when he states that his soul, "instructed by God", was freed from "the slavery in the world". Christians militantly defended free will against determinism of every kind. The whole theology of Origen is centered on two principles: the goodness of God and the freedom of his creatures. [2]

In the history of pre-Christian philosophy there is one eminent figure who defends the freedom of the will; this is the founder of the New Academy, Carneades. Christian apologists constantly utilized his arguments against astrology, divination, and determinism in general. [3] They insisted that, as he had said, "there is something in our power". Man is not the slave of his environment, but under God its master. In other words, man cannot be reduced to nature, for he, not nature, was made in God's image. God is free; therefore man is free. "All things are yours, and you are Christ's, and Christ is God's" (1 Corinthians 3 : 22–23).

Among the earliest Christians the question of the factual or non-factual nature of the miracle stories which proved the reality of divine freedom does not seem to have arisen. Certainly those who handed down the tradition of Jesus' miracles never doubted that they took place. We should not imagine, however, that attacks on them were lacking. The apostle Paul is concerned in the fifteenth chapter of 1 Corinthians to prove the possibility of Jeus' resurrection by a series of natural analogies, and this method came to be employed for most of the miracles. Here we see the attempt to "prove" the truth of stories to which proof was really irrelevant. It is an attempt to interpret in terms of nature events originally regarded as transcending nature. And by thus reducing miracles to nature Christian theologians tended to lose the element of divine freedom which the stories were intended to portray.

We cannot entirely agree with the analysis of Reinhold Niebuhr,

---

[1] See p. 203.　[2] J. Daniélou, *Origène* (Paris, 1948), 204.　[3] D. Amand, *Fatalisme te liberté dans l'antiquité grecque. Recherches sur la survivance de l'argumentation antifataliste de Carnéade chez les philosophes grecs et les théologiens chrétiens des quatres premiers siècles* (Louvain, 1945).

who speaks [1] of miracle stories, or of some miracle stories, as "the
effort to certify this triumph [of Christ] through specific historical
details", and claims that it is "the expression of a scepticism which
runs through the whole history of Christianity".

> Christ cannot be known as the revelation of God except by faith and
> repentance; but a faith not quite sure of itself always hopes to suppress its
> scepticism by establishing the revelatory depth of a fact through its mira-
> culous character. This type of miracle is in opposition to true faith.

Niebuhr's statement is itself an expression of scepticism, but we may
ask whether it is sceptical of the right things. Does not the Christians'
scepticism show itself in the attempt to prove the factuality of miracles?
The miracles themselves we should regard as the more or less spontaneous expressions of faith.

Nor can we agree, on the other hand, with the English theologian
Alan Richardson, who says [2] that "belief in the historicity of the
Gospel miracles.... comes when we decide to accept the testimony
of the apostles concerning the things which they saw with their eyes
and which they heard and handled concerning the Word of Life".
He adds that these miracles "were mere empty portents to those who
had not that gift of sight". This statement begs the question of
whether the "portents" actually took place or not, and it assumes
that "faith" alone can determine questions of historical evidence.

Other theologians are more thoroughgoing in their discussions of
miracle stories. Rudolf Bultmann, for example, declares [3] that the
New Testament needs to be pruned of its mythological features so
that its existential message will be comprehensible today. Miracle
stories are mythological.

> No one can use electric light and the radio, or rely in cases of sickness
> on modern medical and clinical remedies, and at the same time believe in
> the New Testament world of spirits and wonders.

Thus even the resurrection of Jesus is not an historical event; only
the "Easter-faith" of the first disciples is historical. Bultmann regards
the listing of witnesses to the resurrection by Paul as the beginning
of a tragic decline. Paul is trying to "prove" something which cannot
be proved. We have seen in the course of our investigations how

---

[1] *Faith and History* (New York, 1949), 148.   [2] *Christian Apologetics* (New York,
1947), 172.   [3] „Neues Testament und Mythologie", in H. W. Bartsch, *Kerygma
und Mythos* (Hamburg, 1948), 18; cf. also A. N. Wilder in *JBL* 69 (1950), 113–27.

futile such proofs are. At the same time it must be admitted that to prove that miracles cannot take place is almost equally difficult.

The solution which we find most satisfactory is that provided by Richard Kroner in his little book, *The Religious Function of Imagination* (New Haven, 1941). He declares that miracles "happen on a level of meaning where the laws of nature have no place at all".

> Miracles can be verified or rejected by means of scientific thought as little as the laws of nature can be comprehended with the power of religious imagination; they occur and are meaningful in a sphere quite different from that of science and thought. [1]

Kroner proceeds to praise such exegetes as Origen because in their method "the same religious imagination which originally received and produced the content of the divine revelation is also at work". [2]

Our analysis of the relation of early Christianity to natural science leads us to conclusions like those of Kroner. We are forced to disagree with the main thesis of Wilhelm Nestle, whose valuable work *Vom Mythos zum Logos* we have already mentioned. In it he sets forth the thesis that mythical expression and logical thought are absolutely opposed. Originally men thought only in mythical forms, but eventually their minds developed to the point where they could abandon myth and employ logic. Once they raised the question of truth or falsity, they had to give up the myths. Elsewhere, in his brilliant analysis of the principal objections of ancient thought to Christianity, [3] Nestle argues that Christianity cannot be regarded as the heir of Greek philosophy, for Celsus, Porphyry, and Julian attacked the irrational faith of Christians, especially when it was expressed in ideas of creation *ex nihilo*, miracle, and resurrection. Christians believed in an omnipotent God who transcended the order of nature. All this is completely un-Greek. [4]

We should hold, on the contrary, that Greek and Roman ideas of nature and the order of nature were subjective and fluid and that they seemed more rational than they actually were. We should claim that Christians were able to attain a more comprehensive understanding of human nature because of the central place which they gave their mythology, and that they were better able to defend human freedom on their theological grounds.

[1] *Op. cit.*, 42–43. [2] *Ibid.*, 44. [3] *ARW* 37 (1942), 51–100, esp. 70–88. [4] Nestle in *RAC* I 953–54; cf. E. Ivánka, *Hellenisches und Christliches im Frühbyzantischen Geistesleben* (Vienna, 1948). See chapter 9.

On the other hand, we must admit that the church fathers in general were too much under the spell of Greek rationalism to be able to avoid rationalizing their own myths. They had to treat the miracles of faith as if they were events subject to sense-perception. Perhaps their treatment was in part due to pressure from the non-philosophical *simpliciores*. [1] In any case, by such "misplaced concretion" they lost the values they were trying to defend.

These miracle stories were actually symbols, stories conveying pictures of the freedom and the power of God, who was at work in human history and would ultimately vindicate those who trusted and obeyed him. They were not "mere" symbols, for to the religious imagination they were truly miracles, awakening in man the response of faith. They transmitted their power to the believer by freeing him from slavery to his environment and from slavery to "fact". They enabled him to say with the apostle, "I can do all things through him who strengthens me". The believer could not have said that his statement was literally or scientifically true. He had to recognize that he lived both by reason and by faith, both in the flesh and in the spirit. His mind was, so to speak, both Greek and Hebrew, both scientific and imaginative. Pohlenz has summarized the difference thus: [2]

> For the thought of the Greeks the idea of "nature" is the point of departure and the final term. For them it is the power which governs the great events of the world according to its own eternal laws; it also determines the being of mankind and is the norm for its way of life; and therefore morality is nothing other than the full unfolding of man's rational nature. The native language of Jesus had no word which corresponds to the Greek idea of "nature", and for him the world was the work of God. He created it out of nothing (an idea untenable for Stoics as for Epicureans) and appointed it for the course of events. Not man's own reason but God has proclaimed to man what he is to do and to leave undone, what is good and evil, what is morally right.

The early Christian, who was the heir of both world-views, lived in a perpetual tension between the two. Sometimes he exaggerated the claims of imagination; sometimes he rationalized its product into what he thought was fact. If he neglected either element he distorted the meaning of his religion. He lived within nature and was subject

[1] On this pressure cf. H. Delehaye, *Les légendes hagiographiques* (ed. 2, Brussels, 1906), 56. [2] M. Pohlenz, *Die Stoa* (Göttingen, 1948), I 401.

to its laws. He had also a life beyond nature which he lived by faith. He could not deny either nature or supernature, either the world or God. The ways in which he tried to combine the two points of view constitute the story of the relation between early Christianity and natural science.

# ADDENDA

p. 24. For the (physical) "legislation of nature" cf. Vettius Valens, p. 344 : 1 Kroll.

p. 97. Note that Justin also speaks of the "extension of the hands" (cf. Galen, cited pp. 12—13) and the cruciform shape of the nostrils.

p. 106. Hippolytus' knowledge of philosophy is not entirely doxographical; it leads him into error, as when he identifies the system of Basilides with Aristotelianism (*Ref.* vii. 14—19) and that of Valentinus with Pythagorean Platonism (*Ref.* v. 21—28).

p. 120. Not all philosophical writers reject comfort; compare Posidonius in Seneca, *Ep.* 90 : 7 (A. D. N.); but for the later period Seneca's criticism is perhaps more typical.

p. 130. On fate in Alexander cf. R. A. Pack in *AJP* 58 (1937), 418—36 (A. D. N.).

p. 172. I find a similar criticism of Grundmann's view in E. Lohmeyer, *Das Evangelium des Markus* (Göttingen, 1937), 112 n. 2.

p. 212 n. 5. On this subject see now H. J. Schoeps, *Vom himmlischen Fleisches Christi* (Tübingen, 1951), with my review in *ATR* 1952.

p. 220. When Synesius (PG 66, 1085 C) says that „God does not make public exhibitions or work wonders", his sentence cannot be treated as general principle; cf. Chr. Lacombrode, *Synésios de Cyrène hellène et chrétien* (Paris, 1951), pp. 111, 115, 118—119, 121, 177; Id., *Le Discours sur la Royauté de Synésios de Cyrène* (Paris, 1951) 59 u. 109. (J. H. W.)

p. 267. Niebuhr has discussed this subject in more detail in *JR* 21 (1951), 155—68.

# TECHNICAL TERMS

# BIBLICAL PASSAGES

## A. OLD TESTAMENT

## B. NEW TESTAMENT

275

## C. JEWISH AND CHRISTIAN APOCRYPHA AND PSEUDEPIGRAPHA

# SUBJECTS

# ANCIENT AUTHORS

Horapollo, walking on water impossible 178

Hyginus, death of Odysseus 60 n. 3

Iamblichus, God and nature 26, origin of universe 39, miracles of Pythagoras 62, of Abaris 72 n. 6, against sense-perception 75 n. 4, credulity 75—76, divine omnipotence 132, criticizes virginal conception 174

Ignatius, resurrection 230—31, new star 264

Irenaeus, uses doxography 80—81, criticizes philosophy and science 102—3, creation 147, pillar of salt 183, miracles 190—91, resurrection 231—33, 248—49, 256—57

Jerome, rationalizes myth 48 n. 1, uses Pliny and Galen 118, parallels to virginal conception 173, resurrection of flesh 260—61

John Chrysostom, miracle 212—14

Josephus, quotes Agatharchides 50 n. 10, eschatological miracles 166, doubts women sleep with gods 177, Noah's ark extant 183, credibility 183—84, criticizes Apion 187, no resurrection 223, angels' diet 228 n. 5

Juba of Mauretania, in source of Celsus 108 n. 3

Julius Africanus, rationalizes myth 48 n. 1, science and magic 109—11

Julius Ceasar, no wonder stories 57

Julius Marathus, source of Suetonius 176

Julius Obsequens, *Book of Prodigies* 57

Justin, law of nature 24, science and philosophy 96—98, eclecticism 97, creation 141—42, Noah is Deucalion 164, miracles 189—90, angels' diet 228 n. 5. resurrection 231, 239

Juvenal, *aretalogus* term of abuse 156

Lactantius, rationalizes myth 48 n. 1, Euhemerism 50 n. 3, science 113—14, use of Cicero 114, creation 147, miracle 210

Leo (Pope), relation of human and divine 198

Leon of Pella, Euhemerism 49

Leucippus, necessity not defined 19, criticized 113, 147

Livy, scepticism 57, 66, Mars not father of Romulus 174—75, political origin of Numa story 175, no ascension of Romulus 179

Lucian, scepticism 71—73, favors Epicurus 73, uses doxography 80, ridicules science 85, admits Christians opposed charlatan 120, "wonders" 155, ridicules walking on water 178, satirizes flight of soul 180, footprints of Heracles 183 n. 3, encomium and history 186

Lucretius, compact of nature 25 n. 1, scepticism 56, science 83, criticizes omnipotence 128, parallel to Clement 197, on dissolution 240 n. 2

Macarius Magnes, divine omnipotence 132

Manilius, origin of universe 37

Marcion, criticizes virginal conception 177, miracles prove divinity 188—89, 201, rejects resurrection 250—51

Marinus, credulity 76—77

Matris, used by Diodorus Siculus 53

Maximus of Tyre, like Origen on prayer 16 n. 6, 201 n. 1, cites Pherecydes 35 n. 1, credibility 69, against sense-perception 75 n. 4, regular order of generation 130 n. 3, medicinal lie 204 n. 7

Ptolemaeus, Stoic definition of law 21 n. 4

Pythagoras, criticizes myth 43, legendary miracles 62, 75—76, 93, 200, followers accept miracles 73, called son of Apollo 174, resurrection 236

Pytheas of Marseilles, rejected by Polybius 52, generally suspect 81

Quadratus, miracles prove divinity 188

Quintilian, refutation of myth 59, Jews superstitious 187 n. 1, credibility 194 n. 3

*Scriptores historiae Augustae,* uncritical 58

Seneca (rhetor), ocean cannot be crossed 94

Seneca, nature is God 10, prayer 11 n. 1, instinct in animals 16 n. 1, causation 30, textbook 79, future of science 84, eclecticism 97, divne omnipotence 129, "miracles" 167, weight of water 178, elephant and man 202 n. 3, analogies to regeneration 236, 238, pain brings death 243 n. 6

Sextus Empiricus, teleology and chance 31, regularity of nature 32—33, no criterion in history 60, sense-perception of animals 99, used by Hippolytus 105, parallels to Theophilus 143, cited: 9 n. 1, 31 n. 11, 34 n. 2, 51 n. 4, 60 n. 2, 5, 98 n. 5, 99 n. 2, 105 n. 2, 114 n. 5, 186 n. 4, 201 n. 3, 242 n. 6

Soranus, nature, rejects "sympathy" 12

Speusippus, calls Plato son of Apollo 173

*Stoicorum veterum fragmenta* (ed. v. Arnim), cited: 8 n. 1—6, 21, 21 n. 2, 22, 30 n. 7—8, 31 n. 1, 9, 32 n. 2, 33 n. 2, 37 n. 2—5, 8, 10, 47 n. 2, 61 n. 3, 92 n. 4, 107 n. 7, 184, 184 n. 7, 198 n. 8, 200 n. 1, 205 n. 4, 236 n. 1—3, 5, 247 n. 3

Strabo, criticizes Theopompus 50, use of Posidonius 54, criticizes Homer and Eratosthenes 54, criticizes Euhemerus 54, notes collection of miracles 70, "wonders" 155

Strato, nature 7—8, causation 21, rejects teleology 31, his experiments neglected 79, criticized by Stoics 82, rejects immortality 102, criticizes divine omnipotence 128

Suetonius, marvels 58, portents at birth of Augustus 176—77

Tacitus, miracles 58, Jews superstitious 187 n. 1, doubts phoenix 239

Tatian, scepticism 24, criticizes science and philosophy 98, *On Animals* 98—99, relation to Celsus, Origen, Arnobius 99, creation 142, no stress on miracles 190, resurrection 231, 246—47, human freedom 266

Tertullian, criticizes Aristotle 16, criticizes laws of nature 24, Euhemerism 50 n. 3, magic 61 n. 4, science 112, against Hermogenes 143—45, criticizes Marcion on miracles 189, miracle 193—96, phoenix 240, proof of resurrection 240, 256—58, pain brings death 243 n. 6, soul leads flesh to sin 249 n. 6, teeth do not decay 253 n. 3, simple believers 259 n. 2

Theagenes of Rhegium, allegorical method 49

Theodoret, miracles 213—14

Theon (rhetor), refutation of fiction 59, uses Palaephatus 59, myth 203

Theon of Smyrna, textbook 78, relation to Anatolius 116

Theophilus of Antioch, Euhemerism 50 n. 3, conversion 72 n. 5, uses doxography 80, Greek learning conjectural 88 n. 4, science and philosophy 100—2, creation 142—45, Noah is Deucalion 164, miracles 190, resurrection 238

Theophrastus, nature 7, law of nature 22, teleology 31, on Plato 36, acquitted of impiety 44, rationalizes myth 46, originates doxography 79—80 "botanical folklore" 215 n. 1

# MODERN AUTHORS